U THRIVE

How to Succeed in College (and Life)

DANIEL LERNER AND
ALAN SCHLECHTER, MD

Little, Brown Spark
New York   Boston   London

Little, Brown Spark
Hachette Book Group
1290 Avenue of the Americas, New York, NY 10104
littlebrownspark.com

First Edition: April 2017

Little, Brown Spark is an imprint of Little, Brown and Company, a division of Hachette Book Group, Inc. The Little, Brown Spark name and logo are trademarks of Hachette Book Group, Inc.

The publisher is not responsible for websites (or their content) that are not owned by the publisher.

The Hachette Speakers Bureau provides a wide range of authors for speaking events. To find out more, go to hachettespeakersbureau.com or call (866) 376-6591.

The VIA Classification of Character Strengths on pages 61–62 is © copyright 2004–2017, VIA Institute on Character. Used with permission. All rights reserved. www.viacharacter.org

The ESS is protected by international copyright: ESS © MW Johns 1990–1997. Used under License. For more information on the ESS and its conditions of use, please contact Mapi Research Trust, Lyon, France. https://eprovide.mapi-trust.org

Many thanks to Professor Carol Dweck and Nigel Holmes for the use of the image on mindset on page 83. Used with permission. All rights reserved.

ISBN 978-0-316-31161-8
Library of Congress Control Number: 2016953524

10 9 8 7 6 5 4

LSC-C

Printed in the United States of America

To my parents, Martin and Mimi Lerner,
who showed me what it means to thrive.
To Erin and Julian, for reminding me how to do so
every single day.

—*Dan*

To my very own Giving Tree:
Susan and Bruce Schlechter
To my inspiration: Maisie and Marlowe
And to my greatest treasure: Carlyn
All my love and Thanks, 1418

—*Alan*

Contents

Contents

Authors' Note

The information cited in this book is based on more than 350 sources that the authors believe to be reliable. We invite you to visit www.uthrive.info for all references and a full bibliography.

U THRIVE

Introduction

My mission in life is not merely to survive, but to thrive; and
to do so with some passion, some compassion, some humor,
and some style.

—*Maya Angelou*

At its very best, college offers us the opportunity to turn
dreams into realities.

College is about possibility. The moment you set foot on campus, you will be in the middle of one of life's greatest turning points,
taking your first real shot at being an adult. No matter what your
roots, cultural background, or financial status may be, college holds
the promise of rich experiences, lifelong friendships, and an amazing
chance to pursue your passions. This is where you can find your
voice, determine your path, and begin to unlock your true potential.
In short: college is a game-changer.

Yet for many, college is more about surviving than thriving. It
can be a slog through stress and anxiety. It can be four years spent
worrying that you might not be up to snuff, make the grade, or reach
the bar set by your parents, your peers, or yourself. For a growing
number of today's students, college can be discouraging rather than
inspiring, making them feel like they aren't in line for a fulfilling
future, causing their dreams to slowly evaporate until *poof*...they
seem completely unattainable.

Every year, more than 4.6 million students begin their freshman
year at colleges and universities nationwide, spilling onto campuses

with high hopes, overstuffed duffel bags, and a unique mash-up of bravado and bewilderment. As mental health experts and instructors of the largest elective class at New York University, we know that look well. We see it on pretty much all 450 faces in our lecture hall on the first day of school, and we feel you. After all, you just spent the past twelve years busting your humps for this, constantly reminded along the way what a great accomplishment this would be, what a major milestone it is, how leaving home is this magical rite of passage. All of which is true. But you are also leaving behind a lifelong support network of families, friends, and communities for the unknown, which makes this step in your life as scary as it is exhilarating—an emotional bungee jump into the Grand Canyon.

We are going to show you how to minimize the fear and maximize the thrill.

The guiding principle of *U Thrive* is simple: with proper preparation, you can thrive in college. Period.

Based on our course The Science of Happiness, you might consider this the ultimate study guide. A cheat sheet for the most wonderful, complicated, fascinating, and maddening subject you've ever encountered. The crash course in the one subject you need to master to squeeze the very best out of the years to come.

That subject? You.

We could drop charts right here showing that optimistic freshmen tend to have substantially higher GPAs and better social experiences, graphs indicating that hope results in greater academic and athletic success, and diagrams revealing that positive emotion predicts greater accuracy and speed in the face of stressful situations. We'll get to all that, but first, let's just quote a few of our several thousand students who have been generous enough to give us a 99 percent approval rating:

- "I so wish I had taken this class when I was a freshman!"
- "I never thought that I would be able to truly pursue my passions. Thank you for showing me that it is possible."
- "This class has changed how I experience college. Now I love it even more *and* I am doing better in my classes than ever!"
- "Every time that I have this class, I know that the rest of my day is going to be that much more awesome."
- "The Science of Happiness saved my life."

And a common one . . .

- "You guys have GOT to write a book."

So we have. And here it is.

U Thrive is meant to be a reference book, a workbook, and even a journal of sorts. Just like in our class, we want you to be informed, entertained, and engaged. The exercises we provide will help you with challenges and make the most of the opportunities ahead.

As a child and adolescent psychiatrist, Alan has spent more than a decade helping young adults deal with their challenges, while Dan's expertise in positive psychology and strengths-based performance coaching has focused on helping people realize excellence and reach their unique potential. It is with these complementary skills that we strive to address both the tough times and the incredible opportunities that abound in college, sharing the theory, science, and application of thriving. Weaving research into story and practical application, our style and our focus on experiential learning seek to both inform and transform, turning fear into excitement and anxiety into possibility.

The education system spent the past twelve years preparing you to get into college, but what about actually *being* there? Even the most mundane things about school will be radically different: Raising your hand to ask a question in a lecture hall full of two hundred strangers is a far cry from being in a high school English class with a bunch of kids you've known for years. How you are perceived, not to mention how you perceive yourself, can also shift when you enter a more competitive academic arena and possibly slip from the ranks of well above average to just average or even well below average for the first time in your life. Moreover, the toll college takes on your body is as taxing as the one on your brain: most of you will sleep less, eat more poorly, and exercise less often. Oh, and if you don't, people (including yourselves) will think you're slacking.

In high school, you worked incredibly hard to achieve this goal. You built a solid foundation for studying, critical thinking, and test-taking, developing the habits that secured you a coveted spot at a great school. That's something to be proud of, but unfortunately, that awesome tool set isn't enough to guarantee that you'll thrive in college once you've unpacked your bags. College presents a wealth of new stressors—academic and social expectations, a seemingly endless parade of important choices, and the newfound power of autonomy, to name a few. Suddenly, no one will be around to make you go to class. Or to bed, or to dinner. The ability to regulate your sleep and eating habits will be put to the test. Innocuous decisions—Spanish or Russian? Sorority rush or student government?—take on new (and sometimes crushing) weight. The statistics show that the vast majority of students (at least 83.7 percent of you) will feel overwhelmed.

That's the least of it: A study of 16,760 college students in the United States found that in the past twelve months, 79.1 percent had been "exhausted (not from physical activity)," 59.6 percent felt "very sad," 45 percent found that "things were hopeless," and 31.3 percent had been "so depressed that it was difficult to function." Issues ranged from academics (44.7 percent) to intimate relationships (30.9 percent) to personal finances (34.8 percent). One study of over 16,000 students found that psychological well-being tends to be at its lowest point right about (wait for it... wait for it) now—or at least the moment you enter college. While anxiety peaks during the first semester of *each* year (Whoa! New dorms, classes, professors... again!), the most challenging time of all is your first year, from prepping and packing for campus through the end of your freshman-hood.

These numbers can seem daunting, but they do have a bright side: they show that you are not alone.

During the first class of each semester, we ask our students who, during their time in college, has felt stressed out, or overwhelmed, or has experienced anxiety. As one arm becomes two, two doubles to four, and four becomes a vast majority, the result is not embarrassment for any one student but relief for the group, as head turns, eyes scan, and the truth that they aren't alone becomes easy to visualize. It is a part of the reason that we include polls such as those cited above as reading assignments (and why they are laced throughout this book). Through the good and the bad, *you are not alone,* and knowing that there are others—*many* others—who share your experience is the most powerful force we know to help you thrive in college.

We want you to understand how to develop mindsets of growth, success, and resilience so you can nurture inspiration instead of fear. We know you will have a better chance to make the most of these four years if you understand what willpower really is, how it works, how you can strengthen it, and when it is most likely to be tested (dating, eating, drinking, studying, procrastinating, and oh yeah, wasting time on the Internet, just to name a few). We will teach you why choice is difficult, how too much of it can be detrimental, and how you can set yourselves up to make good decisions even when the stakes are high. We want you to be able to recognize bad stress and good stress, and learn how to set a routine that encourages more of the latter and less of the former. Have you ever been "in the zone"?

In "flow"? There's a science behind that, and practices that can get you there more often. We want to help you identify anxiety and depression (in yourselves or others), and will offer scientifically grounded ways to reduce the risk of their becoming serious.

We will cover how positive emotions help you be more creative and feel more relaxed, and allow you to perform better under pressure, be it onstage, in class, on the field, or on a date. Why do college students who are optimists tend to get better grades, have a more satisfying social life, and succeed at a higher level in almost all pursuits (*and* have a higher average salary seventeen years later)? The answers lie straight ahead—including how to muster optimism when things get tough (and yes, we'll talk about why a touch of pessimism can be helpful as well).

Rough roommates? It's in here (Chapter 2). Find out how to cultivate healthy and awesome relationships. Page 31. Are you dating, or trying to psychoanalyze a Person of Interest? *Why is he so quiet, why doesn't she ever stop talking? Why hasn't she texted me back? Does he like me, or was he just being polite?* We'll teach you how to handle those kinds of thinking traps on page 91.

Is the Freshman Fifteen real, and does it apply to more than what happens when you eat waffles and bacon every morning for an entire semester? What happens when you take a fifteen-minute nap while studying? Or a fifteen-minute walk? What can fifteen minutes of breathing practice a day do for your grades, your mood, your relationship, and/or your focus (none of these answers are on page 15, but they are on pages 163, 190, 204, and 217)? What are the seven things you can do to help you get a good night's sleep, and why does that matter anyway? Page 218.

We'll walk you through the specific steps to lay the groundwork and develop the mindset for becoming an expert in your chosen field while you're pursuing your degree. How do you find a mentor? Give and receive the right kind of feedback? What kind of passion leads to success in both life and school, rather than burnout and depression?

But enough with the questions, already! Let's get these answers rolling.

PART I

STRIVE TO THRIVE

Life is traveling to the edge of knowledge, then a leap taken.
—*D. H. Lawrence*

Picture the moment you were accepted to college. What is the image that stands out? A fat envelope bearing the return address and embossed logo of your dream university, waiting for you on the dining room table? How did you feel? What was the very first thing you did? When we ask our students that question during the first class of the semester, some of them tell us they jumped up and down with excitement, others say they sat down and cried. Like all of them, you probably remember feeling somewhere between thankful and relieved.

That "Whew, I did it" relief no doubt turned to anticipation over the summer, whether you spent those few months working to make some extra cash, enjoying a family vacation, or hitting the road with friends to catch your favorite bands on tour. You shopped for clothes and dorm gear. You pored over course descriptions, plotted out your fall schedule, and daydreamed about who you might become, given this big chance to reinvent yourself.

But at some point, it had to hit you. That slightest kernel of anxiety, that briefest flash of doubt: "Do I really have what it takes to thrive in a whole new world?"

Absolutely.

Everything seems to have changed: your surroundings are different (where are the skyscrapers/cows/beach/sun/snow?), your community is different, and so is your crew. But the elements you need to be at your best haven't changed: from the technical skills and habits you forged in high school, to positive emotions, healthy relationships, engagement, meaning, achievement, and physical vitality, everything you need is at your fingertips.

At some point during your childhood, someone asked what you wanted to be when you grew up. Whether you answered ballerina, doctor, astronaut, firefighter, president, wizard, or rhinoceros, think about what factors led you to your decision.

It's tempting to say something easy, like you were picturing a job that would make you *happy*. But while happiness is certainly a piece of the puzzle, it's not enough to explain why we want the things we want. The ambitions you had as a child—or at any age—are far richer and more complex than a simple smile on your rosy little mug. Your dreams of being a ballerina were not just about pirouetting across a stage, but also about wearing beautiful costumes and sharing it all with an audience. Childhood fantasies of fighting fires revolved around being a hero sounding the siren on your big red truck, but you also saw yourself as brave (and had a cool Dalmatian as your sidekick). And before civics class so rudely introduced the concept of democracy, your childhood self likely envisioned the joy of free amusement parks and drinking fountains filled with lemonade when you got elected president — but also a sense of accomplishment, and people to share it all with.

No matter what you chose, what you were imagining was far more complicated than just "happiness." Yes, today you picture plenty of *positive emotions,* and you may see yourself being super-*engaged,* both in your classes and in your *relationships* with other people. As you immerse yourself in the subjects and activities you adore, pursuing your goals carries more *meaning,* and you relish a sense of *achievement* on the field, in the lab, or in the classroom.

We didn't just pull these elements out of the blue. This combination of the conditions that promote thriving was developed by Martin Seligman, the University of Pennsylvania professor who is known as the father of positive psychology (and whom you will get to know quite well in the chapters ahead). Seligman has assembled them into the acronym PERMA, which stands for **P**ositive emotions, **E**ngagement, **R**elationships, **M**eaning, and **A**chievement (some suggest that "sex" should be a part of this matrix, but that would make it SPERMA . . . and that would be awkward).

When you think about it, very few of our ideal visions of "happiness" are all about the smile. No matter what you are doing or how you refer to it — crushing it, killing it, owning it — you are at your best when you are enjoying *all* of the elements above. And when *that* happens, you've transcended happiness. You are *thriving.*

We tell our students to go through their college careers thinking of each part of PERMA as a single bucket, and that they should remain vigilant that none of the buckets ever go dry. Being the unique little snowflakes that you are (yeah, yeah, we know, our students groan, too), each one of you will need to fill them to different levels in order to thrive. When things are tough, it's time to check your buckets to see if any are empty: maybe your workload has you neglecting your relationships, your work is super-meaningful but recently you haven't found yourself laughing very often, or — one that comes up a *lot* in class—your need for accomplishment has been so dominant that there is not another drop in *any* of your other containers.

Happiness, friendship, and doing something you love: three of the simplest things that have been essential to helping you thrive since the day you were born. That won't change in college or beyond, but while it's simple to identify those three goals as important to your well-being, they're not always easy to achieve. That is why in this first section of *U Thrive* we are going to begin by learning how you can make the most of your positive emotions, have fulfilling relationships, and tap into the flow of doing what you love.

Buckle up. It's time to thrive.

CHAPTER 1

Positive Emotions: The Science of Happiness

All men seek happiness. This is without exception.

—*Blaise Pascal*

We do a lot of things for happiness, but what does happiness do for us?

There is a reason we hurl marshmallows at all 450 of our students before the class on positive emotions, and why last year we prepped everyone for the final exam by turning the volume all the way up on some hip-hop and surprising them with a whipping, Nae-Nae-ing, jerking, twerking, Harlem Shaking, popping, locking, *and* dropping performance by an NYU dance major who goes by the name of ZebraKid, who finished with a sick backflip that sent everyone into a frenzy of cheers. It's the same reason that you should think about how you're going to raise *your* mood before every opportunity and challenge that your campus is sure to offer. And it is for this exact reason that we are going to ask you *right now* to walk through the exercise below:

For the next thirty seconds, please think of the happiest memory you can.

Seriously—as soon as you finish reading this paragraph, set your timer, close your eyes, and think about a moment or an experience that brought you real joy, laughter or elation, or a deep sense of serenity. Put yourself back into that experience. Try to recapture the sounds and smells, picture whom you were with and how you expressed your feelings. Did you fist-pump? Grab your bestie for a bear hug? Laugh so hard you snorted? Perhaps you just sat down to take it all in, closed your eyes, or even cried.

Take your time. Thirty seconds. We won't even write anything on the rest of this page.

(We'll wait. It's worth it. You'll see.)

★   ★   ★

In so much of our culture, we have been led to believe that success (both in and out of the classroom) comes before happiness: "When I ace my midterm, I will be happy," "When I make the team/band, I will be happy," "When I get that guy/girl, I will be happy." But the whole premise behind this logic is seriously flawed. Reaching our goals does not automatically flip on some circuit breaker labeled HAPPY LIFE. Getting accepted to college is considered one of life's great achievements, right? Yet unhappiness (and even depression) for you and your peers is at an all-time high: in 2014, college freshmen in America self-rated their emotional health at just 50.7 percent, a 2.3 percent drop from the same group just one year earlier.

If you are deferring happiness until after you hit your career goals, consider the findings of Lawrence S. Krieger, a professor at Florida State University, whose research on students and professionals alike exposes issues that arise with the mindset of "success first / happiness later." "Law students are famous for busting their buns to make high grades…thinking, 'Later I'll be happy, because the American dream will be mine,'" writes Krieger. "Nice, except it doesn't work." A study of more than eight hundred white-collar professionals shows that lawyers—among the highest paid of all professionals—have the lowest well-being, not to mention the highest rates of alcohol and nicotine abuse.

Still stuck on the idea of playing the long game for the big bucks? *CNN Money* recently published an article about unhappy millionaires, concluding that "the pressure that comes with success can be a driving factor in depression." When the objective is to *thrive*, however, happiness comes along for the ride, calls shotgun, and relegates pressure to the backseat. British business tycoon Richard Branson underscored the power of putting self before success when he told a reporter: "I know I'm fortunate to live an extraordinary life and that most people would assume my business success, and the wealth that comes with it, have brought me happiness. But they haven't—in fact it's the reverse. I am successful, wealthy, and connected because I am happy."

Science is not only debunking the myth that greater success leads to greater happiness, it is flipping that long-held formula right on its head.

You . . . The Younger Years

Four-year-olds are awesome research subjects for a number of reasons: they never show up hungover to a study (at least not in our experience), they have no idea that one-way mirrors exist, and they share a multitude of similarities with one another, making them— minus the occasional tantrum—a marvelously uncomplicated sample group. Proof: Every four-year-old in the world loves marshmallows and cupcakes. Every. Single. One. Thus it was with exactly this group of thumb-suckers that in 1979, John C. Masters, R. Christopher Barden, and Martin E. Ford studied how positive emotions affect our ability to function.

All of the kiddos in this study were given a set of blocks and a series of puzzles that challenged their building and spatial skills. We're not talking about reconstructing the Eiffel Tower to scale here: just straightforward "see picture, build picture," and other standard day-in-the-life-of-a-preschooler activities. Some of the tykes were allowed to simply begin the exercise, while others first had to spend thirty seconds thinking of something that made them sad. A third group was given the same blocks and the same instructions as the rest, with one *seemingly* minor additional task: before they were allowed to begin building the structure, they were prompted to think of their happiest memory for thirty seconds (ring a bell?). Now, these were four-year-olds, so what could their "happiest memory" possibly have been? Playing kickball at recess? Pudding for lunch that day? Watching *Frozen* in full princess costume for the forty-seventh time the night before?

Whatever their positive memories were, the impact was astounding: the preschoolers primed with happy memories were 50 percent faster and more accurate in their solutions than their negatively primed peers, and over 30 percent better than the children who tackled the task without any prompts. Let's say that again: *simply being primed with positive emotion dramatically improved these children's performances.*

Of course, none of you reading this are four years old (if you are, you are *way* ahead of the curve), so we don't blame you for wondering how this could possibly apply to a mature, intelligent college student who would much rather dance around an eighty-foot wooden man in the Nevada desert than eat pudding. This very well may have been along the lines of what researchers at Cornell University were wondering, too, when in 1997 they decided to replicate the study, swapping out the juice-box crew for doctors. Three groups of internists were given a case to diagnose. The first group was simply instructed to commence, while a second group was asked to think about humanism in medicine before beginning the task at hand. The last group was given a bag of candy. Why? Simple—to raise their spirits before they went off to make their diagnoses. (They had to hold off actually eating their treats until later, lest the sugar compromise the study.) It turns out that regardless of whether you're in the playroom or the emergency room (or, as you will soon find, the classroom), a little positive priming has significant implications: those physicians who were primed with positive emotion correctly diagnosed the symptoms almost 20 percent faster and more accurately than their nonprimed peers. Would you prefer a doctor who is more accurate and gets to the bottom of things more quickly? Bring a bag of candy.

The Positive Advantage

Positive emotions prime you to perform at your best. Whether you're howling with laughter or just chilling, positive emotions make you better at almost everything you do. Good feelings are a fantastic learning aid: they help you retain more information and stay on the ball in group discussions; they improve your test scores and your grades; they boost resilience and help you deal with stress more effectively.

The two studies we've already discussed aren't the only ones to back these findings up. In another study, students asked to think of their happiest memories for forty-five seconds retained more words while learning a foreign language, while a group of high school juniors and seniors primed in exactly the same way not only answered more questions on a standardized math test but got a higher percentage of them correct.

More focused on creativity than calculus? Four studies of more than two hundred undergrads at the University of Maryland found that students who were positively primed (i.e., with gifts of candy or a few minutes watching comedy bloopers) tested better at creative problem solving and word games.

Of course, opportunities in college extend far beyond the classroom, and the benefits of positive emotions come right along with them. It might be a no-brainer to suggest that happier people enjoy more *new* friendships, but it turns out that happier people spend more time socializing, enjoy their time more with acquaintances and best friends alike, and are perceived as more appealing and inviting. Even the rocky patches can be navigated more smoothly, as happier people are more likely to talk their issues out, while their more negative classmates tend to duck and hide, a reaction that rarely has a happy ending.

Positive emotions can even give you a competitive edge. *Sports*

Illustrated recently explored the trend toward more positively oriented NCAA coaching styles and found that one of the reasons that the longstanding tradition of abusive leadership seems to be coming to an end is that many players perform better when engaged in a manner that encourages positive emotions (not to mention suffering fewer injuries).

One way that positive emotions help us is by changing the way we perceive the world. Scientists at Brandeis University showed a series of slides—each with multiple pictures—to college students and, using eye-tracking technology, found that those undergrads primed with positivity could recall the images both in the center and on the periphery. Their negatively primed peers? They seemed to register only those pictures in the middle. Put simply, their brains functioned in a different way to change how and what they saw. The theory behind this has to do with our evolutionary hardwiring—being positively primed sends us the message that we're not in danger, allowing us to relax rather than be focused on fight-or-flight. For athletes, achieving this broader perspective means seeing and taking in more of the field, more of the action, your teammates, and scoring opportunities. Breaking away from the tunnel vision of negativity can open creative playing fields, too, as one drama major who took our class discovered.

When we introduced the topic of positive coaching style, Blake raised his hand and said he had just realized that every comment his acting professor gave after scenes in class was critical (to everyone). No praise whatsoever. Blake and many of his fellow students were getting discouraged but didn't realize that the relentless litany of what they were doing *wrong* wasn't helping them do much *right*. Contrary to the pop charts, what doesn't kill you *doesn't necessarily* make you stronger. Blake's drama prof sounded like he needed some priming himself, and we gave Blake a strategy: he approached his professor, thanked him for all his great constructive comments, and, explaining that he was eager to make the most out of the opportunity to work with this professor, asked if he wouldn't mind also telling Blake what he was doing *right* if Blake sought him out after each class. The professor readily agreed, and Blake benefited from both honest criticism—which was easier to receive now—and the positive reinforcement. To make the most of their hard work, Blake and some classmates made a practice of sharing peer feedback after each class as well: three good things that they saw in one another's work *and* three places to grow.

Different Strokes for Different Folks

News flash: it's not all about smiling. There are a variety of ways to express positive emotions, and researchers have weighed in with love, contentment, joy, interest, hope, pride, determination, and inspiration, to name just a few. Nurture the ones that work best for you, and the benefits will blossom. Many of you may find that you can improve your mood by slowing down (through meditation, getting adequate sleep, and reducing your caffeine intake, to name a few options). Others can elevate both their mood *and* their game by focusing on what they're passionate about (choose classes that fit your interests, not just your schedule, and seek out experiences that will blow your mind, like admiring spectacular fall colors, great art, or the performance of an awesome athlete). Each of us has a variety of ways to raise our level of positive emotions; the more people and experiences you explore, the longer that list is likely to become. Not to sound all weird about it, but get into a relationship with yourself: pay attention to what makes you happy, what delights you, and offer yourself those gifts.

Keep in mind that your emotional experience isn't a simple binary equation of "Joy = YAY! Sadness = BOO!" Due to a major issue that affects us all (it's called being human), the odds are pretty solid that you spend most waking hours juggling good stuff and bad stuff like Jo-Jo the plate-spinning circus monkey. Your new roommates might be your dream crew...but you just got the "I want to date other people" text from your boyfriend. Classes rock...but you are totally homesick. You just met the girl of your dreams...but she's going abroad in two weeks. You are ecstatic about starting college...but insanely nervous. How do you even start to process all these conflicting feelings? Know this much for starters: "To be or not to be (happy)," that is *not* the question. It's closer to when you add up the good stuff and the bad stuff, how are you doing?

From Knows to Nose

A young woman is lying on a table with her head tilted back and what looks like a turkey baster held just inches from her nose by a rubber-gloved hand. The young woman? A college student. The baster? Packed with rhinovirus. No, she was not being turned into a rhinoceros (that would be some straight-up Harry Potter action right there). This image comes from a Carnegie Mellon University study on how positive emotions can affect immune systems. The young woman was being infected with the common cold.

Before getting a kitchen utensil shoved up the nose, she and every participant in this study had been assessed for their levels of positive and negative emotions. After they were infected, they were kept in quarantine for five days, having their cold symptoms measured throughout (by some lucky research assistant tasked with weighing all their snotty Kleenexes). The outcome was astounding. Those participants with higher positive emotions were only half as likely to get sick, and if they did, they experienced milder symptoms *and* recovered twice as quickly as their more negatively affected classmates. Happiness not only supercharges our brains, it seems to do the same with our bodies.

(If you would like to get a sense of your current state of emotions, head

over to www.uthrive.info and click on the link for the PANAS scale. Putting a pin in the map can help you know where you stand and track any changes you are striving to make.)

You Leave Me Breathless

After teaching over three hundred classes, Dan still gets nervous before standing in front of the room. His heart pounds, his breathing quickens, and if he is in a particularly rough place, he might even be grumpy with Alan. Seeing as speaking in public is the number one phobia in the United States (and we imagine it's high on the list for our non-American readers as well), we aren't surprised by the response when we ask our class how many of them dislike public speaking and almost every arm shoots skyward.

Performance under pressure probably isn't anything new for you, but college ups the ante to a level that would make Channing Tatum's chiseled chin quiver. From now on, every single grade you receive is forever on the record for future employers and grad school applications. An essay written for an internship application can be pivotal to your future. Big games, big dates, interviews, tryouts, performances, and tests can mean a megadose of tension, fear, and even anger, which in turn will trigger a rapid heart rate, quickened breathing, jitters, foggy thinking (less oxygen to the brain), and poor decisions.

Luckily, our positive emotions love a good challenge and continually find ways to help us navigate such challenges with greater ingenuity.

Research psychologists love to scare the hell out of their college student subjects (it's hilarious...you people will do pretty much anything for extra credit or a few extra bucks). In 2004, once Barbara Fredrickson and her colleague Michele Tugade had the participants in their clutches, they sprang this on them: "You have sixty seconds to write a three-minute speech that we will then film and show to millions of people...BWAHAHAHAHAHAHA!!" We paraphrase (and exaggerate), but you get the point: yikes. While the students may not have verbalized their reactions, their bodies spoke loud and clear: researchers found that participants' heart rates and blood pressure went through the roof. When they found out one minute later that they would not actually have to follow through on the panic-prompting task, though, *the students with higher levels of positive emotion recovered from the shock twice as fast as the others:* their cardiovascular systems snapped back to baseline while the negative folks were still clammy-palmed and breathing hard. Whether you're facing a tough exam or locking eyes with a hot classmate, positive emotions respond to an array of challenges, automatically amping you up or cooling you down as the need arises.

You've Gotta Take the Bad with the Good

Don't get us wrong, it's not about wandering around campus radiating sunshine with a smile plastered to your mug 24/7. There are very important reasons to have negatively oriented emotions (plus, that nonstop grin can get pretty creepy). Heck, we wouldn't even be here without them. After all, when our berry-gathering, cave-dwelling ancestors came face-to-face with something that found *them* delicious, it was that healthy dose of fear that kicked their loinclothed butts into gear. So while your Chem 101 final might not threaten you with physical harm, a touch of nerves can serve as a signal that you want to keep your nose in the books. When it comes to sharing your space with a roommate, the hundred-yard stare that prehistorically meant "I am going to club you in the head with a blunt object because you are from a different tribe" may now translate to "Dude, I am perturbed that you keep eating my cereal and if you do it again, I am going to exact passive-aggressive revenge on your Twizzler stash."

We could say the same about relationships or pretty much any other pursuit: you may not welcome negative emotions, but an upside of your dark side can be the useful reminder to deal with your issues before they get out of hand.

The evolutionary link between negative emotions and survival also means that those emotions tend to "weigh" more than our positive experiences. We're willing to bet that the last fight you had with your boyfriend or girlfriend stuck in your head more intensely than the last time you kissed, just as the game you lost or poor grade you received bugged you far longer than the pleasure you enjoyed from the win or the A$^+$. Florida State professor Roy Baumeister and his colleagues found that having a pleasant day doesn't color tomorrow at all, but after we have a nasty one, the next morning our blueberry muffin doesn't taste as good and we drive more aggressively on our way to work.

One of our favorite illustrative studies comes from the wonderfully named Dr. Hi Po Bobo Lau at the University of Hong Kong. After prompting subjects to think very intensely about a range of emotions, he asked how much they would be willing to pay to relive each one. The results:

$44.30 for calm tranquility
$62.80 for excitement
$79.06 for happiness
$83.27 to *avoid* fear
$92.80 to *avoid* sadness
$99.81 to *avoid* embarrassment
$106.26 to *avoid* regret

Bottom line: bad experiences can hurt more than good ones can help, so finding more opportunities to enjoy positive experiences may be necessary to counteract—and outweigh—the inevitable bad experiences that are coming down the pike.

When the Bottom Line Is a Dollar Sign

If you're not already supporting yourself, you may be soon, and it turns out that while money might not buy happiness, happiness has great earning potential. Not only are happier people more likely to graduate from college, but researchers at the University of California, Berkeley, and Stanford University found that positive emotions can lead to higher pay just eighteen months after you receive your diploma, while a University of Illinois study concluded that happiness in college freshmen was a predictor of higher income nineteen years down the line. Don't get us wrong — it's not that employers are just throwing money at your smiling face while you kick back with a bag of Cheetos and watch YouTube videos all day. Instead, your good humor helps you score gigs that put you in a better position to succeed, no matter how you define success. Grads with high positive affect not only tend to land jobs that have more autonomy, meaning, and variety, but they find their work more satisfying, *and* the work they produce satisfies their managers! Bosses rate their happy employees higher in quality, productivity, dependability, and even creativity. You're happy, they're happy, and your bank account is happy. Win, win, *cha-ching*.

The role of happiness in success has become so notable that some of the most prestigious business schools in the country are prepping future managing directors to be advocates of well-being in the workplace: NYU's Stern School of Business features a class on the application of positive psychology in the work environment, some of the Wharton School's most popular courses explore topics such as altruism and happiness, and Stanford University recently hosted a conference titled "Compassion and Business." Even the most sought-after dream-job meccas out there are actively trying to boost employee happiness. Google's pool and Ping-Pong tables, massage chairs, and video games are there for the same reason that Yahoo allows workers to bring their dogs to work and that Patagonia lines its hallways with surfboards (and encourages employees to use them): *happiness impacts success for employees and organizations alike.*

Paul Zak, the director of the Center for Neuroeconomic Studies at Claremont Graduate University, tested the idea that happiness really impacts the bottom line, and found that at Zappos.com, joyful people were more productive, created environments that allowed them to be 22 percent more innovative, shed the stress of work more than 200 percent better than their less joyful colleagues, and were 17 percent more satisfied with their lives overall. Happy people don't just earn more — they give more, too, volunteering in greater numbers and spending more time than their less happy pals on charity and community service groups.

No one builds a skyscraper from the roof down. Just as pouring a strong foundation allows us to construct ever larger and more magnificent buildings, human beings who build on positive emotions have opportunities to develop richer, more meaningful, and far more successful lives. All too often it's tempting to wait for the A, the job, or the win before we allow ourselves to feel good. But believing that positive emotions are meant to come as a result of our efforts is akin to telling your study partners they're going to do a great job on the test after the prof has already said "Pencils down." We operate at a higher level when primed with positive emotions, not simply when they hang tantalizingly as future possibilities. When you make happiness your first priority, you'll enjoy (and we mean really enjoy) the ride ahead, and be more likely to get where you want to go.

And yes, we're absolutely positive.

Opportunities for Action

Exercise: The Attitude of Gratitude

Dan once had an athlete client who never thought he was good enough (even though the stats and victories showed otherwise) and was terribly unhappy because he was no longer having any fun playing the sport that he'd once loved. Brett was constantly complaining about everything, which annoyed his girlfriend to no end and was putting their relationship in jeopardy. Dan suggested setting a rule stipulating that the first three things out of Brett's mouth when he saw his girlfriend after practice or games had to be aspects of work for which he was grateful (he could then complain all he wanted). It was tough at first, but as it became increasingly routine, not only was it easier to find three things, but Brett starting noticing more frequent positive experiences throughout each day. He began to enjoy his work far more, and his girlfriend began to like *him* far more as well . . . it bled over into his life seamlessly.

Gratitude not only qualifies as a positive emotion, but is also one of the most powerful and wide-ranging we have tested. Consider the benefits with which it has been associated: higher GPA, better social integration in college, lower levels of stress and depression for first-year college students, and even better quality and quantity of sleep.

All it takes is five to ten minutes each night before you close your eyes to write down three things that happened during the day that you're grateful for, and why. It could be as simple as "I am grateful for my friend Sarah, because she put that C-minus on my lit paper into perspective when I was freaking out," or "I am grateful for the sweet email my godmother randomly sent me because it reminded me that I am loved." Period, the end.

The first few nights may be a challenge (you'll be thinking,

"What *am* I grateful for anyway?"), but as keeping a gratitude list becomes a habit, you—like Brett—begin to scan for good things automatically every day, so you not only see more of the great(ful) things in life but rewire your brain in the process. And for those particularly challenging days, you will have built up a go-to resource for reminding yourself of what's good in life. One of our students, an aspiring lawyer named Lily, had to force herself to do this at first, then decided to keep going for months after the weeklong exercise ended. "I truly feel a tangible increase in my well-being and resilience to stress," she reported. "It's been really interesting doing the exercise for so long, because I try not to write the same thing every night, so I end up coming up with creative things I wouldn't expect from myself, like the existence of TED Talks, snail mail, my guitar, etc."

Exercise: The Good Day Experiment

Chris Peterson of the University of Michigan found that by better understanding what makes their days "good," people can replicate the activities that move the needle on their overall happiness. Spend a week recording the good stuff in your life as you go through the day, and when you notice patterns starting to appear, consider which ones you can reliably schedule. If someone compliments your outfit or raves that your hair looks good that day, righteous. But this might not happen every day (if it does, bravo!). Instead, stage-manage what you know will deliver some happiness. If exercise coincides with your best days, be sure to get that on the schedule more often; if it's music, make a habit of listening on your way to the day's first lecture; set an alert on your phone to reach out to your BFF on the regular. Don't wait for happiness to come to you; it's not a ginormous care package that falls from the sky and lasts for life. It's something you learn to recognize, seek out, and gather, whether it's by the teaspoonful or the truckload.

Exercise: Consciously Kind

Whether you're involved in community service on the weekends with your sorority or fraternity or doing a special deed to surprise and delight your roommates on a daily basis, the feel-good effects of kindness flow both ways. UC Riverside professor Sonja Lyubomirsky found that people who perform one large or five small conscious acts of kindness throughout just one day experience a boost in happiness that lasts for months afterward. "Conscious" is the key word here; it's not just about congratulating yourself after the fact for holding a door or picking up a classmate's dropped book. It's about thinking in advance of a nice thing to do for a friend ("It's the Frappuccino fairy!") or family member (call your grandpa—he'll love hearing your voice!) and then savoring it as it happens. Novelty can intensify the benefits, so switch up your acts of kindness (give a friend an amazing hand massage, let somebody go head of you in the cafeteria line). Try performing five conscious acts of kindness on just one day each week, planning what you will do in the morning and then asking yourself "What did I do today that was kind and how did it feel?" when your head is hitting the pillow. Let the best response you got be the scene you replay in your mind as you drift off to sleep. Give a little, and you can get a lot in return.

The Takeaway

The Big Idea

- Positive emotions are performance enhancers for your brain, proven to give you an advantage academically, personally, and professionally.

Be Sure to Remember

- Positive emotions can range from joy to calm and from hope to interest. Finding the ones that fit you best is key to making the most of them.
- Positive emotions "weigh less" than their negative counter-parts, so you will need to nurture multiple good experiences for every one that is bad.
- Positive emotions can help you through the challenges as well as make the most of the opportunities.

Making It Happen

- Every night before you go to sleep, take a few minutes to jot down three things you are grateful for and why they matter to you.
- Track which activities consistently generate happiness in your life, and schedule this activity on a regular basis. Putting it in your calendar allows you to look forward to it immediately.
- During the course of your day, perform five conscious acts of kindness.

CHAPTER 2

Relationships: Getting Connected

I've got a dream too, but it's about singing and dancing and making people happy. That's the kind of dream that gets better the more people you share it with.

—Kermit the Frog

Courtney needed to just let it all out, like...right now. Her boyfriend, Rob, was spending more time than ever with his fraternity brothers, and while she knew that the guys were important to him, it meant that she didn't see him quite as often as she would like. She had met some very cool people in class but had yet to really bond with any of them. Her roommate, Hannah, was supersweet but so quiet that Courtney felt uncomfortable sharing these frustrations with her. Rob had encouraged Courtney to pledge a sorority, which would give her an instant social circle, but sororities didn't feel like her scene. She had always found her crew in dance, where her fellow performers were like family, but that community was so at odds with the Greeks that it seemed like she'd have to choose between the two worlds. Of course, there was nobody better to talk to about all of this than Megan, her BFF from home, but getting more than a text convo going was tough, as Megan was in her own whirlwind of a freshman year, balancing a new job with a heavy class load, and trying to sustain a long-distance relationship with her high school boyfriend, Mike (which, given their two-thousand-mile separation, was unsurprisingly going through a rough patch).

Despite having loads of people around her with whom she could study, dance, date, and party, Courtney found herself wondering if she might ever find a crew of besties, or if she was destined to four years of hopping from friend to friend—or, worst of all, if she would ever really fit in to any of the communities that seemed to be blossoming all around her.

And that was just her first semester.

There is no greater indicator of happiness and success in college than the quality of your relationships. During these next few years, you will become part of the most diverse, fascinating, and colorful community you have likely ever encountered. The people you forge relationships with—whether friend, frenemy, sorority sister, or soul mate—will play a bigger role than you might have imagined in shaping your own destiny. The quality of your relationships will predict whether or not you survive first semester, make it to graduation, and thrive both at work and at home, even in the decades well after you walk that stage with diploma in hand. While many schools are terrific at prepping you academically, we have yet to hear of one that offers an education in healthy relationships.

People who enjoy positive relationships are seven times as likely to be engaged in their work. They also produce higher-quality work, have higher well-being, and are less likely to be injured (yes, injured). It's no surprise that positive relationships distinguish the happiest 10 percent of people, but you're also going to feel psychologically safer and learn more if your social life is healthy. Whether in pairs or groups, students report that doing homework together is more productive than studying alone. We evolved to survive in groups—it seems as though we are meant to thrive in them as well.

Yet a study of more than 150,000 freshmen in 2014 revealed that more students were spending less time with friends than any previous generation in the past three decades. In 1987, only 18 percent of students spent fewer than five hours a week socializing, but today this number has more than doubled to 39 percent. (What's up with that?)

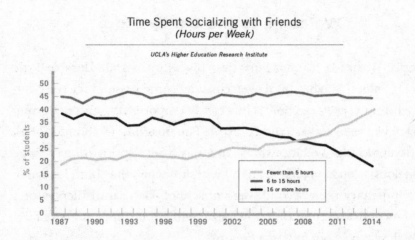

Time Spent Socializing with Friends
(Hours per Week)

UCLA's Higher Education Research Institute

Legend:
- Fewer than 5 hours
- 6 to 15 hours
- 16 or more hours

Simple logic suggests that it's no coincidence the number of freshmen reporting frequent depression has almost doubled in the past five years. And while many of them justify their time alone as a commitment to greater academic achievement, students with poor-quality and low-quantity relationships actually have lower GPAs than their more socially active classmates. Friends can help you deal in those freak-out oh-my-god-I-am-going-to-fail-this-final moments, yet when we ask our students where they go when they are super-stressed or going through rough times, we get a rousing chorus of "Library!" and "Somewhere alone!" and the ever-popular "Under my covers!" Don't count on Student Housing to provide you with positive company: just 17 percent of freshmen click with their roommate…the other 83 percent will be trading theirs in for a different model by their sophomore year.

Roommates, classmates, pals, and partners—we all come to college with the expectation of an array of relationships. In this chapter we will explore what to expect from bromance to romance, what distinguishes the healthy from the not-so-much, and how you can effectively cultivate the former and deal with the latter.

Welcome to the Candy Store

Nerds, Airheads, Runts, Smarties, Big Hunks, and adorable little Sugar Babies. Maybe you'll even consider some Kisses. Like the overwhelming variety of choices in a candy emporium, your peer group has never been so vast and colorful. The possibilities abound for all different kinds of relationships. You may have a spring fling or forge a lifelong friendship, like Dan did with Jon when they both landed in the infirmary their second week of school. Dan sat in silence for a few seconds listening to Jon wheeze, while Jon stared at Dan's face, which was covered in white cream.

"What happened to you, man?" Dan finally asked.

"I was playing rugby and Russ Brightman hit me so hard in the chest that he separated my ribs from my sternum. What happened to you?"

"Yeah...I lit my face on fire trying to do a flaming shot."

The two remain best friends to this day.

So what can you expect, what might work for you, and how can you get the most out of all the different kinds of relationships you will experience in college?

We can all but guarantee that the first person you meet will also be the first one you sleep with. We are talking about your roommate, *of course*, and he or she will determine half of the décor you see when you open your eyes each morning, a fair amount of the music you hear throughout the day, and quite possibly a sizable heap of the resentments you may end up secretly harboring. Your roommate is also likely to see you naked...a lot. Both literally and figuratively. This relationship gives you a chance to become friends with someone who might normally be off your radar—or instantly feel like your separated-at-birth twin. Your roommate can give you—*cha-ching*—an instant social circle! On the days you are feeling lonely (which 50 percent of you reported feeling in the past year), you have a built-in friend to take the edge off.

Your social circle has a significant influence on your thoughts, behavior, and mood. The concept of social contagion is familiar to anyone who's ever ordered an appetizer just because everyone else at the table did, but it extends far beyond our choices. According to research by sociologists Nicholas Christakis and James Fowler, if you spend time with a friend who is happy, you are 15.3 percent more likely to be happy as well. Benefits such as creativity and innovative ideas can also be "caught."

Of course, social contagion works in negative ways, too: Christakis and Fowler found that each unhappy person you hang with decreases your chances of being happy by 7 percent, and when it comes to depression, the number flies through the roof: you are 93 percent more likely to be depressed if a person you are directly connected to is suffering from the disorder. Even the seemingly innocuous stuff is viral: If your roommate shows up packing an Xbox, it is likely to cut thirty minutes off your study time each day and lower your GPA by .2 points. If your roommate is just an occasional drinker, you can lop an additional .26 off your GPA even if you don't imbibe (and .28 if the roommate drinks frequently). If you drink as well, your GPA can get knocked down as fast as the shots you're both slamming, and next thing you know, you're down 0.66. Your roommates (and friends) are going to have an impact on you, whether you like it or not. You may catch some happiness from them, but on the flip side, there are risks of which you should be wary.

The people you surround yourself with are, in fact, your richest and most readily available resource. Together you form an energy reserve of shared experience — all you need to know now is how and when to tap into it. College is famous for weird, wonderful, random encounters, and there's no telling when someone with singed eyebrows will show up by your side and stay there for twenty-eight years (and counting).

Tend-and-Befriend

When we asked our students what they do during stressful times, one junior, Lisa, didn't miss a beat when it came to breakups: "Bed. Under the covers. Usually with cookies." Stressed-out students report holing up in the library, eating their meals with only their cell phone for company, and avoiding the very people who would help them feel better. Placing yourself in solitary during the tough times is like driving *away* from the hospital as your appendix is about to burst. Yet 53 percent of students become so stressed during college that they start to avoid their friends at precisely the moment they should be embracing them.

You may be familiar with the fight-or-flight response to stress and danger (you will be after reading Chapter 8), but it is not your only option: meet tend-and-befriend (T&B), its lesser-known but exceptionally effective sibling. The instinct to grab the person next to you in a crisis is part of your DNA precisely because close relationships can reduce anxiety and depression, bump up your immune system, and diminish physical pain, allowing you to think more clearly and make better decisions.

There is also a preventive component to T&B: A study of more than eight hundred hurricane survivors found that they were four times less likely to develop post-traumatic stress disorder when they had strong friendships. Your tsunami of work may pale in comparison, but its effects can definitely take their toll on your ability to thrive. Indeed, social support systems are one of the most effective coping strategies for stressed-out students.

Dan recalls experiencing T&B on a bumpy airplane ride when the young stranger beside him grabbed his hand and squeezed it really hard for the last thirty minutes of the terrifying flight (her only acknowledgment a very quiet "thank you" upon landing). Alan, being the romantic genius that he is, figured that taking a date to the classic horror film *The Blair Witch Project* would ensure her grabbing hold of him (which might have been successful except that Alan became motion sick from the shaky camera work and threw up). Whether the T&B instinct takes over spontaneously or you deploy it as a conscious strategy, reaching out to someone makes a difference when heavy stress hits.

Support from friends and strangers alike can transform our physical experiences as well. Take pain, for example: researchers at the University of Florida measured the amount of pain experienced by undergrads who were asked to plunge their hand into freezing water for up to three minutes (if they could stand it that long). Some had brought along a friend, while others were paired with a stranger, both of whom were told to act in a supportive way. Another group of subjects had to go it alone, while a third group found themselves paired with a person who was less than supportive. The loners and undersupported groups reported as much as 25 percent more pain than their more comforted classmates. Whether you are recovering from a big night or pushing through a tough workout (or a tough pledge period), study after study shows that having friends around reduces your suffering.

Three weeks into her freshman year, Aleah was stricken by a neurological disorder that landed her in the hospital, unable to walk and suffering from extreme migraines that didn't respond to medication. When she returned to school that spring, she was in a wheelchair. She never missed a single class. Aleah and Alan often seemed to arrive at the same time, and Alan noticed that she went into class more energized each time that he saw her. As she was learning how to walk again, Aleah drew motivation from T&B interactions both big and small.

"Wow, what a concept," she later told us. "I rarely stopped to think about my headache pain, my sore legs, and my next doctor's appointment because I was focused on the friends who visited, the care packages that kept coming, and my puppy, who guarded my bed and knew not to bark and wake me. I could marvel at the kindness of complete strangers, standing in the rain to hold the door for me, at the receptionist at physical therapy who knew I loved chocolate and made sure to find out what my favorite candy bar was so that she could hand me one every time I finished a hard session."

On Romance: From Slow Dance to No Pants

"I think about romantic relationships like maps," said Eli.

During the opening of our class on relationships, we had just asked students what qualities had been key to their best dating and romantic relationships, and Eli's hand shot up.

"I am a big hiker," he explained. "so mountains are kind of my thing. When I look at maps I see an endless array of amazing paths that are waiting for me to explore. It's just like relationships—I can't wait to get out there and see what each one holds."

Dan turned to the class and asked three questions:

"Who here wants to go hiking with Eli?" A bunch of hands went up and Dan joked that Eli was going to have a great semester.

"Okay, and who here is more of a city mouse than a country mouse?" Not surprisingly for a classroom of NYU students, a wide majority raised a paw.

"Who here has no preference?"

Almost nobody stirred.

"That's what I am saying," chimed in Eli. "When it comes to something so personal, people have their preferences, but everyone wants to experience the world."

There is a whole world of romantic relationships out there — the question is, how do you navigate the possibilities to make it work for you?

Not all romantic relationships are alike: some are meant to last an hour, some a night, and others all four years on campus (or longer). Whether you look forward to debating existentialism together until dawn or binge-watching the latest Netflix series, whether you crave commitment or prefer to keep it casual, the most rewarding relationships are going to be the ones in which you feel the most comfortable. That may *sound* simple, but figuring out what you want isn't always easy.

Your ideas of what romance should look like are influenced by what you saw growing up at home, your friends, and of course almost every sitcom or movie you've ever watched. Your personal fairy tale is reflected in what you text, tweet, Instagram, or Snapchat. Suggestions of what you should expect in a relationship seep into nearly every song you hear: a recent survey of Top Ten charts for country, pop, and R&B found that 92 percent of the songs mentioned sex. From dating to mating and all the reindeer games in between, not much is left to the imagination these days. So while it will come as no surprise that college students have serious trouble putting their FOMO on the subject to bed, we hope that some straight-up stats will help you understand that no matter your preference, you are not alone.

Eighty-five percent of your peers believe that everyone else is hooking up on a regular basis (from making out together to waking up together), but in reality, the number is far lower. In a 2015 study of 22,000 undergrads, a mere 8 percent said they *only* hooked up. Ninety-five percent of women and 77 percent of men preferred dating. Seventeen percent of female students wanted *more* opportunities to hook up, and almost 50 percent of men wanted the same (shocking, right?), yet more men (70 percent) than women (66 percent) wanted long-term relationships (shocked again!). Whether your preference is for Mr. Right or Ms. Right Now, he or she is out there and looking for you, too. Finding each other will likely take some trial and error, not to mention a few pints of Cherry Garcia.

When it comes to romance, there is no consensus on how to even define it, much less a compass for finding the perfect partner. Ever had a friend who became fixated on someone and was convinced they were soul mates after a weekend hookup, only to discover weeks into the relationship that The One was more lust than love? Expectations create unnecessary pressure and can lead to the most common response to a hookup: regret and/or disappointment. In one study, by the end of college, 72 percent of all college students had at least one sexual regret, and we're not talking about the missed opportunities. We aren't saying flings are wrong—you just need to figure out what's right or wrong for *you*.

No Easy Answers

Love and romance have captivated poets and scientists alike since the beginning of time, yet neither can definitively explain matters of the heart. No subject generates as many fraught questions or as few evidence-based answers. A student named Jean joined the group clustered around Alan to ask questions after class and wanted to know what she should do about her boyfriend, who had cheated on her over the summer. She still really liked him and the boyfriend wanted them to stay together, but she had this gnawing pit in her stomach. "Would it help if I cheated on him?" she asked. (Two male students immediately raised their hands to endorse this.) "Nooo!" Alan replied. As far as we know, there is no study on the benefits of "revenge cheating." As a therapist, Alan has seen enough cases to conclude that cheating generally pronounces doom and gloom.

College happens to be a hotbed of cheating, with over 65 percent of students reporting some infidelity. About half of students reported ending their relationship due to the wandering eyes (and hands) of their partners, but who knows what the number should really be, since only one-third of undergrads tell their partners when they have strayed. There are few greater ways to destroy trust and damage your partner, and we have yet to meet a student or patient who has improved his or her relationship by cheating.

But not all questions we get about romance are so dark! Take one of the most clichéd clichés in the book: *Opposites attract*. What does that even mean—jocks and geeks won't be able to keep their hands off each other? Classical violinists and thrash metal drummers are hooking up? Entirely possible. It can be a rush to be with someone who has characteristics you don't, though there is some evidence that clashing personalities are at risk for a future apart (it's tough to find a happy medium when a homebody shacks up with a die-hard partyer). But no matter what any online quiz, dating site, or self-proclaimed expert tells you, there is no formula for finding the perfect significant other. If such an equation existed, it would be at the top of every news feed, every day. Forever. If you are looking for love, no matter what your personal definition, here are a few pearls of (evidence-supported) wisdom to keep in mind.

It's More Than Skin Deep

You can find lots of studies about the value of beauty, but attractiveness actually has a fairly low correlation with well-being. For the supermodels and actors out there whose looks define their careers, this may be different, but for the majority of us, our looks do not determine our job, net worth, or happiness. Tempestuous, brooding, and mysterious may work on-screen, but if you are looking to be more than just friends, smiling people are seen as being more physically attractive, intelligent, and competent. Even the genetically blessed among us can find benefits: studies show that when we smile, we are seen as more eye-catching than other "attractive" people who don't. It's not as important to *be* beautiful as it is to *feel* it.

Thrive at Five

If you want to thrive in the world of coupledom, the magic number is five. University of Washington psychologist John Gottman, who has analyzed thousands of couples over the past two decades, has found that when it comes to physical and verbal interactions, those couples who had at least five positives (for example, a nod, a smile, or a sweet "You looked amazing last night") for every negative (such as crossed arms, rolled eyes, or a snide "Is *that* what you're going to wear?") were in it for the long haul. Less than 5:1, and the relationship will likely hit some turbulence, and by the time you get to one negative for every positive, you've got a 94 percent chance of crash-and-burn. Will you argue? Yes! Have rocky patches? No doubt! But knowing that you thrive at five can encourage you to consider the downsides of a critical word and value the upside of a kind comment.

If you find yourself picking away at your partner, stop and consider whether your 5:1 ratio has room to handle that stress. Do you really need to critique the way he smacks his lips when he eats ice cream (true case)? If so, tread lightly, but pour on the positives like chocolate sauce. Greater than 5:1 may not make a relationship perfect, but it can certainly stabilize it. Finding more positive experiences and making more positive comments to your partner are sure to build a stronger bond, and you'll both reap the rewards.

Friends with Benefits

If you are thinking we left out an important category, you're 100 percent wrong. Friends...with benefits. In a study of more than seven hundred undergrads, approximately 20 percent of exclusive relationships start out as FWBs. In a separate study of FWBs, about 25 percent of men and 40 percent of women expressed hope that their relationship would become more exclusive and committed as time went on. Like many aspects of romance, a dose of honest communication can move you ever closer to thriving.

It's Not You, It's Me

Have you ever used the classic breakup line "It's not you, it's me"? It may sound like a cop-out, but there may be more truth to it than you think, and it can be a great cue for some introspection. Part of building a healthy relationship is understanding the conditions under which *you* thrive. Eli's maps offered a world of possibilities, but his attention was drawn to the mountains and trails, for they held the greatest promise of adventure. Relationships involve a good deal of exploration, but knowing how you thrive solo—at ragers or small gatherings, with Biggie or Beethoven, at football games or fine art exhibits—is key to building something special. Just a bit of reflection about your own preferences can move you from "It's not you, it's me" to happier statements about "us."

Why Can't You Be More Like Me?

Wouldn't life be simpler if everyone were more like you? If your roommate were more like you, she would study with classical music playing softly in the background (or crank death metal as loud as the speakers can go). If your date were more like you, she might appreciate a quiet evening together (or embrace a night of party hopping). If your professors were more like you, they would give you a few minutes to think about an answer before expecting you to answer it (or let you talk it through aloud).

But here's the thing: they're not you, and forgetting that fact can get in the way of some potentially great friendships. Is he really *that* stuck up (or is he just quiet)? Does she *ever* stop talking (or does she think more clearly when she speaks)? Can he possibly be *such* a loner (or does he wear headphones in your dorm room because he needs to wind down from a busy day)? Understanding and appreciating how people prefer to engage can help you turn the most puzzling person into a perfect pal.

You Say Tomato, I Say Nothing

Let's rewind to first grade, when the teacher writes a simple equation on the board, turns around, and asks the class, "What is one plus one?" Before she can even finish the question, several hands shoot up into the air, straining to reach as high as possible, while monkeylike sounds of "Ooh! Ooh! Ooh!" escape from enthusiastic little mouths. When called on, one of these six-year-olds might launch into a finger-illustrated discourse: "Well, let's see, okay, one and one isn't one, because that would just be this finger, but...," and while he's thinking out loud, the kids not making monkey noises are watching the scene unfold, thinking, "Oh, come on, Brad...why are you always unloading your crazy brain out loud?! Just give us the damn answer." When the quieter kids are called on, their answer is "[pause to think...pause to think...no squealing or writhing in seat] Two."

Welcome to "Why can't you be more like me?" the prequel.

As the years go by, both types of kids blossom. They may develop rich interests ranging from arts and music to athletics. They might mature into responsible young adults who form relationships in different ways. Who knows...maybe they will even go to college. Yet, while they may no longer feel the need to make monkey sounds when they know the answer, the extrovert's preferred style won't change, and neither will the quiet contemplation of the introvert. Understanding the distinction between the two can spell the difference between loving and loathing your roommate, your study partner, or the person you just started dating.

Most people define extroverts (Es) as folks who are really outgoing, and Introverts (Is) as those who tend to keep more to themselves. While these characteristics are indeed spot-on, the terms also describe where people prefer to get their energy, how they recharge, and even how they process their thoughts and feelings. Es and Is have gas tanks that are drained and replenished in diametrically opposite ways. A super-busy day (classes, interaction, and general campus business) can be premium fuel for Es, while Is may require lower-key activities to top off their tanks. Is like to work alone or in small groups, often in a quieter place for better concentration. Es prefer to collaborate on larger teams, thriving in spaces where there is plenty of activity. The perfect party for an I may include a few close friends, some quiet music, and an evening of board games, while the invite list, atmosphere, and activities for an E are—as one clearly E student recently shouted in class—"Everyone, loud, and a *lot* of dancing!" And if you have ever gotten into an argument with your opposite type, this is likely how it went down: the E announced that if you would just let them say "one more thing" (and it's never just one more thing), everything would be made totally clear, while the I sat there thinking, "If you say one more thing to me, I am so out of here." *Kaboom.*

Understanding how your friends prefer to process is key. Don't take an introvert's silence as a personal affront, or think that an extrovert's motor mouth is a form of attention seeking; these may just be clues to how they thrive. Considering another person's preferred style of communication can be a first step into their shoes, turning conflict into understanding, and opening up a world of relationships for everyone.

Building Your Positives

In her wonderful TED Talk "Saving the World vs. Kissing the Girl," former president of United Artists Pictures Lindsay Doran points out, "Audiences don't care about accomplishments. What they care about is the moment afterward, when the accomplishment is shared." It turns out that undergrads share good news, too, big and small, eight out of ten days, and if you want to experience more positive emotions in your relationships, how you respond to those around you can make all the difference.

University of California, Santa Barbara, psychologist Shelly Gable has shown that only one type of response boosts both participants: active constructive responding (ACR). Imagine how you would feel if you shared your college acceptance with a friend and they reacted like this:

Active constructive responding: "That's amazing! What did the letter say?! How does it feel?! What are you most excited about?! Tell me everything!"

Pretty awesome, right? They're stoked, you're stoked, and you get to recelebrate the whole wonderful experience!

Now imagine if their response was more in line with one of the following three styles:

Passive constructive responding: "Cool. You must be stoked."

Passive destructive responding: "Hmmmm...dude, check out this text I just got."

Active destructive responding: "Whoa. I heard that school is super-competitive and crazy hard. Are you sure you're smart enough? What if you can't hack it? That's really far away from home, too. Gooood...luck."

ACR is a win-win. The others, not so much. In a study at Florida State University, Sarah Woods and her colleagues taught ACR to a group of undergrads and found that within four weeks of using it, they felt increased gratitude and closeness in their friendships. In another study, students reported feeling happier and more satisfied with their lives when people responded to their success with the active and constructive style. In some cases, sharing good news felt even better than the experience itself.

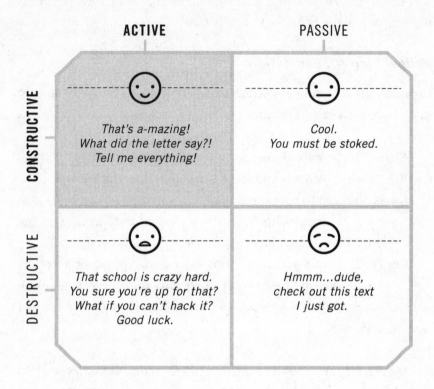

Friendships Worth Fighting For

You can go all ACR and cheerlead, listen, observe, and thoughtfully respond your heart out, but every relationship goes through tough times. Unless you are next in line to be the Dalai Lama (and if you are, *namaste* and you are invited to lecture in our class anytime you would like), you are going to lose your temper, or respond poorly to a friend who does, and when you do, *sha-pow,* it is *so* on. Based on more than forty years of research, the University of Denver's Prevention and Relationship Enhancement Program (PREP) can help you to identify your triggers and turn down the heat before you boil over.

These are PREP's four warning signs that the conversation is moving below the belt:

Yellow Flag #1: Escalation

Escalation is any moment when two people are raising the level of negativity with each response:

> Chris: You promised me you were going to clean today.
> Em (louder): What is your problem? Chill, Martha Stewart.
> Chris (louder): Excuse me if I don't like living in a pigsty! Is it so hard to just pick up your dirty clothes and garbage so my boyfriend doesn't have to step over them? It's gross!
> Em (yelling): It's my room, too! Why don't you paint a perfect line in the middle so you can stick to your perfect side with your perfect boyfriend and let me wallow in my sty if I want to!

Bigger, bigger, *BOOM!* Escalation can feel good at first, when you are all fired up and righteous, but when you calm down, you get the guilty, emotionally messy hangover and feel stupid about things that are tough to take back.

Solutions

Turn up the humor, turn down the volume, and speak from the heart.

- *Humor:* Crack a joke, tango with your pillow, do your best Sia impersonation. Making your friend laugh is like hitting a reset button. And don't forget that positive emotions change the way we think... and can prime us to find solutions.
- *Honesty:* A heartfelt "Hey, this is hard for me and I don't want to yell" can bring you both down to earth and stop an argument in its tracks.

- *Volume:* When you lower your voice, the person you are fighting with is more likely to lower theirs as well.

Yellow Flag #2: Invalidation

Invalidation happens anytime you demean the other person or minimize what they are saying. There are extreme forms of invalidation, like "That's stupid." But there are also subtler ways, such as "That's so obvious" (said with eye-roll). One type of invalidation that can take a conflict to the next level is when we use "never" or "all the time." "You always do this" means you are attacking *them,* not addressing the incident, and that is a deep hole to dig yourself out of.

Solution

Speak for yourself.

Begin your statements with "I" (followed by your feelings) rather than "you" (followed by accusations): "I'm frustrated that the dishes weren't done, I thought we all agreed to pitch in" sounds a lot better than "You're such a pig." This way, you ratchet down the aggression and avoid character attacks—and you're a lot more likely to end up with a clean sink, too.

Yellow Flag #3: Negative Interpretation

Negative interpretation is when we assume the worst about someone's actions.

Unanswered texts from a friend (clearly you are no longer important) or your study partner's lukewarm comments that your work is "fine" (obviously polite-speak for "You're a useless idiot") are prime opportunities to find insult where none was intended. If you're that gifted at mind reading, you need to set up a toll-free number and a PayPal account, ASAP. For the 99.9 percent nonpsychic majority of us, though, relying on runaway assumptions is a recipe for disaster.

Solution

The only mind you should be reading is your own.

Negative interpretation is often the projection of your own fears and worries, so leave the other person out of it and turn the lens on yourself. When we stop assuming we know what others are thinking, we create space to consider other scenarios that won't damage the relationship. Rein in your imagination and rationally consider three alternative positive scenarios (for a step-by-step process, have a look at the ABCDE method in the optimism exercises on page 114). Taking time to consider the less hurtful alternatives can not only help you deal in the moment, but can kick off a habit that will be beneficial in the long term as well.

Yellow Flag #4: Withdrawal

Withdrawal is simply refusing to participate in an important discussion. This creates a dynamic where the other person becomes the pursuer, and it is usually the beginning of a cycle.

> Carlos: What's up? You've been really quiet with me this week.
> Lane: It's nothing.
> Carlos: C'mon. Something's up. We should figure it out before it gets bad.
> Lane: All good. Gotta roll. *(Lane then avoids the discussion... forever.)*

Solution

Kick the habit.

- *Withdrawer:* Talk. Withdrawal can turn into a bad habit because it feels so much better than confrontation. And whether it was your intent or not, it's exciting to be pursued. You need to make a difficult (and yet obvious) decision to pro-

tect either the habit *or* the relationship. You might find it helpful to begin with these words: "This is really hard for me. I
tend to withdraw from conflict, so be patient..."

- *Pursuer:* It takes two to play at this game, and if you are the
  cat to your friend's mouse, you can just...stop...chasing. Let
  your friend know that you are ready to talk when she is. If
  you've done her wrong, apologize and give her the space to
  forgive. As for the great fear: What if the silent treatment
  never ends? If she's more invested in the silent treatment than
  in you...it's on her.

The Relationships That Lead to Great Jobs and Great Lives

Richard J. Light, Harvard University professor and the author of
Making the Most of College, has long asked incoming freshmen, "What
do you see as your job for this term?" After letting the students
meander for a while, he hits them with one of the best-kept secrets of
finding success in college and beyond: Get to know a prof and make
sure that a prof gets to know you. A 2014 poll of more than thirty
thousand college graduates found that the odds of being engaged at
work postgraduation doubled when they had a professor who cared
about them as a person. When they enjoyed a professor who made
them excited about learning *and* had a mentor who encouraged their
goals and dreams as well, their odds of thriving in *all areas* took
nearly the same leap.

Of course, for your professors to care about you as a person, they
have to know that you exist. At the beginning of every semester, we
encourage students to come say hello, and we make time for office
hours or a chat and stroll across campus, and at least 25 percent of
our crew of 450 take us up on the offer. Some come to discuss topics
in class, or for advice about pursuing related careers. Others take

Alan aside to ask for help with their own mental health issues and challenges, or spend time with Dan to explore how they can integrate diverse interests or pursue excellence in a healthy way. Many just come to get to know us.

You can also try your coaches or advisors, or even someone you've long admired or think is a long shot. When he was in grad school, Dan emailed a request for a few minutes with K. Anders Ericsson, the father of the 10,000-hours theory of expert development and an enormously influential psychologist. Ericsson's enthusiastic response (seven minutes later) was "Dan, I will probably learn more from you than you will from me." A lot of your potential mentors feel that way. For many of us, great relationships with students go well beyond talking at you from the front of a classroom. Step up to introduce yourself, and we can both learn a lot about college *and* life.

Opportunities for Action

Exercise: PREPare (Not) to Do Battle

One or two of the PREP warning signs above probably prompted a solid "Whoa...that's totally me." Let's prep you to deal with the yellow flags next time they appear. Write down your go-to warning sign: _____.

When was the last time it showed up?_____
_____
_____.

Write down the three things you could have done to either prevent the warning sign from happening or stop it once the ball was rolling:

1. _____
_____
_____.

2. _____

_____

_____.

3. _____

_____

_____.

Awareness is the first step toward creating change, and looking at your past patterns can help you identify your triggers and potential solutions. Set rules for what you are allowed to do during your next conflict and leave that danger sign out. If you are a withdrawer, choose to sit down and participate. If you are an invalidator, try to avoid accusations and generalizations about the other person. A clue for observing these statements is whether or not you are using the word "you," as in "You always do X, you are X, you think X." Describe their behavior and your reaction to it ("When you do X, I feel Y") and it is much less likely to come off as an invalidation.

Every time you catch yourself mind reading, take a minute to think of alternative scenarios. To defuse the escalation bomb, strategize in advance. You will take deep breaths. You will not "rehearse," or spend your time preparing to defeat your opponent. Heck, stop using the word "opponent" and trying to win, and start trying to *understand:* you're a friend, not a frickin' gladiator.

Learning how to handle conflict is a lifelong practice, so start now. Healthy arguments hold the promise of hurdles overcome together, friendships bonded richly, and of course, the opportunity to laugh about things down the road.

Exercise: Build the Positives

Celebrate a victory with a friend—be it over a burger or on a stroll between classes—and you can elevate the experience from good to Greatest of All Time. If your friend has aced a test, has nabbed an internship, or is just sharing the news of a good day, play it up and join in the jubilation. It's a win-win: encouraging discussion, engaging enthusiastically, and helping to actively celebrate someone else's great experience can generate the benefits of positive emotion for everyone involved.

If you are unsure what type of response style you are using, or recognize yourself in any quadrant that is not ACR, try these simple steps to make a habit:

1. Set a goal for yourself to respond in the ACR style at least three times each day for a week. You can set yourself up with opportunities by asking people how they're doing or how their weekend has been.

2. Be an active celebrant by keeping eye contact and showing genuine enthusiasm (*yes, you should put your phone away!*).

3. Celebrate with them ("That is great!") and ask at least two questions that help them relive the experience ("How did you feel?" "What was the best part of it?").

4. Keep track of your daily count. Even better, write about each conversation at the end of the day in a journal. You'll soon begin to notice that by giving these gifts to your friends, you are cementing the friendships.

The Takeaway

The Big Idea

There is no greater indicator of happiness and success in college than the quality of your relationships.

Be Sure to Remember

- Positive relationships predict greater engagement, higher-quality work, higher GPAs, higher well-being, greater self-esteem, lower rates of depression, and a better response to stressful situations.

- Our friends can give us far more than the common cold. Be they good or bad, mood, habits, health, and even traits such as creativity are viral.
- Finding the right mentor (one who cares about you as a person and/or shares your interests) results in greater well-being and success in work and life both during *and* after college.

Making It Happen

- When your friends bring you good news, make a point of celebrating it enthusiastically and asking them questions to help savor it.
- Reach out to people precisely when stress makes you want to withdraw. Instead of shutting everyone else out to do nothing but study (or hiding under the covers after a breakup), make friends your go-to move.
- Write a detailed letter of gratitude to someone who has had a positive influence on your life. Send it to them, or if you can present it to them in person, even better. (Visit www.uthrive .info for the full exercise.)

CHAPTER 3

The Engaged Life: How Your Strengths Can Help You Soar

> We're so engaged in doing things to achieve purposes of outer value that we forget the inner value, the rapture that is associated with being alive, is what it is all about.
>
> —*Joseph Campbell*

John was no stranger to success. Exuberant, intense, and bright, he had captained his high school baseball team to the regional championship, had been admitted to a number of top-tier schools, and was electrified by all that college had to offer. But by the time he arrived for his sophomore year, he found himself, for the first time in his life, directionless. John had stepped away from playing baseball; he realized that days at school that were once so engaging had become a grind; and it seemed that the harder he tried to seek out fulfilling activities, the more they eluded him.

"I thought college would be the answer to everything I'd been through to get here, but I frequently checked out of classes. Plus the pressure to choose a major, pressure about a career path—basically pressure to succeed—was deflating," he explained. "Without a sense of engagement, the day-to-day didn't carry much significance. I felt smaller. I struggled hard."

Two years later, John is killing it. He has created his own major (The Power of Story and Critical Pedagogy), is a head RA, and is having a blast coaching baseball for city kids. What turned the tide? John realized that he had been relying on "outward definitions of success" rather than looking inside to engage his personal strengths. Once he stopped "going through the motions" and followed his gut instead of adhering to some invisible set of one-size-fits-all guidelines, the narrow door of success he had been trying to squeeze through was flung wide open. College is no longer about "what major" or "what job" he should be chasing. Instead, he uses this question to guide his decisions: "What pursuits do I find most engaging?"

Once he had his picture of success in a frame that fit, the next steps became more tangible. Success is easier and more natural to achieve for John now. It's more gratifying as well. Today John is living the engaged life.

The engaged life emerges when we are using our strengths and talents to meet challenges. Learning something new, demonstrating bravery in word or deed, working closely with others, appreciating something of great beauty, and simply being kind are just a few pathways. When we are engaged with our highest strengths and talents, it even has its own term: flow. Just as John discovered, without engagement in our life, we often feel adrift, but when we cultivate this element of well-being, we can truly thrive.

This chapter will help you understand how to cultivate an engaged life on campus and off. The studies, stories, and solutions will give you a window into the lives of college students who have realized benefits such as:

- Deeper levels of concentration
- Greater levels of personal initiative
- Greater motivation to learn
- Higher levels of performance
- A sense of authenticity ("the real me")
- Happier lives

In the process of writing this book, we reached out to the more than four thousand students who have graced our classroom over the past five years, asking them what topic in our course had the most positive impact on their college experience.

The results weren't even close.

Stories about engagement flooded our inboxes. As one student summed up: "Putting my strengths to use has helped put me in the best place that I've ever been...a strong, independent, resilient woman." This chapter will provide the blueprint that will help you join the ranks of college students who enjoy the advantage of living a fulfilling, gratifying, and truly engaged life.

You've Got Talent

Maybe you're athletic, or you can draw, or you can move like Beyoncé. A talent can be any skill that comes more easily to you than to most people, and it could have been one of the first things in life that garnered you a lot of praise. It also may have led to your earliest experiences of engagement. Being told that you were good at something likely pushed you to dive in more deeply, try to improve, and hone your focus. Identifying an activity as something that "feels right" is a sign that you are engaged.

But full engagement requires more than just talent.

Michael Jordan is famous for his basketball skills, but what propelled him to be the greatest player of all time were the character strengths that he employed throughout his life. After he didn't make the varsity team at Laney High, it was bravery that compelled him to quit crying in his room and get back on the court. When we are truly engaged with something, we concentrate on the process rather than on the outcome, a state for which Jordan was famous. Throughout his career, perseverance pushed him to be the first at practice and the last to leave. This was reflected in Jordan's most famous statement:

"I've failed over and over and over again in my life. And that is why I succeed."

You wouldn't be in college if you didn't have a talent. But if you want to *become* talented—if you want to live an engaged life—for that you will need your character strengths.

Character Strengths: Strong Inside and Out

In his 1999 inaugural speech as president of the American Psychological Association, Martin Seligman (yes, the PERMA guy) called psychology "half-baked" because of the field's near-exclusive focus on illness, and failure to consider "what makes life worth living." Seligman and the University of Michigan's Chris Peterson then set about leading over fifty scholars in the study of more than 250 cultures, societies, and religions to create a system for classifying human strengths that were ubiquitously valued. This would culminate in *Character Strengths and Virtues (CSV)*, a seminal work in positive psychology and an eight-hundred-page tome that can serve as a guide for anyone who is striving for optimal development. At the heart of it all are the twenty-four strengths of character: two dozen pathways to engagement.

Identifying Your Strengths

Marlowe, who took our course in the fall of her junior year, had so many interests that she was scared she would never be able to settle on just one. "I was intensely interested in the music business," she said, yet "I found myself registering for courses in art history, but all the while was totally immersed in the study of French language, and was constantly thinking about how to make travel a part of my life." Like many students, Marlowe was having a hard time identifying her strengths, much less pursuing them with any sense of direction.

To resolve this conundrum, Dr. Ryan Niemiec, education director at the VIA Institute on Character, recommends a three-step process: awareness, exploration, and application. So, first things first: Do not pass go, do not collect $200...dare we say, don't even turn the page until you become aware of your strengths and familiarize yourself with how they suit you. C'mon, we don't ask much of you; in fact, this is the only assessment we will ask you to take all book long. Head over to www.uthrive.info and take the free VIA Strengths Survey (did we mention free? Because it is). It should take ten to fifteen minutes, but the benefits will begin the moment you get your results.

When Marlowe took the survey, she found that her top strength was "love of learning." Then it hit her: "I didn't have a disorder and I wasn't lost—I was simply at my best when I was learning new things. Just being able to name it gave me real freedom to be comfortable in my own process, and school has been SO much more satisfying ever since."

Marlowe's experience is hardly unique: simply identifying one's top strengths (AKA *signature strengths*) has been shown to increase college students' confidence and sense of purpose. While it's a shame that only about one-third of people are familiar with their strengths, given their accessibility and clear advantages, we can't urge you enough to get to know yours and make the most of them.

For the 99 percent of you who didn't jump online to take the survey, please see the complete list of character strengths below. Take a look and check off the five that stand out as feeling like "the real you." Look for options you might use to describe yourself when you have been at your very best.

The VIA Classification
of Character Strengths

★ **CREATIVITY:** Thinking of novel and productive ways to do things.

★ **CURIOSITY:** Taking an interest in ongoing experience; finding subjects and topics fascinating; exploring and discovering.

★ **JUDGMENT:** Thinking things through and examining them from all sides; not jumping to conclusions.

★ **LOVE OF LEARNING:** Mastering new skills, topics, and bodies of knowledge (related to the strength of curiosity but goes beyond it to describe the tendency to add systematically to what one knows).

★ **PERSPECTIVE [WISDOM]:** Being able to provide wise counsel to others.

★ **BRAVERY:** Not shrinking from threat, challenge, difficulty, or pain; speaking up for what is right even if there is opposition.

★ **PERSEVERANCE:** Finishing what one starts; persisting in a course of action in spite of obstacles.

★ **HONESTY:** Speaking the truth but more broadly presenting oneself in a genuine way and acting in a sincere way.

★ **ZEST:** Approaching life with excitement and energy; not doing things halfway or halfheartedly; living life as an adventure.

★ **LOVE:** Valuing close relations with others.

★ **KINDNESS:** Doing favors and good deeds for others.

★ **SOCIAL INTELLIGENCE:** Being aware of the motives and feelings of other people and one's own comfort.

The VIA Classification
of Character Strengths

(continued)

★ **TEAMWORK:** Working well as a member of a group or team.

★ **FAIRNESS:** Treating all people the same according to notions of fairness and justice; not letting personal feelings bias decisions about others.

★ **LEADERSHIP:** Organizing group activities and seeing that they happen, and at the same time maintaining good relations within the group.

★ **FORGIVENESS:** Forgiving those who have done wrong; accepting the shortcomings of others.

★ **HUMILITY:** Letting one's accomplishments speak for themselves.

★ **PRUDENCE:** Being careful about one's choices; not saying or doing things that might later be regretted.

★ **SELF-REGULATION:** Regulating what one feels and does; being disciplined.

★ **APPRECIATION OF BEAUTY AND EXCELLENCE:** Noticing and appreciating beauty, excellence, and/or skilled performance in various domains of life.

★ **GRATITUDE:** Being aware of and thankful for the good things that happen; taking time to express thanks.

★ **HOPE:** Expecting the best in the future and working to achieve it.

★ **HUMOR:** Liking to laugh and tease; bringing smiles to other people; seeing the light side.

★ **SPIRITUALITY:** Having coherent beliefs about the higher purpose and meaning of the universe; having beliefs about the meaning of life that shape conduct and provide comfort.

Signature Strengths: Which Strengths Help You the Most?

Those strengths that will help you be at your best—those that were most helpful in the studies and student stories alike—are called *signature strengths*. Most people have between three and seven signature strengths, and you'll find them among those ranked at the top of your assessment results. If you have any doubt about which are yours, walk through your top strengths with these questions in mind for each:

- Do you feel particularly excited when putting this strength to use?
- When you use this strength, do you feel like "the real me"?
- Do you have a strong desire to use it frequently?
- Does your energy get renewed when you use it?
- Do you feel particularly happy, enthusiastic, or even ecstatic when this strength is part of your process?

If you are beginning to see a connection between using your strengths and being your best, you are not alone. A recent study led by Lucy Hone of nearly ten thousand New Zealanders found that people who were highly *aware* of their strengths were 9 times more likely to be thriving than those who did not share such awareness. Even better, those participants who frequently *used* their strengths were 18 times more likely to thrive than their peers who rarely put them to use.

Waaiiit a Second—How Can THAT Be a Strength?

More often than not, people find top strengths that they have trouble seeing as their own—or even as strengths at all. For example, take a guess at what strengths predicted military performance in West Point cadets. *Bravery? Self-regulation? Perseverance?* Yes, indeed. But we have yet to hear any student *ever* guess that a key predictor for accomplishments as a leader is *love*. Yes, *love!* After initial hesitancy, soldiers realized that one of the only things powerful enough to make one risk their life for another would *obviously* have to be love. Beyond bravery or justice, it's the love they have for the person right next to them. Oh, and a bonus question: What strength predicted the greatest loyalty to their commanders?...Wrong. No. Try again. No. Third time's the charm? No. We say no three times because there is no way that you guessed *humor*—which is the answer. We can all be leaders in our own way: Gandhi may have led through love or spirituality, Steve Jobs through creativity, and Barack Obama through hope. So before dismissing a strength, think through times when you have been at your best—they may be a key to how you shine.

What Do I Do with My Lesser Strengths?

Alan's lowest strength was forgiveness. Now, Alan is a child and adolescent psychiatrist, constantly talking to parents and children alike about forgiveness as an essential component of relationships, but there it was on paper, his lowest strength of all. It made instantaneous sense: the family Alan comes from holds grudges like a judge handing down a sentence—twenty years to life, minimum, no parole. Does this connect with anyone? Note that we describe forgiveness as Alan's lowest strength—not as a weakness. Strengths are measured by degrees, not as absolutes. You can have a lesser strength, one that is lower on your list, but it's always there when you really need it.

Alan realized that a life with little forgiveness was getting in the way of his relationships and began to concentrate on exercising this strength more often. Some worry that working on a lesser strength will be painful or won't bring any of the benefits you get from working with your signature strengths; after all, there is a reason it's down there at the bottom. But in a study of undergrads at Lewis-Clark State College, researchers saw that this does not have to be a chore. Students were randomly assigned to work on two of their top five strengths, or one top strength and one in their bottom five. Both groups found the same increased life satisfaction. Something has to be at the bottom of the list, but if you feel a lesser strength is diminishing your happiness, remember: it can be improved. Pair the lower strength with one of your top five, and not only can it move on up, but your well-being can rise with it.

From Exploration to Engagement

Getting a handle on your strengths is step one, but the real adventure begins when you start to explore them in greater depth. This not only helps you understand the strengths, it also helps you understand... you, and not just any you, but you at your best.

Exploration can begin by getting an outside perspective. When Damon, a student in our class, received his VIA results, he couldn't see how any of them applied to him at all. In fact, he told the class that he thought them so ridiculous, he'd shown them to his girlfriend to get a good laugh. She'd taken one look at the results, pronounced them dead-on, and proceeded to tick off a list of examples demonstrating each one of Damon's top five strengths.

Sharing the language can help, too. Whitney convinced her parents to take the assessment. "The conversation about how we have seen our strengths play out was one of the best that we had in years," she reported. "My dad reminded me that since I was little, I wanted to take care of everyone around me. I figured that was just what people did, but his insights showed me how I always thrived when using my love and kindness. Since then, I've been volunteering at shelters more often and have made a point to send a note to someone that I love each morning. It's an amazing feeling."

Talking, reflecting, or even journaling about how your signature strengths played a role when you were at your best can be a step toward understanding how to use them to their utmost—and a leap toward living a life of engagement.

To Engage Fully, Apply Liberally

Not using your strengths is like carrying a tube of sunblock with you but never putting it on. Having first assessed each participant for their strengths, Alex Linley and his colleagues asked 240 second-year college students to write down their "top three goals" for the semester. Primed with examples such as "Attend most of my lectures," "Have fun and enjoy myself," and "Stop drinking alcohol during the week," participants were clearly instructed that the goals must be personally meaningful. It turned out that signature strengths accounted for more than 50 percent of the reason that they reached their goals.

But the engaged life goes deeper than just realizing goals. Shannon spent a semester applying her number one character strength—"bravery"—in a number of ways. "First I engaged in physical bravery—biking over bridges in NYC and bouldering. I had so much fun and felt a real high from the adrenaline rush I got from both of these activities. I also felt very proud of myself after doing hard bouldering runs, as I was simultaneously engaging in perseverance, another one of my signature strengths." But Shannon took it a step further, applying her bravery in new and varied ways, like calling the son of a recently deceased Holocaust survivor she had befriended. "It was hard to call a complete stranger, but it turned out to be a really great conversation that I got so much out of," Shannon said. "Mrs. Reizman was truly an amazing woman. It was nice to have a little closure speaking to her son. I am glad that I called him, because even though it was scary, it was the right thing to do."

If your goals are more personal than academic, consider Sarah, an army veteran who took our course one summer, expressing her number one strength ("love") by designing a "strengths date" for her artist boyfriend. Having taken the VIA assessment, they discovered that his number one strength had been "appreciation of beauty and excellence," so Sarah took him to breakfast at a particularly lovely restaurant before surprising him with a day at the Metropolitan Museum of Art, followed by a walk in neighboring Central Park. They finished their day by watching the sun set from the highest building at NYU. Sarah's report: "Best. Date. Ever." You can use your signature strengths to make the most of your relationships, be your best in the classroom, or enhance your life in every other way. At the end of the day, your strengths can lead to both happiness *and* engagement—literally: we had a student who credited his bravery for asking his girlfriend to marry him ☺!

Flow: Knowing It, Sowing It, and Growing It

Imagine becoming so engrossed while volunteering at a soup kitchen that you become oblivious to the meal *you* skipped. So intensely focused while listening to a piece of music that you lose track of time. When you are utterly absorbed in what you are doing—exercising a signature strength such as kindness or appreciation of beauty and mastery, skiing or knitting a sweater—when all distractions have melted away and only the present place, time, and action exist, you are in flow. This is what psychologist Mihalyi Csikszentmihalyi has termed "the optimal experience."

As a ten-year-old boy during World War II, Csikszentmihalyi was imprisoned with his family in an Italian POW camp, where he found his escape from the everyday fear and misery by discovering a talent for chess, concentrating on the game for hours at a time and slipping into a totally different world. After the war, he observed this quality in people around him—artists and people who went rock climbing: when people pursued their talents or interests under certain conditions, they discovered a unique type of fulfillment. Csikszentmihalyi went on to devote his life to studying engagement.

Flow has been linked not only with the development of skills and higher levels of performance, but also with greater positive emotion and life satisfaction. Harvard University's Teresa Amabile has found not only that people are more creative when they are in flow, but also that their heightened state of creativity on one day continues into the next.

Whether we are studying psychology, cycling in spin class, or cogitating on what to spell in Scrabble, when we are using our highest strengths and talents and *the level of challenge meets the level of our skill* (see the "Flow" graph), we become so absorbed in the process that our attention is focused like a laser. Too little challenge and we are bored, too much and we feel anxious, but when we find the sweet spot, we enter flow.

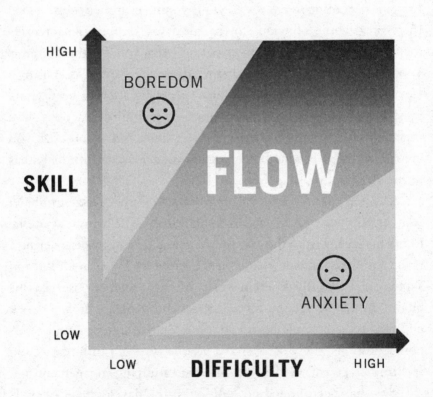

If staying in the zone were simple, we would all just live there, but as your skills improve, the challenges need to keep up, and that means flow is very fluid. Finding the right level of opponents or teammates is key, and for solo pursuits, you need the feedback and goal-setting that will push you far enough to keep you flying high. Skill level and challenge are essential characteristics of flow, but they are not enough. To ensure that you can reach the highest levels of engagement, you also need to focus on the *process* and your *absorption*.

Process

A flow activity is not done for the applause, not to get to the finish line, not because your parents told you to, and not because it feels good, but because the process—the moment-to-moment actions you take—fulfills you. If you are playing a game, you are immersed in the moment, not focused on the outcome. If it's an instrument, there are times when you feel like nothing exists but the music. If it's work—a job, an internship, or a volunteer position—your responsibilities are just the right blend of fascinating and challenging. It's a pursuit you've chosen yourself: if you *choose* to go for a run, on go the headphones and off you go into flow, but if someone were to *force* you to run against your will, time would slow to a crawl (and you might as well). When we do what we love, flow is rarely far away.

Absorption

In flow, you are in a state of total absorption, concentration, and attention. You are so focused that you lose track of time and may not even hear when people address you (you realize that you didn't glance at your texts, despite feeling your phone vibrate). You forget to eat or just don't care to. To achieve this state, you need to be locked in with clear goals, whether that means hitting shots, communicating in a foreign language, or preparing for an art history exam. If you aren't clear what you are trying to accomplish, it's very hard to find the flow.

Junk Flow: The Candy That Rots Your Brain

If you are reading this thinking, "Wait, I become absorbed when I watch TV! Isn't that flow!?"—the answer is no. No one gets up after bingeing on TV for five hours, brushes the orange Dorito dust off their belly, and exclaims, "Whoa! I feel *amazing*! What a rush!" Television is a type of *junk flow*. There is literally no challenge level, and instead of feeling invigorated, studies of junk flow find, folks feel more apathetic. Just as a Snickers bar has a few redeeming peanuts, junk flow activities have an element of flow, but sorry, they don't truly satisfy.

Opportunities for Action

Exercise: Never Stop Exploring

Take ten minutes and write about a time when you were either at your very best or at your most resilient in the face of challenge. Explore the experience in great detail, making a point to focus on:

- where you were;
- whom you were with;
- what you were proudest of, both in the process and in the outcome;
- *and* how your strength played a role.

With greater awareness of how your strengths have played a role when you were at your best, the opportunity to appreciate their power—and *your* power—is that much riper, and your motivation to use them and your clarity about how they work will be stronger than ever.

Exercise: It's Time to Apply

Studies show that applying a signature strength daily in new ways leads to benefits that include increased well-being and fewer depressive symptoms for as long as you keep it going. Review your list of signature strengths and then set the goal of using at least one of them daily in a novel way.

1. If humor is a strength, go to a comedy club, try improv, or volunteer at a home for the elderly with the sole purpose of making people laugh. If it's curiosity, try a new food or visit a place on campus you've always wondered about. If you are still stumped, check out Tayyab Rashid's *340 Ways to Use VIA Character Strengths* (www.uthrive.info).

2. Simply observing someone who exemplifies one of your signature strengths can be elevating. Who is that for you? If you can hang out with them, great, but if not, check out a biography or watch a character on film. For ideas, check out Ryan Niemiec's *Positive Psychology at the Movies* (www .uthrive.info).

3. Choose a class or an activity where you can more actively apply a signature strength. For example, with bravery, you might plan to speak up more frequently or challenge assumptions (nicely, please!). If teamwork is a strength, be sure to start a study group or actively look for classes that emphasize group projects. Planning which strengths you will use can help you make the most of them.

The Takeaway

The Big Idea

Knowing, exploring, and applying your talents and signature strengths provide the pathway to living an engaged life.

Be Sure to Remember

- Engagement may not always include positive emotions, but it is no less fulfilling and is a key to thriving.
- Just like muscles, your signature strengths grow stronger the more you exercise them.
- Peak engagement (flow) is achieved when our highest strengths and talents meet just the right level of challenge.

Making It Happen

- Pinpoint your signature strengths by taking the VIA Character Strengths Test (www.uthrive.info).
- Watch films, read books, and observe role models who exemplify your signature strengths. You can find a comprehensive list at www.uthrive.info.
- Experiment with your signature strengths by using them in new ways in class, with friends, and anywhere else you can. For suggestions, check out Tayyab Rashid's *340 Ways to Use VIA Character Strengths* at www.uthrive.info.

PART II

OPPORTUNITIES (AND BARRIERS) TO CHANGE

My experience is what I agree to attend to. Only those items which I notice shape my mind.

—*William James*

It's finally winter break; you and four friends pile into the car to take a road trip for a long-awaited weekend of skiing and snowboarding (and general shenanigans). It will be well past midnight before you arrive, but your crew will be set to hit the slopes first thing in the morning.

You and your friends decided to take turns driving, and you drew the late shift and now find yourself maneuvering an unfamiliar two-lane road, winding precipitously to the top of the mountain. A recent heavy snow is promising for tomorrow's adventures but less ideal for a dark night at the wheel. The only light comes from your car's headlights, which occasionally illuminate snow-capped signs warning you to watch out for falling rocks, and every so often reflect off a guardrail that seems far too small to keep you from plunging over the precipice into the valley below. The stereo is on full blast and your friends are chatting loudly, but you just peer forward, taking deep breaths and occasionally using your sleeve to wipe moisture from the window.

Thankfully (and with no small measure of relief), you make it safely to your cabin. The next morning at breakfast, something strange happens. While your friends are all cracking up over the conversation from late last night, you draw a complete blank. How is it possible that you were in the car with them the whole time but the only things you recall are snow and nerves?

It's because, as William James put it, your experience is what you agree to attend to — and you were attending to different things (like not dying). While your friends focused on the conversation, your mind was locked in dead ahead, hands tightly gripping the steering wheel and eyes peering intensely at whatever was illuminated by your headlights. You were directing your attention, and in turn your attention shaped your experience. Whether it's on a nerve-racking midnight drive or a normal day on campus, where you focus your attention is key to how you navigate your life.

Atteeeeeeeen-SHUN

Fortunately, not all of life is a nonstop, white-knuckled, heart-pounding drive through blizzards (at least we *hope* not). Most days we just walk down the street with plenty of sensory information competing for our attention — people, traffic, ads, smells, and music being just a few.

But while your senses tend to be casual observers of the world, certain encounters can be so overwhelming that they appear to be seared into your brain. Like the time you glanced directly at the sun, and that big ball of fire burned itself right into your retinas. For a few moments, whether you kept your eyes open or closed, your vision was tinged by an afterimage of the sun. A similar phenomenon happens with our attention, and it's called the Tetris effect.

In Tetris, the most popular video game of all time (and one of the most addictive), different-shaped blocks fall from the top of your screen, and your goal is to fit them into horizontal lines. Every time you complete a line, it disappears. More shapes fall, you make more lines, and your life is slowly overtaken by colorful little pixels. It's a simple concept, but 425 million downloads can't be wrong.

In a study that sounds pretty pleasant to participate in (it beats getting low-grade electric shocks or being told horrible news just so the experimenters can watch your reaction), college students were paid to play the game for several hours each day over the course of a week. It turned out that the longer they played, the more deeply the game lodged itself in the participants' minds. Users imagined blocks as they went to sleep and started visualizing things in everyday life that could be connected into a single, Tetris-like horizontal line. One participant reported snapping out of a near-trance to find herself rearranging cereal boxes in grocery stores, and visualizing the rotation of certain buildings to fit between others as she gazed at the city skyline. In other words, intense and lengthy sessions of Tetris not only shaped the study participants' attention while they were playing the game, but also spilled over into their everyday interactions with the world around them.

You may be exposed to a huge variety of stimuli every day, and most will fade quickly. Yet similar to the afterimage of the sun or Tetris, the places where you focus your attention intently—the terrible grade you just received or the great date you are walking home from (the next morning)—will also stick in your mind. When we give our attention to a particular experience, our focus will shape the way we see, think, feel, and experience life.

The Fast Track

The morning after you arrive on the mountain, you're riding up the ski lift (feeling very lucky to be alive) when you notice something interesting: even though the slopes are hundreds of feet wide, most skiers seem to follow just a few narrow tracks. Why don't they spread out and enjoy the open space? Then you recall your own experience sledding as a kid: you always barreled down the well-traveled tracks because they were way faster than trying to plow through the untouched snow. Turns out that your brain works the same way. As neuroscientist Norman Doidge illustrates in his marvelous book *The Brain That Changes Itself,* the more we revisit a path (think multiple hours of Tetris), the more likely our brain is to repeat the pattern. We have control over the design of our brain's highway system. Changing our thoughts and behaviors leads to physical, concrete differences in our brains and influences those thoughts and behaviors to come (like setting up a path down the ski slope). Thirty years ago, that idea would have gotten you laughed out of a room (well, not any room, but definitely a room full of neuroscientists). Today, it's a fact.

The cells that transmit information in the brain are called neurons. When a neuron "fires," it transmits an electric impulse along its length to the next one, and so on, until the message gets where it's going. Like the snowy track that gets increasingly packed (and correspondingly faster) with every ski, snowboard, or sled that hits it, neurons that fire together, wire together. Every time we focus our attention on the same things, think in the same patterns, or take the same actions, those same neurons fire, and once fired, they trigger thousands of other neurons. The more they fire, the more neurons they become wired to, and before we know it, we're repeating the actions without even thinking about them. This type of automatic cruise control is what makes you always put on your left shoe before your right, or always fasten your seat belt before turning on the engine when you get into the driver's seat.

Thanks to the phenomenon called neuroplasticity, our brains' superhighway can be expanded and rerouted at any point in our life. Don't get us wrong—it's not a simple process. Change isn't always easy, but it *is* always possible. (We'll coach you through the process in chapter 4, "Mindsets: Maximizing Your Mental Makeup.")

The Road Ahead

The great E. L. Doctorow once compared writing a novel to driving at night, observing: "You never see further than your headlights, but you can make the whole trip that way." College is much the same— you choose where to train your headlights, which path to illuminate, as you steadily make your way to the happy ending you want.

In this section we want to set your inner GPS for the most epic four-year road trip of your life. We will share the best techniques for honing your attention and building your resilience. You'll discover willpower's best-kept secret and how to hack it. Most important of all, we'll alert you to the potential rockslides, potholes, and hairpin turns as your journey progresses, and show you how to reclaim your sanity when you feel like you are about to lose it—or feel like you already have.

CHAPTER 4

Mindsets: Maximizing Your Mental Makeup

A mind that is stretched by a new experience can never go
back to its old dimensions.

—*Oliver Wendell Holmes*

Running a mile in under four minutes was supposed to be
impossible. In 1954, the conventional wisdom was that our muscles,
tendons, and bones were incapable of sustaining the pace necessary
for such a feat. But British runner Roger Bannister wasn't conventional.
He believed differently, and on May 6, 1954, became the first human
being to break the four-minute barrier, running the mile in three
minutes and 59.4 seconds. To put this feat into context, Bannister ran
a mile in less time than it takes to poach an egg. It was an incredible
accomplishment, but it wasn't the end of this story. Only one month
after Bannister's landmark effort, the record was broken again.
Within a year, the record was broken four more times, and as of
2016, a sub-four-minute mile has been achieved more than five
thousand times.

It wasn't physical capabilities that constrained runners before
Bannister, it was the mental ceiling they kept hitting. Like so many
limits, the four-minute barrier was all in the mind. Once that barrier
was broken, the imagination of what was possible for the human

body was forever altered—not just for Bannister, but also for those who followed him.

Bannister didn't just break a record, he shattered a mindset.

Mind Games: Challenging Our Limitations

While some of us may not have a mindset regarding the human capacity to run swiftly, there are mindsets that many of us share. A mindset is any firmly held belief about our qualities or what we are capable of, physically, intellectually, or in any other sense imaginable. It is determined by every experience we have ever had: our accomplishments and failures in kindergarten, how our parents praised and punished us, relationships that brought us agony or ecstasy, and every lesson that taught us about our limits, or lack of them. Our mindsets are often called implicit, meaning we are rarely aware of how they were formed and believe in them as truth everlasting. That is, until we bring our attention to them. Your mindset about mindsets is being built as you read these very words (whoa ... meta), and if we've done our jobs, it will continue to develop throughout this chapter.

Our mindsets affect the decisions we make, how we understand our own personalities, our relationships, our levels of intelligence, and even the classes we take and the internships we apply for. They will dictate our potential for change, motivation, behavior, learning style, performance, and potential. Some mindsets provoke a lot of debate (e.g., does life begin at conception or at birth?), but it is the ones that are rarely questioned or contemplated that we will focus on in this chapter. As important as your mindsets are, it can be tough to step back far enough to recognize their role in your life. As with the people who didn't believe the four-minute mile was possible, sometimes your mindset can blind you to your true potential.

With the right kind of knowledge and a bit of practice, you can learn to observe your mindsets, evaluate them, and, as your awareness increases, alter them to maximize your potential to thrive. In this chapter we will also show you how to develop awareness of the thoughts that we don't have as much control over (after all, they are called automatic thoughts). When we confront tough situations in life, these thoughts can turn sour and are referred to as thinking traps. We'll give you some advice on how to pull yourself out of that kind of emotional quicksand.

You can develop mindsets to help you slay challenging courses, recover from a bad breakup, or steer out of any other skid in the road that is uniquely yours. The mindsets you establish now open you up to all the extraordinary people, ideas, and experiences that are available in college, building not just knowledge but a deeper understanding of the "real world" you're on the verge of stepping into.

Fixed vs. Growth Mindsets

For Stanford University's Carol Dweck, there are two essential types of mindsets: fixed and growth.

If you have ever been told (or perhaps have said), "I can't change that, it's just the way I am," you have encountered a *fixed* mindset. If someone can't change whatever "that" is (attitude, ability, belief, you name it), what's the point of trying? None. Drop the mike, conversation over. If we don't believe we can change, there's no reason to try. Feedback? No thank you. Tutors? Waste of pizza money. If the grades aren't good now, they never will be. When someone with a fixed mindset bombs a test, their effort (and often interest) in the class drops with it.

Even when they do well, it is often not enough. During college, Alan couldn't look himself in the mirror if he had less than a perfect grade in hand. He spent a lot of time feeling disappointed. In his senior year, his dream finally came true when a biology exam came back with a score of 105. Better than perfect! Rejoice! But then he noticed that there had been a 20-point curve, and his immediate thought was: "I could have gotten a 120." He quickly threw the test away, but even eight years before becoming a psychiatrist, Alan knew that something was wrong with his reaction.

People with *growth* mindsets are the opposite. Regardless of their results, they are always looking for ways to improve. Smack a student with a growth mindset in the face with a paper full of red ink and they'll respond with a tsunami of effort and tenacity. For people with growth mindsets, a loss is a lesson and a bad grade on a paper is a fine opportunity to practice revision skills. Feedback? Bring it. Challenges? The bigger the better. When you know that you can change, that you can learn, and that you can improve, every challenge is an opportunity.

Now that you are becoming familiar with some characteristics of the two mindsets, have a look at the graphic on the next page.

Given the differences between the two mindsets, it's not hard to figure out that a student with a growth mindset is more likely to thrive, whereas a student with a fixed mindset is going to live in survival mode. Before you despair at having a fixed mindset, it's important to remember that mindsets are rarely all-encompassing. You may see yourself as having a fixed mindset in class ("I can't get any smarter") but having a growth mindset in relationships ("I am really inspired by how she pushes my boundaries"). Most important, mindsets change. By the time Alan reached medical school, his mindset had been altered significantly. On his very first exam, the passing grade was a 67, and Alan received a 67.5 along with a handwritten note by the professor: "You may have passed this exam, but you do not know the material." Alan fought his instinct to crumple up the blue book and browbeat himself, instead searching out a TA so he could learn where he had screwed up and figure out how to be

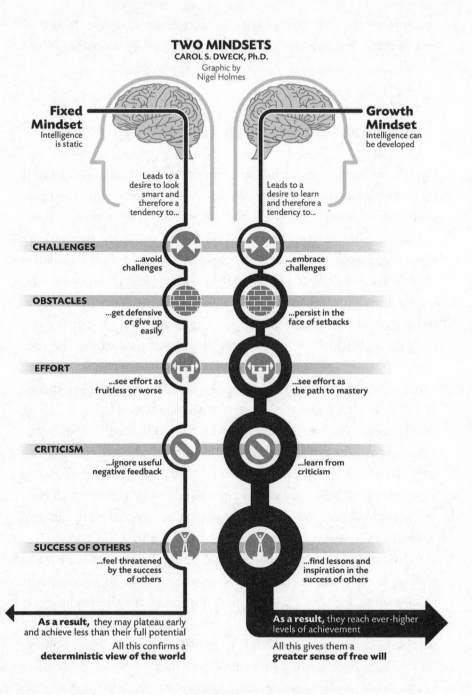

TWO MINDSETS
CAROL S. DWECK, Ph.D.
Graphic by
Nigel Holmes

Fixed Mindset
Intelligence is static

Leads to a desire to look smart and therefore a tendency to...

Growth Mindset
Intelligence can be developed

Leads to a desire to learn and therefore a tendency to...

CHALLENGES
...avoid challenges

...embrace challenges

OBSTACLES
...get defensive or give up easily

...persist in the face of setbacks

EFFORT
...see effort as fruitless or worse

...see effort as the path to mastery

CRITICISM
...ignore useful negative feedback

...learn from criticism

SUCCESS OF OTHERS
...feel threatened by the success of others

...find lessons and inspiration in the success of others

As a result, they may plateau early and achieve less than their full potential

All this confirms a **deterministic view of the world**

As a result, they reach ever-higher levels of achievement

All this gives them a **greater sense of free will**

better prepared for his next exam. Perfection was no longer the be-all and end-all. Progress, it turned out, was just as valuable, if not more so.

Intelligence: How Much Smarter Can You Be?

Dweck has studied the mindsets of thousands of students and found that approximately 40 percent of them have a fixed mindset, 40 percent have a growth mindset, and 20 percent cannot be classified. When we label our abilities, we limit our possibilities, particularly when it comes to intelligence. Saying "I'm a B student" may limit the effort you are willing to put into a paper or the time you spend studying for an exam, since for you, it is a predetermined outcome. On the flip side, students who believe that "learning is about the effort you put into it" will likely find themselves learning anything they set their mind to. They're the ones who come back from a semester abroad fluent in Swedish because they translated every sign, menu, and museum brochure they came across and refused to let their host family speak English. Like your muscles, your brain doesn't gain without pain (or at least strain). You might find yourself puzzling over things a little longer than you'd like to and rubbing off all the vowels on your keyboard as you revise and revise again, but as with any good workout, you'll feel like you have accomplished something when it's over—and you know what? You have.

Our mindsets determine how we define success and failure as well. A great grade feels good to anyone who earns it (as well it should!), but for those with growth mindsets, it's the *improvement* that is the biggest reward, the payoff for the time and effort they invested. Think of "Fixed" and "Growth" as two people at point A on the map, both aiming for point B, where they will receive their grade. *Fixed* jumps into the nearest rental car, hits the accelerator, and zooms up the interstate to point B. *Growth* boards a train and sits next to a native of point B, who tells an amazing story about its history and clues Growth in on a detour to sample the world's greatest artisanal chocolate. Growth gets off at the next stop and heads straight to the shop, falls madly in love with the chocolatier's son, who offers to take her the rest of the way to point B on his Vespa, but they puncture a tire, which the chocolatier's son fixes using pine sap from a nearby tree, who knew? Anyway, Growth arrives at point B three days after Fixed, who has collected his A grade, but that's it. Growth may have gotten an A or a B grade, but either way also found her soul mate, started a GoFundMe campaign that's already raised thousands in venture capital for her line of miracle pine-sap products, and learned so much about point B's fascinating history that she realizes Fixed left his car parked on top of an ancient burial ground and is going to have really, really bad karma for the rest of his life. Growth: winning.

Now, regardless of a fixed or growth mindset, perfect test scores feel great, but if the end result doesn't turn out like they want it to, those with fixed mindsets can struggle to reconcile themselves with failure. Fixed-mindsetters are more likely to feel shame about a bad grade and more likely to want to get rid of the evidence. Without the sense that they can handle challenges and accomplish things, a bad grade must mean that they just aren't that smart, full stop.

To understand your mindset about intelligence, think about that gut-wrenching moment when your SAT scores arrived. Imagine if you had torn the envelope open after all that test prep, your future in the balance, to find (drumroll, please)...a pathetically low score. This CAN'T be right! But wait, there's a second page that lists a high score. You totally crushed it! Until you realize that the page with the higher score has a different student's name on it. It must have been mistakenly folded into your envelope. How would you react?

That's the basic premise of a diabolical scenario that researcher

Ying-yi Hong and her colleagues devised to test the mindsets of undergraduates at Columbia University. Researchers wanted to find out how a person's mindset determined their reaction to an embarrassingly low grade. The students were assessed for fixed or growth mindsets around intelligence and then given an exam. Regardless of their performance, all of the students received low scores but were then "mistakenly" shown an (imaginary) classmate's much higher grade. Asked to reflect on their performance and their plans to move forward, the growth-mindset students were twice as likely to say they believed that even though they'd done poorly, their effort still mattered. Most everyone is going to be humbled at one time or another, but with a growth mindset, there is always another chance at redemption. It's not that intelligence is irrelevant, but if you believe you can become smarter through effort, you are more likely to find the motivation to keep working.

A growth mindset not only helps us make the effort to push *ourselves,* it also makes it more likely that we will reach out for help from *others.* Hong and her colleagues offered 150 Chinese students who were studying at an English-speaking university the opportunity to take a master class in English. That's a no-brainer, but the students with a growth mindset were 20 percent more likely than the fixed-mindset students to take her up on this offer. For those with a fixed mindset, seeking help is an admission that they are not intelligent, and that's something to be avoided at all costs — even if it ends up costing them plenty.

When the Going Gets Tough, the Tough Get Growing

We wouldn't devote a chapter to mindsets if they couldn't be changed (that would mean we had fixed mindsets, anyway).

Mindsets are often shaped without our awareness, but that doesn't mean we don't have a say in changing them, and that other people can't act covertly to change your beliefs—it's called priming. You are being primed constantly by every billboard, commercial, and pop-up ad you see. If you've ever chosen the expensive designer shoes over the knockoff pair with the slightly misspelled label, you've been primed. You are priming yourself when you are getting pumped up (or worrying yourself silly) before a big game, show, or date. When something or someone, including yourself, is preparing you to take a specific course of action, you are being primed.

In another experiment conducted by Hong and Dweck, the researchers tested the effects of priming mindsets. One group of undergrads read an article explaining that intelligence could only shift by 1 or 2 percentage points (a fixed-mindset view), while the remaining participants were exposed to material indicating that we can increase our IQ by 50 percent (a growth-mindset view). Both groups then took an exam, and all subjects received a score that (falsely) put them in the bottom twentieth percentile. The type of priming each student received had a massive effect on how they responded: when offered the option to work on a tutorial that could improve their score on the next exam, only 13 percent of the group who had been exposed to the fixed-mindset readings chose to do so, but a whopping *73 percent* of the students primed with a growth mindset accepted the help.

Exposure to just the *idea* that they could improve changed both their attitude and their action (it's why we hold out hope that this chapter might do the same!). What might it do for you? Jocelyn approached Alan after the class on mindsets because she'd had the revelation that she was 100 percent fixed. Jocelyn was exhausted by constantly trying to prove her self-worth every time she took an exam or handed in a paper. Her writing was especially important to her, and when she got negative feedback on a paper, it felt like a third-degree burn. Jocelyn couldn't hear the feedback; instead, all she ended up feeling was judged. Alan challenged Jocelyn to consider that when people are giving her feedback, they do so simply because they care about helping her improve, and wouldn't invest the time if they didn't believe she could. He suggested that she consider some questions the next time a paper was returned to her: "How do I use these comments to improve my writing? What do they give me the opportunity to learn?" He encouraged her to thank the teacher or TA for giving her the feedback, to shift her perception of them from critic to ally. Two weeks later Jocelyn gave him a thumbs-up and said, "I got a paper back last week and it was awesome. I told myself that it would just be one big opportunity, and that's exactly what it was."

When it comes to understanding your mindsets, once the cat's out of the bag, you can't put it back in. You may now bring your attention to the mindsets that shape your experience and take control of how you succeed in college. By reshaping mindsets, we can reshape our brains, grow our intelligence, experience new challenges, and even embrace some failure.

Mindsets and Relationships

Efforts to change a mindset can not only improve your academic performance, they can pay off in your relationships with friends, colleagues, family members, and romantic interests. Aaron Beck, the father of cognitive therapy, notes that there are people who believe there is something wrong with a relationship if it requires effort. Beck also notes that these people are mistaken. While navigating your relationships shouldn't feel the same as slogging through a tough physics class (at least not most of the time), people who believe in the capacity of others to change are more likely to overcome their fear of conflict and invest the time and energy to work things out rather than walk away.

Of course, when it comes to relationships, our mindsets not only determine how (and if) we deal with the tough times, but also influence who we connect with in the first place. Yes, that hottie you've been eyeing in class looks awesome; yes, they make you laugh; yes, they are fascinating/fun/cool/comfortable to be with. But part of the attraction lies in what you can't see: whom we look for in a partner is closely interwoven with what type of mindset we lean toward.

Just as someone with a fixed mindset seeks validation in the classroom, they may have some of the same demands in relationships. That might influence them to date people who:

- worship them
- give them status on campus
- elevate them in their parents' eyes
- make them look good

If you are spotting a trend here, good eyes: if you are certain you can't change, you might as well find someone who can make you *look* better. You may also notice that none of those attributes have to do with how our fixed-mindset friend actually gets along with the other person (does that seem as weird to you as it does to us?). Arm candy may be fun for a little while, but it's not enough to sustain you. It's tough to grow together when nobody is actually growing.

Speaking of growth, that is (unsurprisingly) the core of what people with a growth mindset value in a partner, often connecting best with those who:

- challenge them to grow
- make them understand how they can improve themselves
- give them experience in understanding others

Not that any of us want relationships to be all challenge all day long, but when we are willing to consider change (and when our partners are, too), we may find much greater success. Take this scenario, for example:

> You: If I'm being honest, I can't get back to sleep when you hit your snooze button like seven times before you get up.
>
> Them: I wish I could do something about it, but that's how I've always been.

This isn't going to be a productive conversation. However, a response such as "I totally hear you. Let me see what happens when I just set my alarm for twenty minutes later" or "Let's see if I can reduce my number of snoozes by a couple every morning" bodes far better for your relationship going forward.

Psychologists Laura Kammrath and Carol Dweck looked at the propensity of undergraduates to speak up when their relationships, both friendly and romantic, get problematic. Low-level disagreements, such as what music to play in the car, didn't reveal much difference between those with fixed and growth mindsets. But when it came to issues that deeply upset one person in the relationship, students with growth mindsets were more likely to speak up, while those with a fixed mindset simply "lost their voice." Fixed-mindsetters were more prone to leave a relationship without trying to improve it. Although there are times when this may be the right move, you want to be making decisions based on conscious choice rather than acquiescing to your fixed mindset.

Relationships can help you thrive, but *only when you let them*, keeping yourself open to — even welcoming — the new experiences and feedback that can help you grow and improve together. Mindsets about what a relationship should look like, or how it can operate, or whether or not you can speak your mind, will help determine how your friends and more-than-friends can impact your life (and vice versa). Growth can be tough, but when you set the right mindset, it can be a total adventure.

Mind the Thinking Traps

Thomas texts Kylie to see if she'd like to hang out on Friday night. Kylie apologizes but says she's busy. When Thomas assumes that Kylie is not interested in going out with him...*ever*...he has fallen into the thinking trap of *jumping to conclusions:* a broad conclusion based on a single event or an inconclusive piece of evidence. When Taylor's roommate walks into the kitchen in silence, slams her books down, and walks out of the room, the first thought that runs through Taylor's mind is "Why is she pissed at me?" Taylor is *personalizing:* assuming that what people say or do is a reaction to us. Thomas can spend the rest of the day, or, perhaps week, reviewing what happened, even though he should simply have responded by asking if Kylie was free on Thursday instead. And Taylor could save herself some anxiety and annoyance simply by checking in to see what's up with her roommate.

How we react to challenging events dictates both our experience and the outcome. These reactions are often experienced as a series of thoughts that appear so spontaneously they are called automatic, and when they are incorrect, like the examples with Thomas and Taylor, we call them thinking traps. Given a bit of distance from the scenarios, they can almost seem silly. But because we have no distance at all from our own thinking traps (not even a centimeter), they can totally overwhelm us, sucking us in like sinkholes.

Thinking traps are not always easy to break out of, because even though they are false, we presume them to be correct. Obviously, there was no scary clown in your closet when you were five, but your belief that there was made the monster real enough, and even now that you're an adult, thinking traps can leave you feeling like you're stuck in a horror movie. The first thing you need to do is shed some light on things with a little awareness. These are some of the most common thinking traps:

Thinking Traps

JUMPING TO CONCLUSIONS	A broad conclusion based on a single event or an inconclusive piece of evidence.
PERSONALIZING	Assuming that a negative response is a reaction to you.
CATASTROPHIZING	When we believe the only possible outcome is the worst thing imaginable.
BLACK-OR-WHITE THINKING	You look at situations or people in terms of extremes: good or bad, success or failure.
MIND READING	We believe we know what others are thinking and assume the worst.
NEGATIVE FILTER	When you can only see the downsides in yourself or in a situation.
LABELING	We talk to ourselves or about others in cruel ways, often using a single word like "I/they are (insert word)."
SHOULD-MUST STATEMENTS	When we tell ourselves how we "should" or "must" be even though it is not how we actually feel.

When you read the list of thinking traps, you might recognize a few or feel like you run through the whole list every day. The higher the stress, the more traps tend to be bouncing around in your head. You can get so caught up in them that it becomes hard to think of anything else, let alone actually deal with the challenge that triggered them in the first place. Now that you know how to recognize them, you can find ways below to dismantle them.

Opportunities for Action

Exercise: Dismantling Your Thinking Trap

Choose the thinking trap that pops up in your head with the most frequency. Below are a series of clues and questions. The clue is there to remind you of the trap, while the question allows you to avoid it, giving you a shot at aligning your thoughts and reality.

Thinking Traps: Clues and Questions

JUMPING TO CONCLUSIONS	**Clue:** Using the word "always" or "never." **Question:** What is the one thing that is truly affected by my/his/her behavior/response?
PERSONALIZING	**Clue:** It's all about me, me, me. **Question:** What are some other possible drivers for their behavior?
CATASTROPHIZING	**Clue:** I'm predicting Armageddon. **Question:** What are some other possible outcomes? If the worst happens, how will I manage it?
BLACK-OR-WHITE THINKING	**Clue:** Using a word like "perfect" or "failure" or "all" or "nothing." **Question:** How can I look at this from a pro/con perspective?
MIND READING	**Clue:** You believe you have telepathy. **Question:** What questions could I ask that would provide clarity?
NEGATIVE FILTER	**Clue:** Negativity takes up the entire map you call a mind. **Question:** What are some of the positives in this situation?
LABELING	**Clue:** We are summing up ourselves/others in one word. **Question:** Describe yourself/him/her with at least three words, no two alike.
SHOULD-MUST STATEMENTS	**Clue:** You are putting an unreasonable demand on yourself. **Question:** Who is to tell me how I should or must be feeling right now?!

Once you have chosen the thinking trap you most identify with, try these two steps to dismantle it:

1. Write down three incidents where this trap has been sprung during the recent past.

2. Commit to staying vigilant for the clue and using the corresponding question for the next week, and track your daily success.

Getting frustrated with yourself is more often a sign that your thinking traps are getting the best of you. Once you finish dismantling your first thinking trap, feel free to move on to the next. As you develop your skill at dismantling thinking traps, you will have the opportunity to live more of your life with your thoughts and not trapped by them.

Exercise: Fixed to Growth

Letting go of our fixed mindsets isn't necessarily easy, but if priming a person with a paragraph can make a difference, imagine what you are capable of now that you have read this chapter. Your imagination is exactly what Carol Dweck wants you to explore in the hopes that you will develop a growth mindset.

Dweck has broken down the transformation from fixed to growth mindset into three very practical steps:

1. Learn to hear your fixed-mindset "voice." This is the voice that reminds you that you are not smart enough, fast enough, or, perhaps, good-looking enough. Try to pinpoint an area where you consistently hear your fixed "voice."

2. Once you hear the fixed voice, talk back! Recognize that you have a choice. You can't control life, but your decisions are up to you; if you hear the fixed voice telling you to give up, or not even try, imagine what a good response would be. If you can't think of one, what would a friend, one with a powerful growth mindset, say to that voice (or to you)? Whatever you are saying you can't do, add a "yet" to the end of the sentence and it is instantaneously more consistent with a growth mindset.

3. Talk back, and take action. Your fixed mindset wins if you don't then take the growth-mindset action. Get feedback,

put yourself out there even though you might fail, and you will become aware of how good these actions make you feel. They are literally win/win—either you do well and learn something, or you don't, in which case you may learn even more. It's okay to have lots of self-doubt even as you move forward. Make an irreversible decision to take the growth-mindset action—the more you do so, the easier it becomes to commit to more of them.

Exercise: Putting On the Growth Mindset

Would you like to change your mindset as easily as you change clothes? In a way, you can. On October 31, you put on the Catwoman, Tarzan, or vampire costume and take advantage of a certain license to act differently. Hiss at strangers or ask to suck their blood if you want. Yodel with abandon.

How we dress impacts our mindsets regarding appropriate behavior on Halloween—and the other 364 days of the year. Studies have shown that college students wearing a white lab coat were found to be more attentive and careful when carrying out tasks compared to their un-coated peers. As we've seen in the studies earlier in the chapter, sometimes the oh-so-slightest mental shifts can change our experience. When we are aware of those shifts, we can use their power to push our brains in productive directions that help us thrive.

One of the most valuable places to put on the right mindset is when we enter the classroom, the library, or any other venue where we are learning or being put to the test. As you approach academic challenges, ask yourself the following three questions to put yourself in the right mindset:

1. What are the materials or experiences that put me into a growth mindset? Is it the way I dress, taking a shower, or going for a jog?

2. What is the mindset I want when I enter a classroom, an exam room, or a space where I will be performing? Is it one expecting to learn something, at least one thing, or is it a mindset of fear—what if I look bad?

3. If that fixed mindset rears its ugly head (in my head!), what is the one thing I can do to remind myself that I also have a growth mindset? (When you know you are entering a stressful situation, try to give yourself a cue that will remind you of your growth mindset—draw a smiley face on your arm, wear a certain piece of jewelry, or put your hat on backward. We can all have a growth mindset; we just need to remind ourselves it's there.)

The Takeaway

The Big Idea

Our mindsets determine what we believe can change and grow, and learn in life: they either limit our potential, or explode it.

Be Sure to Remember

- People with growth mindsets measure their success in their effort and are much more likely to confront challenges and seek help. Fixed mindsets encourage the exact opposite.
- If you believe that people can change, you are more likely to speak up when you need to, essential to growing relationships and dealing with the challenges that inevitably confront them.
- Thinking traps—the small repetitive thoughts that invade our mind when we encounter challenge—reinforce the fixed mindset and can harm a growth mindset.

Making It Happen

- Find out which thinking trap gets you the most stuck and use the appropriate question-key to talk back to your thoughts in a productive way instead of getting into a fight with your own mind.
- To find your growth mindset, get attuned to listening for the fixed mindset voice in your head and make an irreversible decision to take the growth mindset action in response.
- Developing a different mindset can be as simple as trying on a new set of clothing or deciding what mindset you want to wear that day.

CHAPTER 5

Optimism and Pessimism: Making the Most of Reality

Whether you think you can or you think you can't—you're right.

—*Henry Ford*

As the dean of admissions at the University of Pennsylvania, Lee Stetson pretty much had his pick of the best and brightest students from around the world who battled for admission to the elite university each year. When almost 13,000 high achievers applied for a coveted spot in the class of 1987, for example, Stetson chose fewer than 20 percent of them. The rigorous screening created a freshman class that often exceeded the high standards of the school, but Stetson and his team had a vexing problem: 20 percent of Penn's students struggled mightily during their first year of school.

Stetson found himself asking the same question that has run through the minds of many of our students, and perhaps yours as well: what distinguishes the freshmen who thrive from those who flounder? After all, every one of them had gained admittance to school. It wasn't like they hadn't found success in the classroom before. Why would some excel and others fall by the wayside? Stetson turned to famed psychologist and University of Pennsylvania faculty member Martin Seligman.

Seligman, who had made his name by understanding how people learned to become helpless in life, had recently turned his research on its head, asking the opposite question: Could they learn to become optimistic? As he became better acquainted with the three key components that made up the UPenn admittance process (essentially, GPA + SAT + AP results), he suspected that beyond academics, one additional factor might make a difference for young adults dealing with this particularly stressful first year of college: optimism.

For five years, Seligman had been researching the powerful effects of optimism and whether it too was something that could be learned. Having worked with subjects ranging from fourth graders to insurance salespeople and professional athletes, he and his team had found that when measures of talent were held constant, people assessed as optimists rose above expected performance, while their pessimistic counterparts fell short.

Seligman believed that the same would hold true for college students. He was confident that a key difference between those freshmen who thrived both academically and socially and those who didn't was their level of optimism.

His findings would help change the way we look at success and the very nature of the human mind.

Optimism and Pessimism: What's Driving Your Life Experience?

Over the past two decades, optimism—a combination of hope and confidence in a successful outcome—has been found to predict not only higher GPAs and better social experiences, but also a greater ability to bounce back after poor exam results, after losses, and during tough times. Optimists take better care of their health, whether that means avoiding tobacco, drug, or alcohol abuse; maintaining a healthy diet; or exercising regularly. Here's a big one: optimists are better liked than others. Oh, and optimists experience less anxiety in adjusting to challenges such as new jobs or new schools. Interested?

College students in general tend to consider life's glass half full rather than half empty. Studies show they believe they'll be more likely than average to own their own home, have a talented kid, be featured in the media, and travel to Europe. They also believe they are less likely to be alcoholics, break a bone, get into a car accident, or contract a sexually transmitted disease. But before you go skydiving without a parachute, thinking everything is—and will be—just grand (which about 60 percent of you do), let's do a reality check: it can't all be rainbows and butterflies. More on extreme optimism and its pitfalls later, but for now, be advised that trying to just positively *think* your way to success is not a viable strategy.

But if too much optimism tells you that you don't need to look both ways before crossing the street ("because I'll *never* get hit by a car!"), too much pessimism will never let you leave the house ("because I will *definitely* get hit by a car"). While we don't wish to sound pessimistic about pessimism, too much pessimism has been shown to result in lower salaries, less success in school and work, and lower overall satisfaction with life. Even if you don't get hit by that car, pessimism can genuinely be an express lane to depression.

You pessimists probably think we're going to dump on you for the entire chapter. (Nothing *ever* works out for you, does it?) We won't—in fact, we will do the opposite, trumpeting your praises like Kanye showing the love to Beyoncé ("Yo, optimism, I'm really happy for you, I'ma let you finish, but pessimism is one of the best things of all time!"). Pessimists—defined as those with a lack of hope plus low confidence in the future and in successful outcomes—are more likely to think through possible outcomes and prepare for potential issues. They are less likely to engage in risky behavior. Pessimists process poor performances in a way that helps them learn and improve. When properly channeled, pessimism can be a key to better preparation, lower anxiety, and improved performance.

Hold on…there's a *third* perspective. For a solid 24 percent of you it's not about how traffic might affect your day. If you plan to dispassionately process the information available before setting foot in the crosswalk, you may be a realist. Stay put. We'll get back to you.

No matter which camp you fall into, whether you are in the wake of victory or failure, a terrific situation or a tough one, your beliefs will influence what you make of the experience in the moment, and, equally important, what you expect and how you succeed on the road ahead.

We are not going to try to turn you into an optimist, a pessimist, or a realist, but we are going to help you understand the why, when, and how, to cultivate an attitude that can help you achieve your goals and dreams while addressing the challenges in school and beyond. You may think you are without question one or the other (or the other), but, people, this is science, where we measure stuff. If you really want to nail it down, check out the Life Orientation Test (LOT) at our site, www.uthrive.info.

Optimism

Maria was a student in our course who, during the class on optimism, volunteered that she was the first person in her family to go to college. Raised in a rough part of the Bronx, where her parents struggled to make ends meet, Maria had grown up constantly hearing that she shouldn't get her hopes up. But Maria tuned out her parents' dire warnings, deciding to focus on living up to what *she* believed she could achieve rather than on what circumstances seemed to dictate. She worked as hard as she could in school to give herself every advantage possible, pushed forward, she said, by an optimistic outlook that helped her keep her eyes on the prize. That prize turned out to be an academic scholarship to NYU.

Think through any great achievement or proud accomplishment in your life, and we bet you'll find that optimism provided a fair amount of impetus to get you there. It wasn't just the mantra "I think I can, I think I can, I think I can" that pushed the Little Engine That Could over that damn hill; that engine busted its little train ass to get to the top of that sucker. Overcoming challenges requires genuine effort, and optimism helps you see possibilities so enticing that you are willing to go above and beyond to turn them into realities. Whether you are trying to deliver toys to kids on the other side of the mountain, or longing to achieve something in college—a seat on the student senate, a scholarship to study abroad, a coveted internship—your level of optimism can affect your path and ultimately influence your outcome.

A study of more than 2,100 freshmen from the University of Kentucky found that the optimistic first-years were more likely to score higher GPAs, more driven to succeed than their pessimistic classmates, and better prepared to deal with the challenging times that came from being…well…freshmen. They were also more adept at building a support network.

Optimism can help us get others on board (tiny elephants, professors, roommates), providing that all-important social support to get us over the daunting hills. Optimistic freshmen at Rutgers University had larger networks of friends within two weeks of beginning school, and by the end of the semester had higher-quality friendships as well. They adjusted psychologically to their rookie semesters better than their pessimistic classmates, experiencing smaller increases in both stress and depression.

Expecting good things to happen instead of anticipating disaster can improve your love life as well. When we are optimistic that things can work, no matter the context, we are more willing to cooperate, problem-solve, listen, and deal with the barriers and challenges that stand in our way, which leads to happier romantic relationships. Researchers even found that optimism predicted relationship satisfaction that lasted more than two years.

Optimistic Explanatory Style

Five years after being called by the dean of admissions, Seligman was glued to his TV set along with millions of other people around the world as the Summer Olympics got under way in Seoul. It was September 18, 1988, and all eyes that day were on a twenty-two-year-old American swimmer named Matt Biondi, who was widely expected to make history at the epic games.

Many pundits had predicted that Biondi would tie Mark Spitz's record of seven gold medals at a single Olympics. Not just seven medals—seven *gold* medals. A 1984 Olympic gold medalist and three-time NCAA Swimmer of the Year while at Berkeley, Biondi was America's greatest swimmer since Spitz had taken the world by storm sixteen years earlier.

With a nation's expectations on his broad shoulders, Biondi dove into the Olympic pool. Just one minute and forty-eight seconds later, the dream evaporated: Biondi finished a distant third in the 200-meter freestyle.

His second race was even more painful. Whipping the crowd into a frenzy by dominating the field for the duration of the 100-meter butterfly, Biondi was poised for victory when, just a few feet from the race's end, he seemed to just...stop swimming. Rather than taking his last stroke—and the gold that would come with it—Biondi chose to glide to the wall, and in doing so lost the race by just .01 second. Hundreds of millions of viewers watched Anthony Nesty of Suriname win the gold instead. ("One one-hundredth of a second—what if I had grown my fingernails longer?" Biondi would later reflect.)

In Seoul, Biondi seemed to be sinking faster than he was swimming. The buzz from the press, the public, and the swimming community was that the champion might have hit a mental barrier he could not get over.

Halfway around the world, in the comfort of his living room,

Seligman believed otherwise. Despite the crushing pressure surrounding Biondi and the telltale signs of an epic choke, Seligman was certain that Biondi could bounce back and be better than ever. Seligman's extensive research had determined that the way a person explained bad events—known as explanatory style—had a massive impact on how they responded going forward. And Matt Biondi, it turned out, had participated in one of Seligman's experiments just a few months earlier.

Let's say you and your bestie score interviews for dream internships. Both of you are so stoked that you go out and get your hair cut, shine your shoes, pick out your best dress-for-success outfit, and hit the sack early the night before so you get a solid eight hours. Feeling great and looking great, you each head into the interview just knowing that you are the person for the job. Your résumés are flawless, and so are you. You both nail the audish, and it is on.

So when you both get your email the next day from your future employers, you are all but ready to high-five each other and announce to the social media universe that you two rock stars are on the path to glory, when, *bam!* the second sentence hits you like a ton of bricks: "...we have decided to go in another direction."

Dude. Whoa.

Back to square one it is: haircut, shoes, best outfit, quality zzzs, résumé buffed and polished to perfection. Same result. And again. And again. And maybe even once again.

For the optimist, it's obvious how this happened: you tell yourself (and potentially others) that these are amazing companies and there must have been thousands of candidates for each opening. Getting hired the first (or even second or third or fourth) time around would have been incredible, but tomorrow is another day, and if you keep plugging away, you *will* score a primo gig. For the pessimist, it is rapidly becoming equally obvious: you're not good enough to work at this level—maybe in anything you do—so the best action would be to lower expectations.

When optimistic students look in the rearview mirror, bad events may appear farther away than they really are, and thus they declare that the road ahead is clear. The pessimists' rearview, however, is like that scene from *Jurassic Park,* where the dinosaur is right on their tail and getting ever closer—for them, the horror is not only immediately behind them but bound to be blocking the road ahead as well. In other words, when bad stuff happens, people with an optimistic explanatory style (OES) see it like this:

Not me *(External):* Life events stem from external
   circumstances, not from my individual traits and actions.
Not always *(Unstable):* Causes are temporary and likely to
   change in the future.
Not everything *(Specific):* Only a limited part of my life is
   affected.

Someone with a pessimistic explanatory style (PES), however, might look at it like this:

Me *(Internal):* The problem is with me, not the situation.
Always *(Stable):* Causes are permanent and unlikely to change.
Everything *(Global):* Every aspect of my life is affected.

Perhaps you will recognize yourself in the following scenarios:

A bad grade on an exam

The OES:
   "Math has always been a challenge (*not everything,* just math), and that was a particularly tough test (*not me,* the test), but I bet if I study harder I can nail this sucker (*not always,* because I can create change)."

The PES:

"I suck at school (*everything*, not just this test or class). No matter what I do (*always*, I can't do anything about it), I'm never going to be smart enough for this class anyway (it's *me*, not the test)."

A bad day on the field

The OES:

"That goalie was really good (*not me* who was bad, but the opponent who was really good!). It was a rough game (*not always*, and tomorrow is another day), but fortunately, there are plenty of things that are going well in the rest of my life (*not everything*, as friends and classes are going great)."

The PES:

"I just can't score this year (*always*, not just today). Everyone is going to think I'm a loser (*everything* is affected, not just soccer). Maybe I'm not good enough (*me*, not that the opponent was particularly good or I need to train harder)."

A bad day in Cupid's house

The OES:

"Maybe she doesn't want to go out with me because she's dating someone else (*not me*, if she were single she might have said yes!). I can get back on my horse and ask out the cute chick in my chemistry class (*not always*, I will date again in the future). Even though she rejected me, I still look fly and I'm killing it in my classes (*not everything*, there are still other things I've got going on)."

The PES:

"She definitely said no because she thinks I'm gross and annoying (*me*, it's my personality and appearance). My family and friends probably think so, too (*everything*, if she doesn't like me everyone else probably feels the same way). I'll never get a girlfriend (*always*, OMG, I'm totally going to be alone forever)."

The pessimists essentially give up hope for the future, while the optimists see that they can take action and shape their future.

Dan's eight-year-old son, Julian, was having a tough gymnastics meet. He had taken gold at states the previous year and rarely lost, but today he was not on point, and the subpar performance was reflected in his scores. Despite knowing that he was out of the running for an all-around medal, in his last event—*boom!*—Julian nailed a 10.7 on parallel bars, his best score of the season. Bounding off the mat this time, he looked at Dan with a huge smile and said, "Rough day, but we always finish strong, right?" Telling himself that his disappointing performance earlier was the result of a rough moment (*not always*), and that it was limited to certain events (*not everything*), allowed Julian to see the chances he still had to medal in his remaining events and encouraged him to try even harder. Score another victory for OES: his spin was what kept the door open for the eventual win.

Shortly before the Seoul Olympics, Seligman had tested the explanatory style theory on the UC Berkeley swim team by playing one of those devilish little tricks that psychologists seem to love so much: he lied to them. Okay, he had their coach lie to them, giving each swimmer a time for their last event that was slower than their actual time. The pessimistic swimmers swam even more slowly the next time around. But the optimists? Amazingly, they swam even faster than their best times. In other words, bad news doused the pessimists' motivation and confidence, but it stoked the optimists' fire to work harder, knowing that they could absolutely do better. Biondi was on the Berkeley team that Seligman assessed, and yes indeed, he was a damn strong optimist, which meant his explanatory style would put bad events such as his two humiliating losses at the outset of the

Games into healthy perspective. Seligman had reason to believe Biondi was about to come back stronger than ever. And he was right.

Despite his poor showing in the first two races, the doomsday predictions of the press, and the huge amount of public pressure he was under, Biondi went on to win five gold medals—one every day for the next five days—setting four world records in the process.

It's (Not) All Good

So "it's all good" is all good? Not quite. Sit tight.

Too much belief that it is "all good" can lead to some serious issues. Just ask the crew member of the RMS *Titanic* who (in-) famously announced to a boarding passenger, "God himself could not sink this ship!" Oh, that's right, you can't ask him . . . he died four days later. So ask his boss instead: P. A. S. Franklin, vice president of the White Star Line, who, when told that his ship had hit an iceberg and was sinking, declared, "We place absolute confidence in the *Titanic*. We believe the boat is unsinkable!" We all know how that went . . . down.

Not that your college career is headed for a watery grave, but there will be icebergs during your voyage, and *extreme optimism*—simply choosing to believe that you are unsinkable—can lead to some very messy (and equally unhappy) outcomes. Extreme optimists underestimate the risk of health problems and are less likely to quit smoking, are more likely to contract STDs (and less likely to go for treatment . . . ewww), are less likely to achieve their goals, and . . . here it comes . . . have lower college GPAs.

A study of more than 500 students at UC Berkeley found that freshmen with unrealistically high perceptions of their academic ability suffered from decreasing levels of self-esteem as the years progressed. Research on 236 Canadian college students was even more straightforward: those who were assessed as overly optimistic had lower GPAs than their pessimistic peers.

Yes, we *were* trumpeting the benefits of optimism, but if you believe you are completely iceberg-proof (or if you simply choose not to believe in icebergs), there is really no reason to even prepare for them. Surely you're not the person who contracts an STD, so no condoms for you, thank you very much. If you truly believe that you won't get cancer from smoking, why quit? In research that has looked at exactly these scenarios, optimists are less likely to wear 'em, and more likely to smoke 'em — in fact, optimists as a whole are not only less likely to prepare, but more likely to engage in risky behavior in a variety of contexts. (Gambling? Yes, please! In fact, when an optimist loses, he bets even more on the next shot.) So when challenges do befall our overly optimistic pals, they are less prepared to deal with them and thus suffer the consequences far more intensely.

Oh, and as you move toward the inevitable (that would be a j-o-b *job*, people), keep this in mind: a study from Ludwig-Maximilians University in Munich showed that the more frequently grad students had run through positive fantasies about finding a job, the fewer résumés they sent out, the fewer job offers they received, the less success they had in finding work compared with their classmates, and the less money they made. All good? You be the judge.

Pessimism

Pessimists, we're back...and know what? You are *right*! Yes, you! Okay, partially right. Pessimism *can* be a healthy thing. Just as "all good" is overblown, so is "all bad." If you are trying to *prevent* something from happening, pessimism — specifically *defensive pessimism* — can be a lifesaver.

Defensive pessimism is defined as a strategy for managing anxiety by resisting the natural urge to run away from the situation causing distress and instead mentally bracing yourself for the worst. As Dr. Julie Norem at Wellesley College discovered, when people are being defensively pessimistic, "they set low expectations, but then they take the next step, which is to think through in concrete and vivid ways what exactly might go wrong." This helps them plan to avoid the disaster, Norem found, and by directing their anxiety toward productive activity, they end up performing better than they would have if they hadn't used the strategy.

When it comes to your health, for example, a classic optimist might think, "I don't need a flu shot...I never get the flu." But a defensive pessimist is cautiously vigilant, believing they *will* get the flu, and thus are more likely to get the shot.

Defensive pessimism, which helps you see potential downsides, can motivate you to study more (when we believe that the exam will be harder than it is), practice more (because we never believe we are adequately prepared), or even consider more potential pitfalls in anything from road-tripping (we are bound to run out of gas) to dating (breath mint, anyone?).

But defensive pessimists also have a distinctive pathway to raising their levels of performance, as Norem and her colleague Stacie Spencer found during a study of college students playing darts at Northeastern University. They had participants either listen to relaxing audiotapes or visualize themselves missing the dartboard, and found that optimists who relaxed with the tapes performed about 30 percent better than optimists who imagined missing the board. Amazingly, however, the pessimists had precisely the opposite response: defensive pessimists who imagined their misses performed 30 percent better than defensive pessimists who had to relax first! In related research, defensive pessimists who imagined some of the possible issues at the root of their nervousness about public speaking were able to better prepare themselves for their potential nightmare scenarios, i.e., forgetting their lines, dry mouth, or staining their clothes before the speech. By anticipating these issues—strategically placing note cards, bringing water to the podium, or carrying an extra shirt—they not only experienced less anxiety, but also raised their level of performance.

Yet here's the twist: even when they perform at the same level as their optimistic peers, defensive pessimists are *less satisfied* with their performance and rate themselves higher in "need for improvement." Assuming that you prioritize overall life satisfaction over performance, no matter how you slice it, it's a net loss. If you are simply trying to survive, it seems that pessimists may have the upper hand. But given that pessimism can get us to stop trying in tough times and makes us worry more, feel more anxious, and just feel worse, when it comes to *thriving*, you have to look on the bright side occasionally as well.

Realism

Discussing optimism and pessimism without touching on realism hardly seems fair (or realistic). After all, shouldn't we all just be realistic about life's events, opportunities, and challenges? We can all agree that realistically a banana is a banana (provided that it really is a banana) and that 8 a.m. is 8 a.m. (assuming you are in the same time zone). But in an infinite array of matters, it can be awfully tough to agree on what reality actually is. If you and your roommate get into a fight over the definition of a "clean" dish or "reasonable" volume level, is one of you more realistic than the other? Who is realistically hot and who is realistically not? What is success? How soon is "too soon"? Is the glass half full, half empty, or totally full— half with water and half with air? You and your oppositely minded pal are looking at exactly the same scenarios, thinking that one of you (definitely *not* the other person) is being realistic. Often, the issue is one of interpretation, and that is so deeply influenced by every related experience you have ever had that "clean," "success," and "hotness" are too subjective to come under the umbrella of realism. Human beings are loaded with biases, so if you see that ridiculously tough organic chem class as an "exciting personal challenge" and your pal sees it as "living hell," who is being realistic, optimistic, or pessimistic? The realist may believe that optimists are delusional about the amount of skill or control they have over a situation, while others may think optimists have a pretty good grip on reality. It seems that the jury is still (and will always be) out.

There may be an answer that allows us to enjoy the benefits of both optimism and reality. Realistic optimism is a concept that maximizes a positive outlook, helps us anticipate potential issues, and allows us to keep our feet on the ground even when our head is happily in the clouds.

Mental Contrasting: Optimizing Optimism

In their book *The Resilience Factor,* Karen Reivich and Andrew Shatté define realistic optimism as "The ability to maintain a positive outlook without denying reality, actively appreciating the positive aspects of a situation without ignoring the negative aspects." Good stuff, and Gabriele Oettingen, our colleague at NYU and the author of *Rethinking Positive Thinking,* has spent two decades working with thousands of college students to make the most of what optimism has to offer while staying rooted in reality. Her answer is *mental contrasting (MC).* MC is a strategy in which you think about positive aspects of the goal that you have in mind, pinpoint the most positive, dwell on it (visualizing, writing, etc.), and then go through exactly the same process with the obstacles. Think about a number of them, then narrow it down to the most imposing and dwell on those (that is, visualize/write/discuss with others). We'll walk you through the steps in the exercise at the end of this chapter.

Whether the goals are academic, social, occupational, physical, or otherwise, Oettingen has found that a mixture of positive fantasy and cautious reality can lead to remarkably higher rates of success. Students who practice MC score better grades and study more than their classmates who are merely optimistic that their GPAs will rise. Students who practice MC also try harder in class, complete more school assignments independently, suffer less disappointment, and bounce back more resiliently than those who see nothing but a clear path to academic glory. If you're thinking about grad school, think about this: aspiring grad students who used MC to gain clarity about their obstacles had a greater sense of personal responsibility for next steps and felt more strongly about pursuit of the goal.

Far more important, using MC can help you get together with that person you are crushing on! (I know, right? Can you imagine how different high school would have been with this seemingly magical power? Prom?!) Oettingen found that students who practice MC are more likely to find the guts to make the first move.

In a subtle but essential twist on optimism as motivator, it seems that (as with most things in life) balance is key. NYU students who envisioned and wrote down how the *ideal* week ahead would play out— doing well in class, hitting awesome parties, chilling in their favorite way—reported feeling less energized and accomplishing less during the week. Daydreaming can be a great thing, but when our heads get *too* lost in the clouds, our feet don't hit the ground to turn fantasy into reality.

Mental contrasting has been linked to more creativity and even greater acceptance of people who are different from ourselves. You may not be overly concerned about how you will get along with your still-a-mystery roommate, but given the world of new cultures, languages, and ideas that you are about to encounter, a touch of nerves would be totally understandable. From social connections to grades, mental contrasting might come in handy. Read on for how to put it into action.

Opportunities for Action

With four years of amazing opportunities right in front of you, and plenty more down the road, changing your perspective can literally change your life. Here are some ways to make the most of your possibilities and set yourself up to meet the challenges ahead.

Exercise: As Easy as A, B, C, D, and E

It would be a straight-up bummer if we sang the praises of optimism without showing you how to cultivate it in your life. Fortunately, it can be as easy as ABCDE: adversity, belief, consequence, disputation, and energization.

A simple (and global) example of an *adversity* is when you text somebody and they don't text you back right away. Your resulting *beliefs* can then run a huge gamut, ranging from "They must be in class" or "Their phone is dead" to "They hate me" or "They are so rude." (For a hilarious example, Google "Aziz Ansari Texting.") As you can imagine, the *consequence* of your belief is as wide-ranging as that belief, from "No biggie" to "This relationship is frickin' over!"

The key to how this will play out lies in *disputation,* the process of arguing with yourself and raising alternative explanations to shoot down your pessimistic assumptions—"Maybe they don't hate me, but... their phone is in their bag, or on silent, or they're on the other line with their parents, or they're at the gym." Simply thinking through some viable alternatives can change your entire experience, and when you make a note of the shift in your *energy* (literally, write it down if you can!)—"I felt so much more relaxed and far less judgmental. Being more patient really paid off"—you are locking in a whole new way of thinking. Do it consistently, and the process—not to mention an optimistic explanatory style—can become second nature.

You can practice this exercise anyplace and anytime, but to lock it into that brain of yours, we suggest pausing to write out each step:

Adversity: The event that occurred.
Belief: How we interpret that event and what it means about
　　　our future (think about explanatory style—is the event
　　　stable or unstable, etc.).
Consequence: How we feel or act as a result of that belief.

Disputation: Generating alternatives to your beliefs.

Energization: How your mood changed as a result of the
     process.

Practice this exercise at least once a day, and before you know it
you will be seeing the world—especially the challenges—in a whole
new (and brighter) light.

Exercise: How to WOOP It Up

You may have read through the section on mental contrasting thinking, "Ummmm...yeah, guys...I *so* already do that." If you do, congratulations and a hearty mazel tov! That is wonderful, fabulous,
fantastic, and...well...unlikely. Gabriele Oettingen and her colleague A. Timur Sevincer found that only 9 percent of students use
MC spontaneously. If you are looking to turn fantasies into reality,
try WOOP, the scientists' remarkably simple and effective exercise
that can help you get into the flow of MC.

Grab some index cards or get the app if that's how you roll (www
.woopmylife.org).

Now choose any topic—physical, dietary, relationship, job search,
or whatever is relevant to you—and think of a goal you want to
achieve. Jot down your answers in this order:

Wish: What is the challenging goal you are aiming to achieve,
     whether today, next week, in a month, or in a year?
Outcome: How would you feel if this goal were accomplished?
Obstacle: What is standing in your way? What assumptions or
     habits are holding you back?
Plan: What is one thing you can do to overcome your obstacle?
     Not just generally, specifically, in this very moment? If x
     (obstacle) happens, then I will do y (healthy alternative).

Let's say that your *wish* is to get better grades. The *outcome* might be feeling really excited that you are realizing your potential. If the *obstacle* is that your roommates are awesome but not exactly buried in the books (and thus it is tough to get proper studying time in when you are in the room), your *plan* could be to hit the library every day for an hour before heading home to hang with your crew.

Boom. It's that simple. The more deeply you consider each of these stages—really dwelling on them to bring them to life—the better. Pull out your note cards each day to review them. Visualize each element, create a mental video, and play it when your brain needs a mini-break. Share each element with a friend to let them know what you are up to (and maybe even ask them to check in along the way to see how it's going).

The Takeaway

The Big Idea

Your levels of optimism and pessimism will not only affect your path, but will also ultimately influence your outcomes in life.

Be Sure to Remember

- Optimism can be learned.
- A key to managing bad events is how we explain them. Changing your perspective shifts your experiences in the moment and in the future.
- An occasional dose of well-timed pessimism can lead to better preparation and improved performance.

Making It Happen

- Sticks and stones may break your bones, and words *can* really hurt you: when explaining bad events, remember your nots: not me, not always, and not everything.

- Know your ABCD and Es: Identify the ADVERSITY, the resulting BELIEFS, and the CONSEQUENCES of those beliefs. Then DISPUTE your reasoning to consider alternative possibilities and see how that ENERGIZES you.
- Walk through WOOP: What goal do you wish to achieve? How would you feel if the goal were accomplished? What obstacles stand in your way? What is the one specific thing you can do to overcome that obstacle?

CHAPTER 6

Willpower: Doing What You Really Want to Do

Strength does not come from physical capacity. It comes from an indomitable will.

—Mohandas K. Gandhi

Imagine yourself as a four-year-old again. Your busy daily itinerary includes sandboxes, swings, and naps. When you are hungry, people prepare your meals, cut your food, and sometimes even feed it to you. When you are tired, they carry you. When your tummy hurts, they rub it for you. Life couldn't be much better if you were the emperor of China. Yet today your parents have brought you to a room where you sit alone. Your legs swing from the oversize chair, and you take in the space, perhaps making funny faces in the two-way mirror just opposite you (on the other side of which, unbeknownst to you, are cameras and groups of observant researchers). All of a sudden the door swings open, and a kind-looking young woman (is she your new babysitter?) is holding one of life's greatest treasures: a marshmallow. That's right, a marshmallow...and it's for you! What a great place! Nice people and a marshmallow—what more could a kid want?

Yes! Two marshmallows! It gets even better, for as the visitor places the hunk of pillowy goodness in front of you, she says that you will get another one—that's right, a *second* marshmallow, if you don't eat the first one until she comes back—that is, you can either eat the one in front of you right now *or* you can double your sweet pleasure if you can wait for her to return.

This is precisely the study that Stanford-based psychologist Walter Mischel began over fifty years ago. His astounding findings would change the way that we look at willpower.

The kids who were able to delay gratification and wait for the second marshmallow grew up to have higher GPAs and SAT scores (as well as GREs and GMATs) and reach higher educational levels. They used risky drugs less frequently and were far more physically fit than the study participants who couldn't resist the first marshmallow. The first group also thought ahead more, planned more, and were better able to pursue their goals. They became more resilient, self-reliant, confident; they handled stress more effectively and were more successful at maintaining close relationships. They made more money, too. Brain scans confirmed these benefits, showing that the part of their brains used for effective problem solving, creative thinking, and controlling impulsive behavior was more active. Oh, and they had lower rates of felony and misdemeanor charges.

Imagine the next four years with these advantages. It's almost not fair.

So this cute kiddo? He is now Mark Zuckerberg.

And this one? She's behind bars for 25 to 30.

(Okay, we jest. Hey, they well may be after all, but we can't confirm — or deny — that at this point.)

Now, of course this is great if you were a four-year-old marshmallow-waiting champion — but what if you (like 70 percent of the kids in the study) weren't? Are you destined to spend the rest of your days eating the dust of your more self-regulated contemporaries? Doomed to lower GPAs, less confidence and happiness, and a virtual carousel of failed relationships — and bound for the state penitentiary?

Fortunately, there is hope for you (and us) after all. Remember, these were four-year-olds, not masters of the universe. The kids' secrets and strategies for success are not hard to crack and are more than readily learnable.

Willpower is essential to thriving in life. If you want to have a successful college experience — in terms of grades, roommates, dating, friends, health (mental and physical), and happiness (to name a few), willpower is key.

Stanford psychologist Kelly McGonigal defines willpower as

"the ability to do what matters most, even when it's difficult or when some part of you doesn't want to." If this sounds familiar, it's because you most likely would not have gotten into (or stayed in) college without it. Have you ever hit the books when hanging out was more tempting? Willpower. Hit the sack when Xbox, Netflix, or Instagram was just a click away? Willpower. How about skipped a party because you had a game or exam the next day? Done any number of things because you knew they were "right" rather than "fun"? You know what's coming... willpower.

College will test your willpower in ways you haven't even imagined. In terms both of temptations and of potential rewards, it's the major leagues, the big enchilada, the Super Bowl, and the finals of *American Ninja Warrior* all rolled into one. Rather than simply a baby step from what you had to deal with in high school, let's call it what it really is—a quantum leap.

In high school you may have been tempted to party on the weekends. (College: the 24/7 party zone.) To hook up *if* you had a place to yourself, *if* you could find someone. (College: the smorgasbord of opportune sexuality *and* private space.) To binge-watch/game-play/text—until your mom made you hand over your phone. (College: where any and all media are yours—for as long as you like—ooohhh, and check this out... did you know that a guy in South Korea died after playing fifty-seven straight hours of video games?) To sneak a fourth late-night slice of pizza from the fridge. (College: where the cafeteria has all-day make-'em-yourself waffle and soft-serve stations! Right. Next. To. Each. Other.) Even those temptations that you will "never" succumb to are lurking, ready to pounce: 40 percent of college students either began smoking or became regular smokers after arriving on campus. Binge drinking shoots through the roof—its frequency in college is a tremendous predictor of major issues with alcohol in later years—and willpower is what you need to keep it in check. It's not just the easy availability of enticements—good and bad—that test your willpower in college, but the sheer variety as well—every shape, size, color, flavor, texture, and potency as far as the eye can see and in every possible direction. "Just say no" just got a whole lot harder than it ever was before you left home.

Now that you've been stripped of the familiar day-to-day structure once provided by high school, teachers, family, close pals, sports, clubs, and anything else you were involved with consistently, your responsibilities are going through the ceiling just as your support system is falling through the floor. All the precise habits, routines, and influences that helped you to say yes to the good stuff and no to the bad? *Poof*…gone. It's all on you now to choose the apple over the cupcake, a good night's sleep over the girls' night out, hitting the books instead of hitting anything also that starts with the letter *b*. If that's not pressure enough, each decision you make will speak directly to your overall level of both success and fulfillment during these four years. Self-control impacts the degree of depression, anxiety, and loneliness you may feel. Too little willpower can also make you less likely to compromise, more self-indulgent, more likely to act irrationally, more selfish and unfair, and less trusting of others.

But the "choose your own adventure" thrill of college can put you on top of the world instead of through the wringer if you make choices that set you up to thrive instead of merely survive. Higher grades, more frequent goal attainment, more effective problem solving, and greater creative thinking? Greater willpower gives you the advantage.

Resistance Fighters

So now that marshmallows have sweetly illustrated *why* willpower is so important, let's look at *how* it works (and how you can work it).

For that matter, let's not talk about marshmallows. Let's talk about cookies. Yes...cookies. Actually, cookies and radishes. And let's add some college students to the mix—specifically your peers from a Psych 101 class at Florida State University, whom social psychologist Roy Baumeister and his colleagues included in yet another research study.

Upon entering the room, all of the participants were hit by the tantalizing aroma of chocolate chip cookies that had been freshly baked on-site and now sat heaped on plates around the room. The students were divided into two groups. One group—let's call them the Monsters—were told the cookies were all theirs: Munch 'em, throw 'em like Frisbees, hang 'em on the wall like art, rub 'em all over their bodies (we made up those last three, but you get the idea—they were asked to eat at least two or three). But...why were there bowls of radishes in equal abundance? The Monsters were out of luck if they wanted any radishes. It was cookies or nothing for them.

The second group—the Rabbits—were asked to eat a few radishes, but they were forbidden to eat any cookies. (That didn't stop many of them from "picking up a number of the cookies to sniff at," the researchers reported. Oh, the agony.)

After just five minutes to savor (or suffer), the researchers switched gears and informed both groups that it was time to move on to a different study. Removing the food from the room, they handed out a book of math puzzles to all participants and asked them to begin solving them.

What they did not share—and here is where things really get interesting—was that the puzzles were unsolvable.

How many minutes would you work at a puzzle before giving up? The Rabbits gave up in just eight minutes. The Monsters? They persisted for *nineteen*. That's right, nineteen (19, XIX, 5+4+7+3!). The cookie eaters worked more than twice as long before they gave up on the puzzle.

Allow us to put that more precisely:

Radish eaters: 8.35 minutes until giving up
Cookie eaters: 18.90 minutes until giving up

What...just...happened?
It turns out that this is willpower:

Your willpower (and for that matter, Alan's and Dan's, your mom's, your boyfriend's, and that of the girl sitting next to you) is like a muscle. Whether you are resisting cookies, marshmallows, beer, video games, your ex, or your texts, the more you use it, the weaker it gets, until it's all but gone. The radish eaters had depleted their willpower resisting cookies, and thus didn't have the oomph left to stick with the puzzle as long as the cookie eaters did. And just as nos drain, so do yeses: the well-intentioned efforts that you make to push through unsolvable problems, study harder, clean your dorm room, or balance your finances all take a toll on your willpower, too. The more you use it throughout the day, the weaker it becomes, and the less you have remaining when you're having that midnight stare down with Ben (and Jerry's)—give it up and grab the spoon...this sucker was over before it began.

And let's be clear here—almost everything you do requires willpower:

- Getting up in the morning (without hitting your snooze bar eight times)

- Hitting the gym (instead of the couch)
- Paying attention to the prof (not your phone)

And every choice you make—good or bad—continually fatigues that willpower muscle. That muscle wakes up like Lindsay Lohan circa *Mean Girls* but by bedtime is the hot-mess Lindsay Lohan of today.

As the day progresses, your strength is progressively sapped, and after a long, tough one, most of us are far more likely to make poor decisions. Ever have a regrettable fight, regrettable double bacon pepperoni pizza, regrettable sex, or a million other regrettable things? Probably happened later in the day, didn't it? By the time night falls, you may find yourself simply doing nothing at all (some call this procrastination—but we are putting that topic off for later). You may find yourself on a sort of robotic autopilot, zombie-walking back into your suite, sincerely intending to tackle the reading/ writing/'rithmetic that is piling up on your desk (and on your conscience) but discovering that the lure of the couch is simply too much to resist. Your only course of action is to collapse next to your equally zoned-out roommate, reach into the nearly empty tube of Pringles, and have this conversation:

You: Hey.
Roommate: Whattup?
(Twenty-minute delay)
You: Whattup?
Roommate: Hey.
(Ten minutes...)
You: You hungry?
Roommate: Word.
(Ten minutes...)
You: Let's order something.
Roommate: Dude. Yes.

(Ten minutes . . .)

One of you: Dude.

Willpower? Gone. Proactivity? Not happening. And thirty minutes later, no food has been ordered, you are still watching the same dumb show, and the spiral has only gone further downward.

There are both psychological and physiological elements to willpower, which we'll touch on later in the chapter. But for now, be aware that some of the most common willpower vampires include:

- Making decisions
- Low blood sugar
- Multitasking
- Restraining impulses
- Sleep deprivation

Even when we try to do the right thing, we seem to only have so much willpower. As Kelly McGonigal points out, studies show:

- Smokers who abstain from cigarettes for twenty-four hours are more likely to binge on ice cream.
- Drinkers who say no to their favorite cocktail become weaker on a test of physical endurance.
- People who are on a diet are more likely to cheat on their spouse (yes, you read that correctly).

So what the hell are we supposed to do? Are we doomed to either smoke or eat sundaes? Drink or collapse on a run? Wear oversize sweatshirts forever or cheat on our partners?

Undoubtedly, by now you are thinking (because you are a college smarty-pants), "But hey . . . if you guys are telling us that willpower works like a muscle, shouldn't we be able to exercise it and make it buff? Can't we save some for when we need it most?"

That is a great question, and right you are. You *can* pump that sucker up and—like a mental athlete—make it work for you. In fact not only can you make it stronger, but you can also keep some on ice for later.

How can you put this info into action? Well, let's start with a little quiz. Match the following desire to its solution.

Want to quit smoking?	Stop eating sweets for two weeks.
Want to stop texting your ex?	Use hand grips twice a day.
Want to go easy on the partying?	Walk ten minutes twice a day.
Want to develop better study habits?	Do your dishes every night.

Congratulations! You're right!

How do we know? Because unlike Baumeister's devilish "no right answer" scenario, *every* answer is correct (OMG, how awesome would that have been on the SATs?): every single exercise on the right side of the page has been shown to increase our willpower no matter what we intend to use it for!

The more you exercise willpower, the stronger it gets. Of course, it also becomes fatigued and needs rest to recover. As with a muscle, there are simple rules to strength training:

- If you lift too little weight, there is not enough strain, and you will not build muscle.
- If you attempt to lift too much, you will give up and thus not build muscle (and maybe even hurt yourself).
- Lifting an amount of weight that pushes you beyond your current limits (but not too much), and doing so regularly, with adequate periods of rest in between, will develop greater strength.

When studies have simulated tasks requiring little self-control (regularly doing easy math problems or writing a few lines in a journal), willpower did not improve. When students have been tasked with taking on multiple willpower challenges at once (exercise *and* keeping their room clean, managing personal finances *and* dieting, increasing study habits *and* quitting smoking), they have overwhelmingly failed at both. But when students have been tasked with improving *one* area where willpower is needed over thirty days, they have not only improved in that area; they have found greater success when addressing other areas afterward. Because their willpower muscle has been strengthened, it is more ready than ever for the next challenge. The exercises at the end of this chapter will help you craft a workout that is just right for you.

Giving Your Muscle a Rest

To watch the video of the kids who waited for a second marshmallow is to observe a master class in the creative conservation of the willpower muscle. While the bambinos who couldn't wait stared intently at the fluffy little temptations and scarfed them down in an average of under three minutes, the others used remarkable strategies to resist the same urge: they put the marshmallow out of view by placing the paper plate on top of it, or they turned around to face the wall; they sang songs to distract themselves; and some even put their heads down to sleep until the time was up. One little boy's strategy was simple, later explaining that he couldn't eat the marshmallow because it wasn't there: in order to avoid the temptation he had decided to "go to outer space."

According to Mischel, the overarching strategy of those who wait is simple: "The key is to avoid it [the temptation] in the first place." If you can avoid it, "you can study for the SAT instead of watching television."

What are the marshmallows in your life? What are the things that tempt you the most? Food? Social media? TV? Shopping? Take a moment and jot them down and consider, how might you give your willpower enough rest to ensure it's there when these temptations arise? At Kenyon College, swimmers were coached to avoid climbing stairs in order to save energy as national championships approached. Crazy? Maybe—but they won thirty-one national championships in a row from 1980 through 2010. Resting your muscles—whether it's your pecs and glutes or your willpower—allows them to be at their strongest when you need them to perform their best.

Tomorrow, Tomorrow, There's Always... Procrastination

Wait for it.... Wait for it.... Wait for it.... okay... let's talk about procrastination.

A chapter on willpower simply wouldn't be complete without addressing procrastination. College students spend one-third of their waking life procrastinating. Up to 95 percent of them think they procrastinate, and 60 percent believe that their procrastination has gotten to the point of requiring professional help. Seventy percent think they should be branded with the letter "P" as full-on "procrastinators." But procrastination doesn't make you a procrastinator, just like playing basketball doesn't make you a basketball player. When we think of procrastination as just a behavior to change and not a reflection of character or self-worth, we are much closer to being able to create positive change.

Procrastination is when you put off the thing you should be doing. You make this choice thinking it won't hurt you in the long run, and you're right... for a while. Roy Baumeister and Dianne Tice found that college students who procrastinate more at the beginning of a semester feel so good that they actually have fewer health problems than their peers who take care of their responsibilities in a timely fashion. But not so fast with the champagne and confetti. Baumeister also determined that by the end of the semester, not only do the procrastinators retain much less information (we call it renting rather than buying an education), but also their grades are worse. The terrible pressure and stress that build up as the months go by (and the work piles up) far outweigh the earlier gains.

Procrastination Patterns

There are infinite reasons why we procrastinate, but they all have one thing in common—willpower. When our willpower is low, we are much more likely to give in to the impulse to watch TV, surf the Internet (or the ocean if you go to school on the coast), or look in the fridge (for the third time that hour). Everyone gets depleted at one time or another, and the personal routines that ensue often form consistent patterns of procrastination. What's great about patterns, though, is that with a little bit of awareness, we can recognize them and do some useful rearranging.

Mild-impact procrastination (MIP) is when you suffer the consequences of not getting low-priority items done on time. If you put off registering for classes until the only remaining choice is Needlepoint in the Dark Ages, or wait so long to get tickets for a concert that you end up watching it on YouTube, you have symptoms of MIP. When you put off your laundry until you find yourself smelling each item before wearing it, you've got MIP. MIP has a way of making your whole life messy if it's left unchecked. With MIP, we forgo easy action due to a fear of commitment, and the downward spiral begins.

If you start a million projects but finish very few, make plans but never see them through (or find yourself making endless lists on which nothing is ever crossed off), you may be dealing with *behavioral procrastination*. You've got the ideas, but you don't commit to the behaviors that will accomplish them. College offers a million opportunities—you can make plans to start four clubs, complete two majors (and a minor), produce three podcasts, play sports, and sing in the a cappella group but end up wondering how you never actually do any of them. (Dan *did* sing a cappella, but Alan was rejected. Just for the record and all.)

Deadline procrastination is just what it sounds like. You believe that deadlines can be pushed back, stomped on, slapped in the face (with a white glove, like in an eighteenth-century duel), or altogether ignored. Some softhearted teachers may let you slide by, but then you will find one teacher who won't, and she'll deduct a full letter grade while declaring that this is a life lesson. (This is what happened to Dan in college for handing in a paper FIVE SECONDS LATE. Seriously. Hey, Professor Kluge, I just wrote a book. And I got it in on time.)

If you have accepted an invitation when you really didn't want to, you may have been practicing *hindrance procrastination*. At some point in college (we hope), you are going to be asked to hang out, and, while your brain is thinking "OhmygodIamsobusywithEVERY THINGthereisnowaynonononodon'tsayyes!" your mouth is going to say "Dude, totes!" Then you go, but show up late and are . . . clearly distracted. Your friend asks if you are okay and you say "Fine," but in that clearly not-so-fine way. You realize that had you just said no in the first place, everyone would have been better off. So with steely determination, you firmly resolve to do this in the future: from here on out, *No!* will be your middle name.

Unless you say yes again the very next time.

Chip and Dan Heath, the authors of three best-selling books, claim to do their most focused writing on computers that have the Wi-Fi disabled, and the poet Maya Angelou would famously write in hotel rooms only after having all art removed from the walls. If you don't change your pattern, you aren't going to stop procrastinating. Thinking that you can just "try harder" means relying on the same willpower that let you down in the first place. If resistance seems futile, remember the example of the Great Stanford Marshmallow Resisters of 1968: out of sight, out of mind. When you identify the pattern that has the biggest impact on your life, only then can you break it down and begin to develop a new one.

Opportunities for Action

Exercise: Breathe, Move, Sleep

If you've ever had your heart set aflutter, you have experienced a tell-tale physical sign of temptation. When you are on the verge of caving in to a craving (or succumbing to a distraction such as the Internet), your heart rate rises, but its consistency decreases—a cardiovascular portrait of speeding up while losing control. When you are ready to face the challenge, however, the opposite occurs, a slower and more regulated rhythm. Heart rate variability (HRV) is such a strong indicator of willpower that it can allow researchers to predict how people do in the face of temptation. Fortunately, there are a number of ways to increase your HRV so that it helps you keep your cool at times when you feel like you might get all hot and bothered.

- *Twenty breaths:* Breathing to regulate your HRV can work wonders. The University of Pennsylvania's Michael Baime recommends closing your eyes, sitting upright, and taking twenty breaths, counting each one (an inhale/exhale counts as one) and focusing on each cycle intently for about ten seconds each. Doing this in moments of weakness can help you triumph over temptation. Practicing twice each day builds strength so you can stay on the path, not stray from it.
- *Step (or run) away from temptation:* Regular exercise increases HRV, optimizes your willpower, and has been found to reduce consumption of alcohol, caffeine, and junk food; minimize impulse buying, procrastination, and lateness; and increase study habits and money-saving practices. No need to

run a marathon: If you want to hit the gym, great. If it's a stroll around the block, equally great. Just move it.

- *Rested eyes stay on the prize:* The effects of sleep deprivation resemble mild intoxication, and your HRV suffers the same way (bad decisions, anyone?). If you're still working on getting a solid seven to eight, try a twenty-minute nap (tip: Dan swears by his earplugs and takes them everywhere he goes). It has loads of cognitive benefits, and you may notice an instant boost in your ability to stay on task and ignore the distractions.

Exercise: Out of Sight, Out of Mind

We once had a student in class who loved ice cream so much that when we asked the students about their most challenging temptations, she raised both hands and said, "This is Ben and this is Jerry. They live in my fridge. Always." Her solution to the addiction? She simply stopped keeping ice cream in her freezer, forcing herself to walk to the store to buy a pint when she had to have it. Ben and Jerry were a lot less desirable when it became a commuter relationship. If you're glued to your phone, bury it at the bottom of your closet at bedtime instead of keeping it by — or in — your bed. If you're a shopaholic, freeze your credit card in a block of ice. Not only can you save a few bucks (or calories), but you save up your willpower for when you need it later.

Whether it's ice cream or your ex, choose a temptation you would be better off without. Now, strategize. If you walk by the ex's dorm every day, change your route. If you find yourself rereading their texts, erase them all from your phone. (Dan did this once for his best friend. Without telling him. Long term, good. Short term, mayhem.) Move the TV out of your dorm room. Turn your phone off and leave it in the bottom of your backpack during class. Stick to your strategy for one month, then move on to the next temptation.

Studies show that we should be ready for our next challenge after thirty days.

Exercise: Two Wills Are Better than One

Social support can be key to boosting willpower. Whether you want to resist temptations or take more initiative, teaming up with friends makes the going easier.

- *In good company:* Studies show that simply observing people who are exerting their willpower can help raise our own levels. Do you appreciate a friend's habits when it comes to studying or good nutrition? Spend more time with that person.
- *Get a workout partner:* Accountability to others is a key to goal-setting. Find a friend who is looking to build willpower, share your specific goals with each other, and then set a time to check in every day on progress and goals for the day ahead. A quick text or conversation will do the trick.
- *Try a trainer:* Personal trainers aren't just for toning up your abs, they can buff up your willpower as well. Whether it's organization, managing personal finances, nutrition, or any other area you want to improve, work with a specialist once a week, logging your progress each day. Stick with one area of focus at a time (remember, you only have one willpower muscle!).

The Takeaway

The Big Idea

Willpower is a key element of your success in college and life. It affects the quality of your grades, friendships, health, resilience, and happiness (to name a few), and predicts higher salaries and more secure relationships in the years ahead.

Be Sure to Remember

- Willpower is like a muscle: It becomes tired when exercised, and it needs to be conserved and rested. But the more you exercise it, the stronger it becomes.
- Your willpower muscle is depleted by many everyday activities, including making decisions, taking initiatives, multitasking, restraining impulses, and sleep deprivation. Alcohol and low blood sugar can also sap it.
- Procrastination definitely falls under the heading of willpower. Identifying the *type* of procrastination is key to addressing the issue.

Making It Happen

- Treat your willpower like the muscle it is. Work your breath and body and rest up to be the strongest you can be.
- Avoiding temptation is easier said than done, but when you strategize to keep it off your plate, away from your path, or out of sight, you give yourself an advantage and preserve your willpower for when you need it later.
- Teaming up with others can help you be your strongest in the face of temptation. Rally friends, classmates, or professionals to support you.

CHAPTER 7

Choice: How to Make Decisions Like a Champ

(I Can't Get No) Satisfaction.

—*The Rolling Stones*

Once upon a time, buying a set of headphones meant choosing from precisely one option. It was black and flimsy, with round ear pads that were somehow both spongy and sandpapery, and a thin, sharp metal band that clung to your head with the ferocity of a terrified housecat. Fortunately, listeners were distracted from the pain by the crappy, tinny sound with no bass. As horrible as headphones were, listening to music while walking down the street was the closest thing to a miracle that we had experienced since chocolate met peanut butter, and thus college students nationwide were happy shelling out their $12.99 to suffer for their seriously low-quality sounds. After a while, another pair of headphones came out. They were equally poor, equally painful, and equally priced, but these . . . these were silver. Now when we went to the store we had to decide what color to get. We didn't care that we only had two headphones to choose from; as long as we could bump our Beatles, Biggie, Beethoven, or Basie, life was good.

Speaking of beats, a few decades and a few thousand headphone variations later, we were introduced to Beats By Dre. When these first landed, they were the coolest things you could put on your head, and while far comfier and better-sounding than their prehistoric ancestors, the first pair were a solid black. People wanted them so badly they (sorry, we can't *not* go there) beat each other up over them. Until one day, yes, a silver pair emerged. Just like in the old days, there were two options for you to choose between. But then suddenly, wait... are those red? Whoa... blue? Baby, navy, *and* sky? Oh *snap,* are those *gold?* Whether you rocked the green because they brought out your eyes, the custom jobs studded with rhinestones because bling is beautiful, or the wireless model to avoid tangled cords, the choices were exciting and awesome.

What *isn't* so exciting and awesome, however, is the psychological price tag of abundant choice. As you will find out in this chapter, sacrificing one option for another (say, the black for the silver) may not be the cause of too much regret, but when we are faced with forgoing one hundred possible choices, the psychological toll is exponentially worse. Whether you're moving to Mozart or Metallica, the joy that you get from the Beats you *did* buy can be severely diminished by knowing how many others you *didn't.*

More choice is not always a better thing, and too much can be a nightmare. Now let's take off the headphones and move to all of the choices that life is about to lay out for you, because guess what: you may never have more choices in your entire life than you are about to have in college.

In high school, you were told where to sleep, what time to wake up, where to be when, and what you had to do all day. You had a very limited choice of classes, had to eat at your scheduled lunchtime, and may have had parameters around what you were allowed to wear. You even had to ask permission to go to the bathroom.

In college, however, practically everything is a choice. There is nobody there to tell you when (or where . . . or with whom) to sleep. You can develop early-onset arthritis in your fingers just from incessantly slamming the snooze button every morning. You can have tacos for breakfast if you feel like it. You can wear *anything* (or pretty much nothing) and decide whether to go to class or lounge around in bed all day studying the nuances of Netflix. During class (provided you attend), you can go to the restroom anytime you please — and if you don't want to come back, guess what, you don't have to.

All of those choices take place before 10 a.m.

As for the rest of your life, check this out:

- *Parties:* In high school, you were lucky if you had two parties to choose from on a Saturday night, but now even the smallest schools have five times that number and the big universities have too many to count. But more parties are good, right?
- *Dating:* There is a very good chance that your pool of potential partners just multiplied by anywhere from 100 percent to 10,000 percent. That's a *great* thing . . . right?
- *Majors:* Trying to keep pace with a rapidly changing world and job market, colleges and universities are adding new disciplines every year, offering degrees in fields like homeland security and agroecology. The University of Washington offers 227 majors — more than any other US school in 2016 — followed by Brigham Young University with 169 and Ohio State with 153. Most universities allow you to double-major, you can have a major and a minor, and some schools, such as New York University, allow you to design your own. More majors are good . . . right?

On two consecutive Saturdays at a popular public gathering spot in Menlo Park, California, Sheena Iyengar of Columbia University and

Mark Lepper of nearby Stanford University offered people the opportunity to exercise an inalienable right: the freedom to choose.

What did they get to choose? Jam.

The experiment consisted of two displays of jam, rotated hourly, on tables in a large supermarket. On one display, six flavors of expensive jam were presented with an invitation to taste any and all for free. Forty percent of the shoppers who passed by stopped to try a sample. On the other display were two dozen flavors of jam. The colorful bounty attracted the attention of shoppers the way a glimmering lure catches fish: 60 percent stopped for a taste.

So we like having more choice. Big deal.

But that's only half of the study.

Whether they encountered six jams or two dozen, the 249 people who were drawn to the tables averaged around 1.5 tastes of jam. Of the people who sampled the display of six flavors, 30 percent followed up and purchased the preserves. But of the people who were enticed by the twenty-four choices...get ready...a mere *3 percent* followed up by buying any. Yup, even though shoppers were much more likely to be drawn in by the wide array of choices, they were much *less* likely to follow through with a purchase. We may *tell ourselves* that we want more choices in our lives, but our actions say otherwise.

And this is pertinent to you how? If jam is not your jam, then perhaps extra credit will do the trick. Everybody loves extra credit—unless there are too many options. When students at Stanford University were offered six essays to choose from that would help bump up their grades, 74 percent of them leapt at the opportunity. But when students were offered *thirty* prompts, they were much less likely to participate—oh, and for those who did, the quality of their work was far lower than that of their peers who had fewer choices.

Dating runs the same way. The more choices you have, the less likely you are to choose, and when (or *if*) you do, the less happy you are with your dating experience. One study of hundreds of speed daters found that not only did a greater number of options lessen the odds of participants closing the deal for an evening out, but the wider diversity (height, age, educational background, etc.) of their potential matches dropped the number even further. People who look to meet potential partners online expect to benefit from the cornucopia of possibilities, but often end up just plain confused. Swipe left enough and you may find yourself just shutting off the phone altogether.

It turns out that whether we're talking about headphones, jam, grades, dating, or almost anything else in life, more choice may *seem* fantastic, but in fact it's making it harder for you to thrive. Whether material goods or life decisions, when we set ourselves up to pick positively, our freedom to make decisions can lead to greater optimism, excitement, and happiness. Yet when we let choice overwhelm us, we're likely to end up paralyzed and empty-handed. And when we *do* pull the trigger, it doesn't always lead to a better result.

The Challenge of Choice

A downside of choice is not about what you do choose, it's about what you don't. Back in the days of crappy black headphones, there was literally no choice to make, so when you bought your gear, you hadn't missed out on anything. It's like when your parents made your dinner when you were five years old—that's what was for dinner. Period, the end: fish sticks or nothing. But when the silver headphones hit the market, *boom* . . . there was a cost associated with your selection. Whether it's headphones, a party, or a vacation, when you make a choice, you give up the enjoyment you would have experienced from the other pair, shindig, or trip. *The pleasure you miss out on because of what you don't choose is known as an opportunity cost.*

The opportunity cost of the black vs. silver headphones is no big deal, but it's a whole other ball game when two choices become twenty. Think about the multitude of choices you have on campus on any given Saturday night. When you choose that one party over seven others, *and* over two concerts, *and* over three movies, *and* over the football game, *and* over two rush events, *and* meeting that guy for coffee, *and* a chill night at your dorm, your opportunity costs are those nineteen things you are *not* doing. *The pain you feel over what you did not choose is regret — and it only grows the more options you consider.*

If you find yourself feeling nervous about the opportunity cost of your vast range of choice in college, you're not alone. When Louis Harris polled people as to whether they agreed with a statement including "I feel left out of things going on around me," he found that 9 percent of subjects felt this way in 1966, but by 1986 that number had grown to 37 percent. Hello, FOMO (Fear of Missing Out). No matter which activity you choose, those that you didn't choose stick around in your mind, making you second-guess yourself ("Maybe we should have gone to that party...I heard Mike might be there." "This concert sucks, and why am I hanging out with this girl when I could be with my friends having the best night ever?" "Maybe I should check my phone when he leaves the table so I can see what else is going on right now..."). As your doubts continue to mount, the pleasure that your own choice provides declines, and before you know it, what you chose pales in comparison to what you didn't — because there is so much comparison!

Beyond that single Saturday night, think about the expansion your dating pool undergoes as you make the jump from high school to college. As your number of romantic possibilities grows, so does the mental checklist ("Amazing hair, perfect teeth, sense of humor, award-winning genius..."). Throw in dating sites and apps that can screen for certain qualities, and you have a formula that spits out a cornucopia of suitors who meet your specifications. That can be awesome on the one hand, because you can select for common interests (especially if that special person *must* love basketball, philosophy, sushi, and *Fast & Furious*), but on the other hand, it's easy to get preoccupied with the one thing that doesn't seem quite right ("He's *perfect*... other than that thing he does with his toes").

While a larger number of potential partners makes the odds of finding that perfect person even higher, it also leads to an unrealistic expectation of who is "perfect enough" to date. Even if you *do* find someone you're into, your mind might go wandering through the alternatives. If a first date feels good but not stellar, it's easier than ever to move on to the next thing, preventing us from sticking it out long enough to let our date's qualities (or our own!) shine through.

What you do in your free time and whom you do it with can have very real implications for your enjoyment of college, and the choices you make about the classes you take can shape the whole direction of your life. It's a big leap from a handful of electives in high school to choosing from among hundreds when you arrive at college. Even after you've settled on a major, you still have to decide which classes you should take, with which professors, plus what your plans B, C, and D are if you don't get the ones you want. And given that the choices are now all in *your* hands, if anything goes wrong—it's *your* fault for not choosing wisely! Suddenly, the opportunity cost goes from what class you will *not* have on Tuesday and Thursday afternoon to what you will *not* do for the rest of your life. That is a lot of pressure, and it means that as liberating as they are, the choices you have in college can easily feel overwhelming.

Choosing Satisfaction

After just three days of graduate school, Dan felt as if he had been wandering in the desert for forty years. He was physically and intellectually exhausted, didn't know if he was equipped to complete the journey ahead, and wasn't even sure he belonged with this tribe. It was then, one morning at the University of Pennsylvania, that the heavens parted and the angel Barry descended upon him. The angel Barry (better known as legendary Swarthmore professor, author of the marvelous *Paradox of Choice,* and TED Talker Barry Schwartz) came to Dan and his tribe and spoketh to him two words that would change his experience in school and life.

In what could well have been carved on stone tablets, the angel Barry saideth: "And lo, you will have many choices in life, and you shall have but two ways of making these choices: thou shalt maximize or thou shalt satisfice. There is a time for both, but when thou dost satisfice more often, thou shalt find greater well-being."

Even though this message was delivered far less biblically and in a distinctive Brooklyn accent by a guy wearing shorts and slumpy socks, Dan did thus realize that he had been maximizing too often, and he changed his ways to become a satisficer.

And it was good.

Probably, though, you still wonder what maximizing and satisficing are.

That is good, too. A curious mind is a beautiful thing, and we are about to satisfice your curiosity, for *maximizing* and *satisficing* are essential to understand when it comes to managing (and making the most of) the overwhelming nature of choice.

If you have agonized over which headphones (or baseball glove or flat iron or tablet) to buy—and we mean to the extent that you have checked reviews online, spent hours (days even) comparing prices, asked friends for their opinions, and then checked the Internet again before going to buy said item, only to leave the store or your little cyber-shopping cart with nothing, nada, zilch—you have maximized. If those jeans seemed to fit *almost* perfectly, but you were so sure that there must be another pair that might be even better (and maybe cheaper) that you looked for another month before finally making a purchase, you have maximized. If your dating life consists of swiping left a hundred times every night and swiping right about once a month...yeah, you know the drill.

As you may have gleaned, maximizers will settle only for the best quality and the best fit. They will often confirm their selections by finding the best reviews online, and collecting recommendations from friends, and often will buy something only at the best price. Maximizing on headphones? They need the best bass response, the clearest highs, *and* the perfect color...oh, and you need to find them at the lowest price...in the world. You know the coffee maximizers, because they would *never* be seen in Dunkin' Donuts. Internships? They want the hottest industry, highest possible salary, coolest company. Just the right car, just the right club, just the right dorm. When it comes to dating, everything has to be juuuust right: the perfect hair, teeth, smile, sense of humor, and you know...the rest of it, too. Even when they find what they're looking for, they keep their head on a swivel for the next best thing.

Satisficers, however, are willing to be happy with what Schwartz calls "merely excellent" (and what maximizers might label inferior, ordinary, or second-rate). With all of this wonderful choice at our fingertips, why would we ever choose "merely" anything? Why limit our choices and deprive ourselves of the best fit, taste, feel, or experience? What could possibly be bad about wanting the very best? Nothing...until you consider that due to opportunity cost (you know, that tsunami of things that you DON'T choose), the very process of getting exactly what you want might be diminishing your ability to enjoy it.

Schwartz has proposed that the people who suffer the most in a world of so much choice are the people who strive to get the best. What if satisficing with "good enough" turned out to be more pleasurable than maximizing for the "best"?

How to Satisfice (and Be Satisfied)

As implied by the term—a mashup of "satisfied" and "suffice"—satisficers tend to be more satisfied with the decisions they make, specifically because they *do* suffice by limiting their choices. Despite the idea that they may be "settling for less," studies have shown that thanks to lower opportunity costs and less regret, they are subjectively happier with the choices they make. By setting themselves up to consider fewer options, engage in less social comparison (i.e., what grade did *she* get, or what shoes is *he* wearing), and thus agonize less over the seemingly infinite options, they spend less time exhaustively scouring through their search. Not only does this allow them to dampen the regret and quell those nagging feelings of "What if!?," but the time they save can be spent on friends, family, sleep, studying, or any number of valuable alternatives.

How can you become a satisficer? By minimizing the exact thing that gets you into this situation: choice. To achieve their "merely excellent" outcome, satisficers begin the process by setting a "threshold of acceptability," a fancy way of saying standards for what is good enough. Looking for headphones with booming bass? Check. Under a hundred bucks? Check. Wireless? Check. Once those criteria are met, it's easy to make a decision and move on without stressing about it.

Here are a few more basic strategies to help you change the way you choose:

Rules of thumb: Be systematic and practical about how you approach making a decision. For example, try setting your budget before shopping online for that hot pair of kicks. By checking the corresponding search filter (i.e., "$100 or below"), you lower the number of possibilities and right off the bat eliminate pricier choices that might linger in your mind during and after the purchase. If you know you want a backpack rather than a messenger bag, or definitely want black (or blue or red), check those boxes, too, and *boom,* two thousand options become twenty-five. You can't regret what you don't see (and you won't be tempted to overspend, either).

Habits: Steve Jobs always sported a black turtleneck, and Mark Zuckerberg is famous for his gray T-shirt and hoodie. Why? Because their fashion habits freed them up to focus on more important things in life. Whether you are known for an omnipresent tie or a T-shirt, jeans or yoga pants, dressing habitually can minimize choices and leave your brain to ponder bigger and better things. That doesn't just apply to clothes. Committing to a set study period or location every day, or a set snack (which you drop into your bag every morning), can minimize distraction and allow you to focus more fully on what you need to.

Irreversible decisions: When you get to college, there is a magical time the first few weeks of the semester called the add-drop period during which you can swap any classes you're not into. While this is an important opportunity to make sure you love your course schedule, the end of add-drop can bring an accompanying wave of relaxation. Why? Because there's no more choice to be made (and you can finally stop reading ratemyprofessor.com). While making decisions that can easily be reversed feels like a relief in the moment, this may actually interfere with your enjoyment. You may notice the same effect with consumer purchases: knowing that you can return your new backpack for the next thirty days means that rather than being stoked about your new accessory, you spend a month wondering if something better may pop up. Try buying things that are final sale (or making returns tougher by tearing up the receipt). Committing to the decision when you make it can release you from the stress caused by wondering if you should change your mind.

When It's More Than Just Headphones

There are absolutely times in life when maximizing is the wise path to follow: with big life decisions such as medical emergencies, yeah, you may want to get the *best* surgeon. When you get married, you probably want to make sure you're making the absolute best decision about the person who will be your life partner. Yet while there may seem to be some very obvious scenarios—choosing your major and searching for your first job may come to mind—be careful about how you max out. Even on those fronts, what seems like the "best" choice can often leave you less than satisfied.

With this in mind, we share our final study of the chapter, one that will without question apply to each and every one of you. It is sweeter than the jam study and even more valuable than the research on extra credit. This study looks at the inevitable: the first job you will take when you graduate. Whether this is four years or four days away, it's coming, and when it does, you will want to score something awesome. You are going to want a gig that you love, that pays well, that promises great colleagues and a meaningful purpose, and that puts you in a zip code you're stoked to live in. Clearly, if there was ever a time to maximize, this would be it.

Graduating students from eleven colleges and universities, with majors ranging from business to the arts and humanities, participated in a 2006 study by Sheena Iyengar, Rachael Wells, and Barry Schwartz, and many of them did indeed employ maximizing techniques as they sought the ideal job. As expected, the maximizers not only considered more jobs, sought more options, and did more social comparison, but *they also earned salaries that were 20 percent higher on average than their satisficing peers.*

Those maximizers, however, also earned some other things. In addition to the fatter paychecks, they picked up more anxiety, stress, worry, feelings of being overwhelmed, and disappointment in the process *and* (as if it needed to get any worse) were less satisfied overall with their work. The satisficers? They were more content, excited, elated, and happy, and despite making far less dough, they were far more satisfied with their first job.

In their search for "the best," maximizers considered more

possible jobs. Even when they did score the big gig, their high expectations had no way of being met, and they regretted all the choices they didn't make. Faced with what feels like a huge, life-altering decision, maximizing might help you get to the top, but it doesn't necessarily pave a road that leads to happiness or well-being.

Opportunities for Action

Exercises: Choosing Where to Be Choosy

As ironic as it is, the first step toward making the most of your choice is making one: Which decisions are essential for maximizing? Once you know that, you will feel more comfortable satisficing other choices.

In classic pro/con style, make a two-column list: one labeled "Essential" and the other labeled "Wouldn't it be nice." That list on the left probably won't be voluminous, and just seeing these side by side can make you feel comfortable about taking the steps below.

Exercise: Set Yourself Up for Satisfaction

As you well know by now, a key to making the most of the explosive array of choices at your fingertips is making them manageable. Before you make your next purchase, go on your next date, or even choose what you are going to wear, here are three basic strategies to help you find greater satisfaction in your selections:

1. Build your filter: Just as shopping websites offer a filter for your choices, you can do the same online or off-. Think of three things you need to purchase in the next few weeks. Choose two or three criteria (price, color, style, etc.) to apply to the process, and don't waver from the options that result.

2. Create habits: What is one habit (same clothes, snack, place/ time to study) that you can create and commit to right now? Set the habit and stick to it for at least thirty days.

3. Make irreversible decisions: For the next three purchases, try buying things that are final sale (or at least a hassle to return). Instead of saying you might study or work out later in the day, put it in your calendar and make it irreversible (scheduling it with a partner can help). Committing to the decision at the moment you make it can release you from the stress caused by wondering if you should change your mind. Do or do not, there is no try—Yoda said that. *Write down one irreversible decision you can make in the next week (and don't reverse your decision to make that decision!).*

Exercise: Savoring Satisfaction

What are some particularly wonderful decisions you have made recently? Choose three—animal, vegetable, mineral, human, it doesn't matter. What's so hot about what you bought or whom you met? Focus on the qualities that made you congratulate yourself for a great choice—and then write three of them down.

1. _____

2. _____

3. _____

For the next week, every time you enjoy any of the above, remind yourself what got you all stoked when it/they first came into your life. Don't stop there—make a point of prompting yourself as the weeks and months pass, and your choices will give you that much more satisfaction as time goes on. You aren't just savoring people or objects, you are savoring life.

The Takeaway

The Big Idea

An abundance of choice presents opportunities and challenges. How you set yourself up to make decisions can mean the difference between thriving and suffering.

Be Sure to Remember

- Too much choice can be paralyzing: when you are overwhelmed with options, you often don't choose anything at all.
- No matter how splendid your final choice may be, if you consider too many possibilities in the process, the regret over what you did not choose can outweigh the pleasure of what you did.
- Choosing what is "good enough" (satisficing) can be a lot more satisfying than selecting "the best" (maximizing).

Making It Happen

- Create personalized filters such as price range, specific brand, number of calories, or color of the product *before* beginning your decision-making process.
- Set a time limit for your process of choice. Knowing that you have to click "buy" in the next thirty seconds/minutes/hours can help you minimize unneeded deliberations.
- Whenever possible, make irreversible decisions (i.e., no-return policy on purchases, erasing your ex's number from your phone, unchangeable tickets).

CHAPTER 8

Stress: Making It Work for You

One day, in retrospect, the years of struggle will strike you as the most beautiful.

—*Sigmund Freud*

How much stress do you need to realize your potential? (Hint: the answer is not zero.)

Janet, a nineteen-year-old liberal studies major, was constantly "stressed out." She worried about the test next week, about not finishing her paper on time, about going out on a Friday night. At times she felt overwhelmed and couldn't concentrate. Even the things she loved, like crossword puzzles or connecting with high school friends, felt like a demand. She had difficulty falling asleep, worrying about all the things she needed to do. But worst of all were the stomachaches. By the middle of her first semester, Janet woke up almost every morning with a gnawing pain in her belly. If she could just get rid of all the stress, Janet thought, the stomachaches would go away. We teach our students, however, that while stress may be harmful, it comes with some benefits, too. This came as something of an epiphany for Janet, who then made a conscious decision to turn her problem upside down: instead of striving for no stress, she would start using it to her advantage. Janet accepted that stress was going to be a part of her life, and she wanted to get the most out of it.

Type the word "stress" into a search engine, and you'll get more than half a billion results. For college students, the topic is particularly relevant. In fact, 85 percent of college students report feeling stressed every day. The top stressors include:

- schoolwork (77 percent)
- grades (74 percent)
- finances (67 percent)
- family issues (54 percent)
- relationship/dating (53 percent)
- extracurricular activities (51 percent)

There are plenty of things to be stressed about throughout college: finding the right classes, the right friends, and the right place to live. Although you might imagine that it gets easier, stressors appear in different forms with every passing semester. At some point during their undergrad experience, 60 percent of students feel so much stress that they can't get their work done. Oh, and did we mention that higher levels of stress are correlated with higher rates of depression and anxiety?

No, we're not trying to stress you out; good news is what we're about to deliver here. Stress is not the problem. In fact, stress is essential for you to be your very best. It's how you deal with it that may be tripping you up. This can be awfully tough to grasp, given that over the past forty years, the dominant message in the United States has been that you need to either reduce your stress or get rid of it altogether. In a 2014 survey titled "The Burden of Stress in America," by NPR, the Robert Wood Johnson Foundation, and the Harvard School of Public Health, 70 percent of respondents reported that high levels of stress impacted their family life, health, social lives, and work, but almost the same percentage of people felt that at some time over the past month, stress had given them a boost as well. Sure, stress can come in supersize portions that are too much to handle for any healthy person, but stress reduction is only one side of the coin: *the right amount of stress is enhancing.*

Still skeptical? Take a moment and imagine an achievement from your past. It could be the time you ran a 5K/10K/20K, gave a stellar performance to a packed house, or aced a class that pushed you to your limits. Think about the work you put into it, and your emotions during the process. Write down a few sentences describing the achievement and what you did to accomplish it, if that helps it to hit home. Now consider how stress played a role along the way.

Kelly McGonigal, a lecturer at Stanford University, defines stress as any moment when "something you care about is at stake." Whether your moment was a pressure-packed performance (on the field, onstage, or in the classroom), scoring an internship, or getting into college, your achievement was not only highly personal, but likely involved a great deal of stress. That stress was not there solely to make you miserable: it also pushed you to practice, study, and prepare harder, and when the time came, it was exactly that stress that allowed your mind and body to be focused and primed.

In this chapter, not only will we show you how to manage stress, we'll show you how it can help you to be your very best. For many, including Janet, the first step toward managing her stress involved developing a different mindset toward it. Instead of attempting to reject it, Janet figured out that there are moments in life when we need to invite stress into our lives to push, propel, and motivate us. We will look at the mindsets that stress us out and the ones that help us perform better and score higher and keep us feeling more confident. We will show you ways to calm yourself down when you are feeling overwhelmed, but we will also show you how to seek out challenges and overcome them.

Okay, now you can relax . . . but not too much.

Getting to Know You

Before you take advantage of stress, it is helpful to understand your current stress mindset. Using the Stress Mindset Measure below, rate each question as follows:

0 = Strongly Disagree
1 = Disagree
2 = Neither Agree nor Disagree
3 = Agree
4 = Strongly Agree

1. The effects of stress are negative and should be avoided.
2. Experiencing stress facilitates my learning and growth.
3. Experiencing stress depletes my health and vitality.
4. Experiencing stress enhances my performance and productivity.
5. Experiencing stress inhibits my learning and growth.
6. Experiencing stress improves my health and vitality.
7. Experiencing stress debilitates my performance and productivity.
8. The effects of stress are positive and should be utilized.

Add up your answers to the odd-numbered questions and the even-numbered questions separately; how the two balance out will give you a snapshot of your mindset about stress. Is it more stress-is-harmful (odd-numbered questions) or stress-is-helpful (even-numbered questions)? Just as we have a mindset about growth and learning (as discussed in Chapter 4), we have a mindset about stress. The vast majority of Americans score high on stress-is-harmful and believe that stress will bring us down physically and mentally. A minority of people (hopefully a growing one by the end of this chapter) understand that stress can help them achieve peak performance, growth, and learning. The only thing your score on the above test indicates is your *current* mindset, not the mindset you could develop if you're willing to create some change.

In 1908, Robert Mearns Yerkes and John Dillingham Dodson designed an experiment that would begin to tackle the question, "How is stress related to learning?" The researchers tracked mice to see how stress would affect their ability to learn. Simple—yet painful, because how do you stress out mice? You shock them. The researchers set up two corridors to choose from—one painted white and the other black—and if a mouse went down the black corridor, *ZAP!* Yerkes and Dodson observed that given too mild a shock, the mice just shrugged it off and kept on keepin' on—no biggie if they made the same mistake again. Too big a jolt, and the stress left them too frazzled to figure out what had just happened and how to make that not happen again. Those who learned most quickly—indeed, those mice that might need half as much time to learn which corridor to take—did it Goldilocks style: the size of their shock was juuuuust right.

You may not be a mouse, but research shows that you learn like one.

Not that we are suggesting self-electrocution (to do so would be highly unethical—fascinating, but highly unethical), but a just-right dose of stress can lead to your peak performance. Ed Ehlinger of the University of Minnesota studied almost 10,000 students and found that those who couldn't manage their stress (32 percent of them) had a 0.5 drop in their GPA compared to their less-stressed-out peers. Imagine if getting your ZAP on in just the right way enabled you to learn math/English/anything-else-you-want in less time and learn it better.

The Yerkes-Dodson experiments have risen to prominence as the Yerkes-Dodson Law (YDL) and have become the key to understanding the relationship between stress and our ability to change, learn, and perform. The YDL even comes with a handy-dandy YDL curve (see below) that helps us understand how to think about stress in relation to our performance in college and beyond.

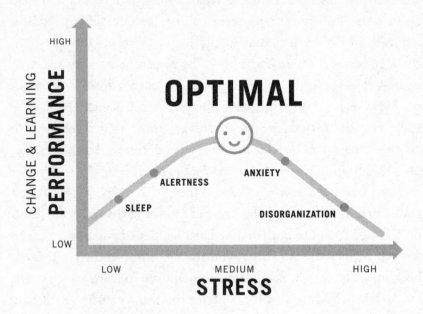

One of the many beauties of the YDL curve is its simplicity: if you have too little stress (the left side of the curve) or too much stress (the right side), you miss out on opportunities to learn, change, perform, or basically do anything in college to help realize your potential. Simple? Yes. Pertinent? Very.

Kristen Joan Anderson, a psychologist at Northwestern University, did her version of the mouse-ZAP study on 100 college students, giving them escalating amounts of caffeine and having them answer questions like the ones in the verbal section of the Graduate Record Examinations (GREs). She found that many college students (and the rest of us), particularly with difficult tasks, perform their best at levels of stimulation that look a lot like the YDL curve (for those interested: about two cups seems to do it).

Interestingly, though, a feeling of control over stress profoundly impacts the effects of being stressed out. A 2015 study about stress and its impact on test scores found that, regardless of how "stressed out" the students really were, if they felt they could handle it, their grades didn't suffer. For Janet, realizing that stress wasn't going to be her lifelong enemy gave her a sense of control. The stress may have stuck around, in varying degrees, but her stomachaches disappeared. How you relate to, tolerate, and manage stress in any given situation dictates how well you can take advantage of it.

Putting Stress to the Test

Stanford psychologist Alia Crum must have been well aware that there are few things on earth that Americans fear more than public speaking when she designed a study to see how college students would react to stressful situations: they had to write and present a captivating ten-minute speech to a roomful of strangers in half an hour. *BOOM*—nightmare! The kicker (if you needed one): they were told that the speech would be videotaped and a group of experts would be available to provide feedback.

Before the task, their stress mindsets were evaluated. For the stress-is-harmful crew, the process proved to be too much. They took a crack at the talk but passed on the potential expert feedback. For the stress-is-helpful peeps? Bring it. They may have taken a deep breath before diving in, but they reacted in a way that took advantage of the promise of growth. Not only did they welcome the expert feedback, but they reported feeling less physically stressed out as well. As Crum points out, the stress-is-helpful mindset rises to meet "the demand, value, or goal" of a stressful situation. You are going to have a lot of different stressful situations in college—social, academic, and personal. Feedback is essential to growth and change in any situation; we talk about it in almost every chapter. The stress-is-enhancing mindset encourages you to seek out feedback and internalize it.

If you landed squarely in the stress-is-harmful mindset, fear not—there is hope for you yet! In another study, Crum chose 388 employees at a company "undergoing dramatic downsizing and restructuring." (To put it in a college context, how would you feel if you heard that a randomly selected 33 percent of students at your school would be kicked out in the next few months? Yeah...ZAP.) Employees were divided into three groups, each assigned to watch one of three short videos on health, performance, or learning. One video focused on stress-is-harmful, one on stress-is-helpful, and the other was simply neutral. Over the course of the next week, those who watched the stress-is-harmful video felt no difference in their work, stress level, or health (likely because a vast majority of them already had the stress-is-harmful mentality). But the employees who watched the stress-is-helpful videos reported greater performance, had a better mood and felt less anxious, and noted that their physical health seemed to improve. Oh, and the videos? They were each only three minutes long. Three! If stressed-out businesspeople who were about to be fired could change their mindsets after watching a three-minute video, there's a good chance that you can as well.

Fight-or-Get-the-Hell-Out-of-Here

It's not just your mind that reacts to stress. Your physical reaction to pressure has been wired into you since the day you were born. Stop for a moment and think about the personal achievement you wrote about earlier, or the last really big test you took (the SAT tends to be a good go-to). Do any of these reactions come to mind?

- Increased heart rate
- Feeling flushed

- Feeling shaky
- Appearing pale
- Breathing quickly

Many people check every box. One study found that certain students preparing to take the SATs reported being so anxious and emotional that their minds would go blank, they became preoccupied worrying about whether others were doing better than they were, or couldn't even concentrate on the test to begin with (all of which influenced their actual scores). What was happening to them? They are human beings. And like every single person since the dawn of mankind, their fight-or-flight instinct was being activated.

The fight-or-flight response is the human fire alarm system that has helped to keep us at the top of the food chain ever since our ancestors first roamed the planet. Lions, tigers, and bears show up at your cave and *ka-WHAM*, that sucker goes off. You start to breathe fast so you can get all the oxygen you need into your blood while your rapidly beating heart is pumping it to your muscles so that you can fight or...yes...get the hell out of there. Your body is primed to react, and your brain is primed to do whatever it needs to survive. As advanced as we are in so many ways, with our shiny cell phones and our fancy computers, our brains are still just like those of our cave-dwelling ancestors. To us, a threat is a threat; our rapid breathing and increased heart rate are the same whether we're staring into the maw of a saber-toothed tiger or the blank page of a calculus midterm. We are primed to fight or book it, yet when it comes to exams, most of us try to ignore the panic and sit, practically motionless. This is part of the *mismatch theory;* what once kept us alive now feels like it is pulling us under. Trying to fight your own internal alarm actually narrows your focus and minimizes your odds of thinking clearly. So, what are you going to do? If only scurrying away scored us an A, we would all just invest in better running shoes—but alas, it doesn't.

Trying to eliminate the fight-or-flight response would be like trying to eliminate our desire for sex. Millions of years of evolution ain't being reversed anytime soon. What we can do is use our big human brains to learn how to manage it, and even make it work *for* us.

If the fight-or-flight response is the overactive kid in the house, constantly in motion and never able to sit still, its sibling is much easier to get along with and far more productive: the challenge response.

The Challenge Response

For most of us, the butterflies in our stomach that come with the big test/date/performance/event are not the pretty little creatures from childhood. They don't land on your shoulder eliciting oohs and aahs as you chase them around the garden. No—these butterflies chase you. They are evil zombie butterflies who cost us about 10 percent of our final SAT score in the previous study compared to the students with less anxiety. But what if the butterflies signaled possibility rather than peril, promise rather than pitfall? What if these little suckers were actually trying to help us do better?

If you have ever prepared to take the field or the stage, or simply braced yourself for a tough conversation with a friend or roommate, you may recognize the challenge response. There is excitement and fear, joy and apprehension, and a nervousness mixed with eager anticipation. Much like the physiological responses that come with its fight-or-flight sibling, the challenge response makes your heart rate and blood pressure rise, but instead of feeling panic and becoming more reactive, you develop greater focus and concentration (sound useful for an exam?). The challenge response is quite a heady cocktail, and if you get it right, it can put you in the headspace to realize terrific breakthroughs. Best of all, you have the ability to influence which response you are going to have.

Opportunities to soar come in many guises, but very few are more pressure-packed than the tests that help determine our future. The GREs are to grad school what your SAT/ACT was to college. More than 500,000 people (69 percent of them twenty-five years old or younger) take the GRE in a year. In a study, Harvard psychologist Jeremy Jamieson, whose research focuses on stress and performance, gave two groups of undergrads a practice GRE. The first group was simply given the test and told to begin. The second group, however, was primed to experience the pressure differently — they were told to read the following paragraph before taking the practice exam:

> People think that feeling anxious while taking a standardized test will make them do poorly on the test. However, recent research suggests that [physiological] arousal doesn't hurt performance on these tests and can even help performance. People who feel anxious during a test might actually do better. This means that you shouldn't feel concerned if you do feel anxious while taking today's GRE test. If you find yourself feeling anxious, simply remind yourself that your arousal could be helping you do well.

The results? The second group scored an average of 55 points higher than their nonprimed classmates (738 to 683). But wait, it gets better. One month later, the same participants took the actual GRE, and the difference between their scores was even greater: 65 points (770 vs. 705).

Can It Really Be This Simple?

Simple, yes. Simplistic, no. The excitement (or dread...what Alan's daughter calls being "nervouscited") we may feel before an exam is the activation of our fight-or-flight response. It turns out that reading the passage shifted the students' mindset so that they reframed stress, feeling less dread and more excitement. This, in turn, led to better performance on the exam. By simply reading and internalizing the paragraph, students swapped out their fight-or-flight response for that much kinder sibling: *the challenge response.*

Opportunities for Action

Exercise: Getting Excited to Stay Calm

If you are thinking that trying to keep calm is the way to go when you are stressed out, welcome to the vast majority. Harvard Business School professor Alison Wood Brooks found that 85 percent of people advise calm in the face of the storm. Yet not only does that not work, it actually has the opposite effect.

In a study using the classic combination of college students and karaoke, Brooks found that telling oneself to chillax is in fact a stress generator. She asked college students to perform karaoke in public, but before they went onstage, the subjects were divided into three groups and primed with one of three ideas: say nothing, say "I am excited," or say "I am anxious." Kind of like in an audition for *The Voice,* subjects were rated for pitch, volume, and rhythm by both computers and researchers (sadly, none of whom resembled Adam Levine or Shakira). The "I am anxious" group scored 53 percent, the lowest, apparently freaking themselves out and showing that certain self-statements can do more harm than good. If they were told to say nothing, their average score was 69 percent.

But the "I am excited" group scored an average of *81 percent.* When you harness your challenge response, you can take advantage of your physiology and your mind, and you can kill it.

Feeling that you have control over stress doesn't mean you stop "feeling" it. The "I am excited" group felt just as much anxiety as the "I am anxious" group and the group that said nothing, but they also felt more capable and were observed by their audience to be more confident. If you need to be intoxicated to perform karaoke, this experiment might not seem believable to you, but Brooks also studied people who had to give a speech or solve math problems. Same results: better performance and an even greater sense of competence.

We are not saying you will enjoy swimming with sharks if you just say "I am excited." There is a time and place for you to actually fight or flee. But the next time something is at stake (other than your actual life) and you feel butterflies in your stomach and your heart pounding, remember that feeling scared and feeling excited often go hand in hand, and choosing one over the other (literally just saying out loud "I am excited") can make all the difference.

Exercise: Take a Deep Breath, We're Going to Vagus, Baby!

The right amount of stress can enhance performance, but there will also be moments when we move past that point and need to take control. Lucky for us, when the fight-or-flight response is going off and we want to tone it down, our bodies have a built-in off switch: the vagus nerve. Your vagus nerve winds through the body, touching almost every organ, and plays an important role in bringing your body to a state of equilibrium. It can signal your heart to slow down, lower your blood pressure, and put a halt to the fight-or-flight system. Thankfully, we have a way of turning on the vagus at will. To begin with, we need to introduce you to your diaphragm:

- Stand up.
- Pull your gut in as far as you can (like you're six years old and trying to hide behind a tree).
- Feel under your rib cage. Dig your hands under there until it is vaguely uncomfortable.
- Now say "Hello, diaphragm."

When you ask most people to take a deep breath, their chest expands. But when you take a *genuinely* deep breath, the belly gets pushed out instead. That is your diaphragm descending to make room for all the air.

This deep breathing is called belly breathing, because you have to push out and make that potbelly every time you take a deep breath in. Breathing deeply and rhythmically in this way activates the vagus nerve, signaling the body to turn off the fight-or-flight response. Belly breathing doesn't come naturally, so it's good to practice in order to train yourself to do it effectively. Belly breathing is easier to do when you are relaxed, so start your training in a calm setting (many people practice before bed).

Try the following steps:

- Lie down on the floor and put something on your belly, like a book.
- Push your belly out and watch the book rise as you inhale and fall as you exhale slowly.
- The exhale should be as long as the inhale. Count to five as you inhale and count to five as you exhale.
- Practice with ten full breaths twice daily.

Breathing patterns can be challenging to change when you are in even minor distress (e.g., your phone just fell into the toilet), but the more you practice, the more like a reflex it becomes, and being able to call on it in tense moments is like carrying around a fire extinguisher for your nerves. The next time your heart is racing out of control before you take the stage, run onto the field, or open the blue book, putting on the brakes can be just a breath away.

The Takeaway

The Big Idea

Stress definitely has some downsides, but it is also essential for developing optimal performance, change, and learning.

Be Sure to Remember

- We each have an ideal level of stress that will produce our highest level of performance in any given situation. You can find your sweet spot—somewhere beyond blasé but short of overwhelmed—when stress hits.
- We all have the capacity to develop a stress-is-helpful belief system.
- Fight-or-flight isn't the only choice. A challenge response produces a similar physical response but replaces panic with focus and concentration.

Making It Happen

- When anxiety rears its ugly head, just saying "I'm excited" can steer you toward your challenge response and the better outcome it promises.
- The fight-or-flight system has an off switch, and it is found in deep, rhythmic belly breathing, but as with the fire drills we performed as kids, the key to using this skill during a crisis is found in routine practice.

CHAPTER 9

Mental Health: Dealing with Tough Times

Inside of a ring or out, ain't nothing wrong with going down.
It's staying down that's wrong.

—*Muhammad Ali*

If you had to wager that one of the three people below would become a multimillionaire, who would it be?

a. A single mother living on welfare, battling depression
b. A young woman with crippling obsessive-compulsive disorder
c. A man who has already destroyed his promising career and is so badly addicted to drugs he ends up in prison

The odds seem against all of them, right? We would understand if you chose not to make the bet.

And yet *all three* of these people are among the most successful in their fields. We've just described: (a) J. K. Rowling (author of the Harry Potter series), (b) Lena Dunham (actress, writer, producer, and director of *Girls*), and (c) Robert Downey Jr. (the highest-grossing actor of 2015 and number five on the all-time list).

The chances of becoming that successful are microscopically small in the first place, even before adding serious adversity to the mix.

So how did each of these people overcome the barriers and setbacks to realize their dreams? They knew how to bounce back—and then bounce higher. The ability to shrug off adversity and succeed in the face of tremendous challenge is called resilience.

Resilience can come from within, but it is also strengthened by the people around us. A support network of friends and family certainly helps, but often, help from a mental health professional proves indispensable. Rowling, Dunham, and Downey had friends and family who bolstered their ability to rebound from their challenges in life, but all three also credit therapy for helping them when they were overwhelmed by depression, obsessions, and drug addiction.

Rowling says her nine months undergoing cognitive behavioral therapy saved her life, and she speaks openly about the challenges she faced. "I have never been remotely ashamed of having been depressed," she said in an interview. "Never. What's there to be ashamed of? I went through a really tough time and I am quite proud that I got out of that."

Dunham has written about the indispensable support of the teachers who helped her cope with obsessional thoughts by allowing her the freedom to ask any and all questions that were crowding her mind. But it took professional help to get her to a mental state where she could succeed.

Downey credits the love and support he received from his wife for finally getting him to find therapy and stick to it. If he wanted to marry her, she told him, he had to be sober. Her uncompromising requirement *and* her support were what Downey needed to truly invest in his mental health and treatment. Downey found a therapist, started a twelve-step program, and began to study meditation, yoga, and wing chun martial arts.

None of these amazing individuals had an easy road to recovering their mental health, but with the power of therapy, each of them managed to muster the resilience necessary to let their talents shine through.

Going to therapy may be one of the most resilient acts any of us can engage in. It's tempting to think mental health issues are relatively uncommon, but 50 percent of people will encounter challenges to their mental health during their lifetime: that's every other person at the football game you're attending, the airport you're passing through, the lecture hall you're sitting in. If it's not you, it's your roommate, classmate, or teammate. Seventy-five percent of all those affected will need professional help before their senior year of college. The peak age for the onset of mental illness? Eighteen to twenty-five. This isn't meant to alarm, but rather the opposite. Mental illness is a part of life. What *is* alarming is how few of us have been given the knowledge and tools to overcome it.

People are designed to bounce back from hard times—the will to survive, adapt, and thrive is in our biology—but when emotional overload leaves you feeling like you've lost your mind, a therapist can help you find it again.

In this chapter we will prepare you to become your own agent of change when times are tough. To take advantage of all the qualities we've covered so far—from optimism, to willpower, to stress management—many of us will first need to overcome the challenges that are created by our own minds. Just as you need an academic education, a physical education, and a sex education, we believe you need a mental health education. If half of all people are going to encounter mental illness in life, we all need to become experts in how to recognize problems early and put ourselves back on the path to mental health.

A Lot of Us Have Been There

When I (Alan) talk about the challenges of mental illness, I'm not only speaking about the rich and famous, I'm talking about me. My junior year of college began with my grandfather's death, and I missed the first week of classes. Campus felt like a lonely place when I returned. My friends didn't know my grandfather and preferred to avoid the issue. I'd have encounters like:

"Hey, Alan, long time! Where have you been, how was your summer?"

"Hey, I got back late because my grandfather died."

"Oh, man, I'm so sorry, that sucks. It's good you're back, let's get pizza later!"

The semester moved on and I wasn't a happy camper, and even though my grandfather had died, I didn't connect his loss with my mood. I went about my life. I took classes. As in every semester before, I developed a crush on a woman. We'll call her Satan (my memory is rusty, but I'm pretty sure that was her name). I was pretty sure she wasn't interested in me, but that didn't stop me from pursuing her. I really liked Satan, and my good friend and housemate— we'll call him Esswipe—encouraged me to go after her. After I spent two months chasing her unsuccessfully, Esswipe and Satan ended up making out on a dance floor. The next day when I confronted him, he was hoping I would be "cool" with it.

I wasn't.

My anxiety went through the roof over the weeks that followed. I couldn't sleep and it was hard to keep food down. At first I couldn't concentrate in class, and then I just stopped going. I finally went to the health center, thinking I had the flu, and was indignant when they suggested I might need to talk to someone about my mental health. *"What idiots!"* I thought. Still, I was barely sleeping, accomplishing no work, and even I realized it was time to go home. I missed two days of classes, but enough family and friends remarked on how unhappy I seemed that when I returned to campus, I found myself in front of the office of Dr. Janet Madigan. Pressing the buzzer to be let in, I felt nothing but doom, gloom, and an enormous amount of anxiety, but the stairs to her office proved to be quite literally the first steps I would take toward finding my mental health.

When Should You Seek Help?

Mental illness is a product of our genetics, our environment, and our behaviors. My issues in college checked all those boxes: I was always an anxious kid, which was genetically programmed into me by coming from a long line of worriers. Had my environment that semester been different, I might very well have developed significant anxiety anyway, but there's no doubt that my downward spiral was spurred by my grandfather's death and compounded by the situation with Satan and my roommate. Instead of trying to change my behavior to pull myself out of an emotional nose dive, I didn't acknowledge that I was suffering. After my grandfather died, I didn't talk about feeling upset with anyone, allowing the negative emotions to grow, and I didn't initially seek help after the incident with my roommate, either. Believing that we are resilient can be a double-edged sword, fooling us into suffering longer than we need to.

Because it's absolutely true that everyone has ups and downs, it can be hard to tell when it's time to send up the flares. So how do you know when enough is enough and it's time to seek professional help? Mental anguish isn't as easy to see and evaluate as physical distress, but there are signs you can look for in yourself. Let's take the two most common mental diagnoses on campus: depression and anxiety. One of the classic symptoms of being depressed is that you stop finding pleasure in the things you enjoy. If you are no longer having fun when you play a sport or an instrument you have always loved, that is an indication that you are more than just a little blue. If you feel so anxious that you stop going out or if you can't concentrate enough to get your work done, it's time to get some help. If your mood is consistently down for more than two weeks, this should definitely be a warning sign.

It's okay for life to be hard, but it's not okay for it to be miserable (for too long). When you find yourself incapable of accomplishing tasks or isolating yourself from your friends—the very people who could help you bounce back—this is a strong indication that it is time for outside support.

Most importantly, if negative feelings progress to the point where you are considering harming yourself, it's time to go to the emergency room. More than 50 percent of college students report having thoughts at some point of not wanting to live. The moment you can even conceive of acting on those kinds of thoughts, you need to seek help. Seriously considering self-harm is the mental health equivalent of throwing up blood. That's a graphic comparison, but it should be. You wouldn't hesitate to go to the ER if you were vomiting blood, and if you are contemplating not living, that's just as serious. If you get to this point, it's time to get to a mental health clinician as soon as possible.

To Go or Not to Go?

Don't get stuck on this question. People usually cite stigma, or shame, as being a top reason to avoid therapy, but that is changing. In a 2014 survey, over 30 percent of college students sought out services at the counseling center. More students are seeking care than ever before, possibly because of anti-stigma campaigns and growing awareness that anything divulged to the therapist will remain confidential under the Family Educational Rights and Privacy Act (FERPA: the law that maintains the privacy of mental health records for college students from all people, including their parents).

Many people mistakenly doubt the value of therapy. When the American Psychological Association asked a thousand people why they wouldn't get therapy, 77 percent responded that it just doesn't work. But research tells us the opposite. Fifty-three percent of people in treatment feel significantly better after just one to eight visits. Researchers who evaluate the effectiveness of various mental health treatments have found that the statistical "effect size" of therapy (a measure of how effective it is) is truly huge, and that it grows over time. In one study, people who had received up to forty hours of therapy found that the benefits continued to grow even after the therapy had ended. In another, the benefits of therapy increased by 50 percent in the nine months after therapy was completed.

For those of you who are thinking the cost of therapy will be too high or it will be a waste of your time (and time is money, after all), another large study found that getting therapy can be thirty-two times more efficient at increasing your well-being than making more money: to create the same amount of change as four months of therapy (for a cost of about $800), you'd need a raise of about $25,000.

Alan Goes to Therapy

Walking up the staircase to Dr. Madigan's office, I was filled with doubt, the feeling that I was not normal, and a certain degree of shame. It was a calm room and I knew she was there to help, but I still sat in that chair feeling like I was facing my nemesis. The hardest part of the session turned out to be fighting the desire to like her. She asked me broad questions about who I was and how I had ended up in her office. I told her the story about Satan and Esswipe, and she wondered if that was really at the heart of everything. For the first time, I realized that I hadn't mentioned the loss of my grandfather. It was a lightbulb moment.

Dr. Madigan helped me feel totally comfortable, and over the course of our first three sessions, I started to feel better. She helped me realize that I had to stop worrying about what was "normal" (I now think that "normal" is a useless word that should be banned). She encouraged me to pursue health both mentally and physically. During our conversations, I came to realize that I had stopped exercising, for reasons I couldn't recall. She helped me realize that my lifelong anxiety had made me spend much of my time keeping people at a distance, afraid they would see what a wreck I really was. I felt open enough to talk about why I had never had a girlfriend and how I might do things differently in the future.

When I first went to the campus health center, I saw anxiety the way I did the flu—something to get rid of, something that needed to be cured. But with Dr. Madigan's help, I developed a different relationship with myself, with the people I cared for, and with the world around me. I came to understand that my anxiety hadn't been caused by a single thing, but by everything: years of being anxious, the loss of my grandfather, feeling lonely, feeling hurt. Most importantly, therapy helped me realize that if I was going to thrive in college, I was going to have to change my mental approach.

I began to resume my life, somewhat shaken but also feeling a new confidence. I had been through the worst but had gained new strategies for handling the world. I went back to the gym. I started to reach out to friends with whom I'd lost touch. Perhaps most importantly, my desire and capacity to create change had taken center stage in my life; in making this my priority, I was learning how to truly care for myself.

You Make Change Happen

Your desire to create change counts for a lot. Michael Lambert and his colleagues at Brigham Young University looked at hundreds of studies to see what factors make therapy effective. The most important variable? You. Lambert estimates that up to 40 percent of your potential for success in therapy is determined by your belief that you have the strengths and skills to create change.

If you want a guideline for how people change, check out this model developed by James Prochaska and Carlo DiClemente. This is a general path toward trying to break habits, whether that means cutting down on drinking, quitting smoking, or just keeping your room clean. Think of something you want to change, and try to imagine making that change in these steps:

- Precontemplation—you are not intending to take action in the foreseeable future.
- Contemplation—you are intending to change in the next six months.
- Preparation—you are going to take action in the immediate future, in at least the next month.
- Action—you have made specific overt modifications in your life.
- Maintenance—you've made your change and now are working to prevent slipping back into your old habit. This stage can last from six months to five years.
- Termination—you have zero temptation to return to your old unhealthy habit. Your room is spotless, there are no liquor bottles in your recycling bin, and the smell of nicotine makes your stomach roll.

Keep in mind that the process of change is not necessarily linear and you may find yourself between two stages. At any step along the way, you might relapse and slide back to an earlier stage of change. That's natural. It takes most smokers four attempts to quit cigarettes, and at first glance this might seem discouraging. But if you have this knowledge while attempting to quit for the first time, a relapse is a setback rather than a total failure. That kind of understanding about the difficulty of change can be essential in getting yourself from maintenance to termination.

If you show up at a therapist's office and believe you are still in pre-contemplation, that is the first thing worth talking about. If you seek therapy and are ready for action, you are 40 percent of the way home.

While your desire to create change is essential, it is not enough on its own to guarantee success. Your relationship with the therapist determines up to 30 percent of the success of your treatment. Lambert asserts that therapist skill accounts for another 15 percent when it comes to predicting a good outcome in treatment. Finally, if you have confidence that you are going to get better, this optimism acts like a powerful placebo: Lambert believes it accounts for the final 15 percent toward your successful treatment. All of the factors leave us with a nice chart that helps us visualize what is contributing to a person's improvement during therapy. Every piece plays its part, but none more so than you.

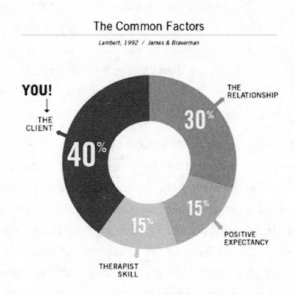

The Common Factors

Lambert, 1992 / James & Braverman

YOU!
↓
THE CLIENT

40%

THE RELATIONSHIP

30%

15%

POSITIVE EXPECTANCY

15%

THERAPIST SKILL

The Common Questions

When a person starts therapy, a series of common questions, answered in advance, might reduce the tension and keep them on the right path.

I'm smarter than my therapist, so how can they help me?

It's okay if you believe you are smarter than the therapist! We might be smarter than our mechanic in certain realms, but most of us still prefer to have a mechanic fixing our car. The important thing is that your therapist has the skills to organize your session in a productive way, much like a trainer in a gym. Their role is to guide you in looking at your thoughts, so that you can challenge yourself and come to a greater understanding but not feel overwhelmed.

Why can't I just talk about my problems with a friend?

Friends and family can give great advice, but there are situations where using them as a therapist is not fair to either of you. Helping family with mental health issues can be like trying to read a map that is so close to your face, it's touching your nose. Proper perspective can only be gained by standing back. You are also more likely to say everything on your mind to someone who has been trained to help others navigate their thoughts and who, by law, must maintain confidentiality.

How do I know if I've found the right therapist?

If you see change after three sessions, you are on the right track. If you aren't seeing the change, let your therapist know. A good therapist should make an effort to mold their approach to your needs. If you start to feel change, keep track of it and keep your therapist in the loop. In one study, people who observed their change and gave their therapists feedback did 75 percent better than peers who didn't take the time to monitor their progress.

If you don't see significant change after five sessions, it's time to find someone else. However, if you go to the next person and the next and there is still no change, consider that—just maybe—it could have something to do with your approach. Some people go to therapy determined to get better, just so long as it doesn't involve changing something about themselves. Therapy won't help people who don't believe change is possible or who think it's the world that needs to change. You need motivation to succeed in therapy, or at the least a desire to develop some of that motivation.

Is going to therapy a sign that I am weak, or will it make me weak?

Going to therapy is an act of bravery. It is the opposite of being weak and, like going to a mental gym, gives you the opportunity to strengthen your mind. Therapy requires that you confront the thing you are most scared of, or the things that make you sad. You may confront fear itself. When the therapist says something you don't like, you need the courage to stay in the session, respond to it, and return! The therapist should make you feel safe, but may need to push you into uncomfortable waters.

"It's Staying Down That's Wrong"

When I (Alan) graduated from college, I had to leave Dr. Madigan behind, but the skills she helped me discover stick with me to this day. Just days after graduating, I finally found a wonderful girlfriend, Agnes, and for that alone, Dr. Madigan was worth her weight in gold (as was Agnes!). I had started to live an examined life, really trying to understand myself. When graduation rolled around, part of me was hoping that I was leaving my anxiety behind as well. I went off to medical school, which, as you may have heard, is not known for being a low-stress environment. Surprise, surprise, I started getting anxious again. But there was a difference this time. After the very first night of not being able to fall asleep, I went in search of a therapist. I made the decision to do whatever it would take to feel good: therapy, meditation, exercise, you name it, I'd try it.

College provides a lot of opportunities to be resilient. That's true for everyone, so remember that your peers are very likely to be experiencing struggles of their own. Don't hesitate to seek out support and camaraderie when you get back a test with a surprisingly low score or put on a show of your artwork and receive challenging critical feedback. But beyond your resilience and the support of your

177

peers, there might come a time when it feels like you've been knocked down and just want to stay there. Some of you will successfully manage on your own, but some of you will not. Remember that you deserve to be healthy, and that suffering in silence is not a badge of honor. The most resilient people understand that seeking help is a way to develop their strength. If you feel like your mental health needs an assist, or perhaps you just feel off, don't wait for it to get better—simply having the desire to change and seek help means you're almost halfway there.

Opportunities for Action

Exercise: It's Time to Go

Even given the extraordinary benefits that therapy can bring, it can sometimes be difficult to resolve to seek help even if you think you might need it. If you are on the fence about seeing a therapist, here are two simple questions to ask yourself:

- What is the risk of going to therapy?
- What are the benefits of going to therapy?

Write down the answers to these questions. We've tried to answer them in this chapter, but we cannot possibly answer them fully for all of you. When it comes to the risks of therapy, it is possible you won't connect with your therapist, you may feel misunderstood, and it will almost definitely be uncomfortable at first. As for the benefits, it could be anything from "this will help me develop a relationship" to "I won't be anxious all the time." When we are really down, we are not thinking with our best mind. We often feel like our worries and anguish are under a microscope and we can see little else, including the things that will help us. Completing this exercise may provide you with some needed objectivity.

Exercise: Making Change Happen in the Session

A good relationship between you and your therapist exists when the two of you agree on what your challenges are and how best to work together to solve them. To find out if you and your therapist are in agreement, we have an assessment created by Dr. Scott Miller, the cofounder of the International Center for Clinical Excellence, to measure the outcome of therapy and the quality of your alliance with the clinician. Before entering the session, look back over the past week, including today, and on a scale of 1 to 5, with 5 being the best, assess how you are doing:

1. With your personal well-being.
2. With your close relationships.
3. With your relationships at work and school.
4. Overall in your life (including work, school, etc.).

Write these down so that you can refer to them in the future. Over time, the scores may come in very handy, giving you an objective measure of whether or not you are improving.

At the end of every session, using the same scale, 1 to 5, answer these three questions to assess the quality of your relationship with the therapist:

1. Did I feel understood and respected?
2. Did we work on and talk about what I wanted to work on and talk about?
3. Is the therapist's approach a good fit for me?
4. Overall, was today's session right for me?

If any of these answers are scoring low, it's a signal of what needs to be discussed with the therapist (for the full scale, check out the link at uthrive .com). Therapists are trained to ask *and* tolerate challenging questions, but if it is too uncomfortable for either of you, it's time to find a new therapist.

The Takeaway

The Big Idea

Many of us have been challenged by mental illness, but with the right awareness and tools, we can find our resilience as well.

Be Sure to Remember

- 50 percent of people experience mental illness in their lifetimes, 75 percent of those by the time they are a senior in college.
- Your belief that you can change is the number one factor that predicts that you will overcome mental illness.
- Your relationship with your therapist is the number two factor that will help you overcome mental health challenges.

Making It Happen

- When we are confronted with mental illness, we are often not using our best mind. If you are reluctant to seek therapy, make a list of the pros and cons of reaching out for help to give yourself some objectivity.
- Before your first session, on a scale of 1 to 5, with 5 as the best, rank how you think you're doing with your personal well-being, with your close relationships, and at handling life in general. Keep the scorecard with you so you can look back and gauge progress as your therapy continues.
- If you are feeling better after three sessions, you have found the right therapist, but by the fifth session, if there's no improvement in sight, time to find a new one.

PART III

STUDENT BODIES

The Church says: the body is a sin.
Science says: the body is a machine.
Advertising says: the body is a business.
The Body says: I am a fiesta.

—*Eduardo Galeano*

Like a magician sawing a person in half, for thousands of years philosophy and religion have attempted to separate the mind from the body. Plato and the Bible both conclude that our body is a distraction (if not something worse) and suggest that if our minds and souls didn't have to deal with our five senses, we could find both peace and purity (although it would make it awfully tough to enjoy a pizza).

Everything in this book thus far has been entirely neck-up, but that is not because we discount the importance of physical health. To thrive in college, you will need your body and your mind, and in this section, we are going to perform a magic trick of our own: we are going to put the body and mind back together.

This reconnection is no simple trick: today's undergrads sleep less, eat worse, and spend more time sitting than any previous generation of students in America. To be fair, college students are just one part of the dismal picture of public health in this country: the United States is a world leader in obesity and also has more than a third of the people with eating disorders, two categories that nobody wants to win. The media portrays very few body types, and most come with chiseled abs, toned legs, and no wrinkles, so it's only natural that when students do worry about their bodies, their concerns are rarely much more than skin deep. The problem with trying to look perfect is that it doesn't mean you're healthy. In fact, the opposite is often true.

We're not trying to lay blame on students for making poor health decisions. Studies have confirmed that our body image and health habits are drastically shaped by what is portrayed in media. In 1995, the ideal female form on the tropical paradise of Fiji was healthily full-figured—but television hadn't yet made its way to the entire island. As TV rapidly entered the local culture, researchers monitored the effects of Western shows on adolescent girls in the Nadroga province. From 1995 to 1999, as the girls discovered *Baywatch*, they also discovered dieting and bulimia. By the end of the study, a whopping 83 percent of those surveyed identified television as having specifically made them want to change their body shape or weight. So, it was no surprise that 62 percent had been trying to diet in the last four weeks and 74 percent felt they were "too big or fat." Over the course of just three years, vomiting to control weight was found in 11.3 percent of the subjects—pre-TV, there had not been a single case reported. We've been watching the tube for decades: it's a wonder we are even alive.

The body of these chapters aims to undo some of the dark magic and illuminate how our bodies and minds codetermine our capacity to thrive. Another hour in the sack (*sleeping,* thank you very much), a few more minutes of elevated heart rate (however you choose to make that happen), and grabbing some grub in the a.m. (or whatever time you wake up) can result in higher GPAs, better concentration, improved learning ability, and an increase in your well-being. And yes, it can even make you more attractive to others.

Hey, we're not trying to preach; it's college, and we are definitely not going to tell you how much to sleep, how or what to eat, or how many steps you should take each day. What we will try to do is show you the advantages of taking care of your body, and the pitfalls that appear when you don't. We'll show you how your body can help your mind get you into tip-top shape and how just a few small habits can go a long way toward ensuring that you thrive.

CHAPTER 10

Exercise: Student Bodies in Motion

The body is the storm-center, the origin of coordinates.... The world is experienced at all times with our body as its center, center of vision, center of action, center of interest.

— *William James*

Gym class wasn't always just about dressing up in unflattering clothing and running around in circles. Back in the day, there was an essential belief that in life we would need both an academic and a physical education, and pursuing one without the other would be like learning addition without subtraction. In 1861, Amherst College created what is considered the first undergraduate PE program, and to administer this program the school did not turn to their greatest athlete, they hired a Harvard physician known affectionately as Doc. Physical education at the time sprang from the belief that the "highest intellectual efficiency can never be reached, the noblest characters will never be formed, till a greater soundness of physical constitution is attained." PE wasn't to "develop sportsmen," but rather to help students "relieve the strain associated with their academic courses." We don't know about you, but that was definitely not our gym class.

Your skepticism about the state of science back in 1861 is warranted. After all, we are talking about the year the Civil War began, when a person's character was still assessed by the bumps on their head, and fevers were treated by bleeding the patient. Although we are glad bloodletting and head-feeling have tapered off, in this chapter we will see that Amherst's initiative was more prescient than they could have imagined. Separating our body and mind means running the risk of limiting our potential and experience in life. Movement and a healthy body (whatever that looks like for you) are elemental in the pursuit of well-being, and essential for you to thrive in the classroom.

Changing your level of physical activity is notoriously challenging. You most likely will not put down this chapter and sprint to the gym, and it's not the Tone It Up girls we're trying to channel here. We draw our inspiration instead from the immortal wisdom of the Beastie Boys, "We need body rockin', not perfection." We will show you how to develop the physical activity that is right for you and how that activity will power your mood, concentration, and ability to learn.

Motion Throughout the Millennia

For tens of thousands of years, our ancestors averaged five to ten miles, on their feet, each day to find food. They foraged for nuts, berries, anything they could eat, all the while making sure that nothing ate them. Movement was inextricably intertwined with human evolution...not to mention sheer survival. In college, it will help you thrive.

Our bodies are primed from the beginning of our lives to enjoy physical activity. When we are active, we release all the hormones and neurotransmitters (dopamine, norepinephrine, serotonin, endorphins, you-name-itins) that make us feel good. It's like a buffet of positive emotions. Exercise, sports, and games focus and absorb you, getting you into flow. Also, if you have been having a bad day, physical activity can act as an amazing distraction from whatever was spinning in your mind moments before.

If you haven't thrown down this book to go rock climbing, that's not surprising. Your behavior is consistent with the frequency of physical activity going on in the United States today: not a lot. Our hunter-gatherer past is long gone, and today all you have to hunt for is your cell phone. A few clicks and your kill (be it pizza, wings, Vietnamese, Chinese, Italian, or Thai) will arrive at the door, plastic utensils included. The world of food is truly at your fingertips. Modern conveniences have slammed the brakes on our movement. Though spending all day sitting is not in accordance with thousands of years of evolution, fewer of us earn a living with physical labor, and the college environment (not to mention the deskbound jobs that follow) encourages us to plant our bodies in a seat, whether during class, at the library, or in the dorm.

Bodies and Brains

You may or may not think of yourself as a physically active person, but we can say with close to 99 percent certainty that as a toddler and as a child, you were moving around constantly. There is a reason you don't see two-year-olds chilling slack-jawed on the couch (and why you *do* see exhausted new parents): thousands of years of evolution. The benefits of moving are innately understood by children: it makes them feel good, it is how they learn, and although they have no awareness of this, it is helping their brains develop. These benefits don't stop when we hit puberty, when we get to college, or when we start collecting Social Security. They are with us our entire lives, but only if we take advantage of them.

Jump Around, Jump Around, Jump Up, Jump Up, and Get...Big Brains

With movement come bigger brains, and bigger brains can come with many benefits, one of them being *"magna cum laude"* embossed on your diploma. Like our Civil War–era Doc, Harvard University's John Ratey is on his own mission to illustrate the power of increasing your heart rate. In his book *Spark,* Ratey tells the story of Naperville Central High School on the outskirts of Chicago. Like most schools, Naperville was searching for ways to raise its national test scores by improving the minds of its students. Often people think higher test scores come from effective teaching or diligent study habits, but Naperville decided to get the gym teachers involved, implementing a program to increase physical fitness in order to improve mental aptitude.

Naperville Central High dramatically altered its exercise program, grading students not just on their athletic prowess (or simply on attendance), but on how long they could keep their heart rate in an elevated zone. The school equipped every student with a heart monitor to wear during gym class, and provided more activities from which students could choose. Sports were made more aerobically challenging by making teams smaller to encourage more movement. If sports weren't your thing, walking was just fine. Even *Dance Dance Revolution (DDR)* was an option. Physical activity didn't stop after gym class—DDR and treadmills were available before and after school and even before particularly demanding classes. If you're wondering why any of this mattered, here's your answer: Naperville students are among the 230,000 students around the world who take the TIMSS (a test that ranks nations in terms of math and science). Before the phys ed initiative, Naperville's scores were on par with the United States average: eighteenth in math and nineteenth in science worldwide. After the new athletic program was implemented, Naperville's rankings went through the roof: sixth in math and first in science *in the world.*

It's not that every student had to run the mile in under four minutes to stimulate their brains; it's that they kept moving. When we exercise, a protein called brain-derived neurotrophic factor (BDNF, or what Ratey refers to as Miracle-Gro for the brain) is synthesized, causing our frontal lobes to get pumped up like the bulging biceps of a professional body builder. Frontal lobes are where you find your willpower, your ability to focus, learn, and even ponder the nature of life. BDNF gets its biggest bump from aerobic exercise — the kind of activity that requires a lot of oxygen to keep you powered, including jogging, riding a bike, swimming, and most importantly, walking — and as the students at Naperville showed, that can add up to a cornucopia of benefits.

There is growing evidence that exercise does more than just grow your brain. Done at the right time, exercise improves your memory. In a recent study on undergrads in the Netherlands, seventy-two students were asked to memorize ninety pictures over a period of approximately forty minutes. Participants were randomly assigned to three groups. One group was given a thirty-five-minute workout session immediately after being shown the pictures. Another group (the control group) watched nature documentaries for three hours between seeing the photos and their workout session. And the final group was asked to hang out for four hours before being given their own thirty-five-minute workout. Two days later, the three groups were tested on their recall of the ninety pictures. The folks who worked out after the four-hour delay remembered 10 percent more of the material than their counterparts. Improving our recall is not just about adding more Miracle-Gro to the brain; it's knowing when to add it.

Movement for the Masses

Emil, a student who commuted to our class from outside NYC, approached us at the end of the semester to share his experience with physical activity: "I am not an athlete," he said. "Can't throw a ball, always hated gym. But I like to walk, and since we covered exercise in class, instead of taking the subway from Grand Central, I walk the two miles here and back. I lose some time but feel great and am more alert in class when I get there." Many of our students tell us they don't feel like athletes, but we all have the ability to be active. Walking or sprinting, dancing or playing ball, growing your brain isn't about getting fit for the Olympics, it's about finding the exercise that fits you.

Plenty of people don't feel naturally inclined toward physical activity, or at least don't consider themselves athletic, and we are giving you license to blame it on your elementary school gym class. Unfortunately, PE can be a difficult environment: everyone wants to win, and your physical appearance (or performance) may relegate you to getting picked last for everything, every time. The more frequently this occurs, the more likely it is that the last-picked kid will develop an aversion to physical activity. These kids begin to "self-handicap": when a student does not feel good about their ability on the court, they are more prone to find a way to get off it. These experiences can add up to a profound impact on their self-esteem, often leaving them with a mindset that physical activity should be avoided.

We aren't gym teachers, but we would like to personally apologize to everyone who had bad experiences growing up in PE, because it did you a great disservice. Not only that, we are going to do something about it. Yes, we are offering a makeup class that's all about you! The best part? This new opportunity gives you the power and ability to shape your own relationship with physical activity and how it can make you look, feel, and engage with your body.

Getting going may be as simple as changing the way you think about being active. Just as you have mindsets regarding stress, and can change those mindsets, you have mindsets about the body and what it means to exercise. Researchers Ellen Langer and Alia Crum had hotel maids reframe the way they think about the walking, bending, and cleaning they do every day. They pointed out to the cleaning staff that throughout the day, they were also accomplishing a considerable amount of physical exercise: every fifteen minutes spent changing linens burned forty calories, vacuuming for fifteen minutes another fifty, and cleaning a bathroom knocked off sixty. Cleaning fifteen rooms in a given day, the 2,250 calories they were burning easily exceeded the surgeon general's recommendations for being active. Four weeks after elevating their awareness regarding physical activity, the housekeepers were found to have decreased weight, body fat, and blood pressure. The control group, which was similar to the subjects in every way (age, weight, activity) but did not receive this intervention, showed no changes in health.

How does this magic happen? There was no increase in reported exercise outside work, nor any increase in workload, and yet the subjects were getting a different, healthier result, simply because they had changed their mindset regarding exercise. It may be the power of the placebo effect. As Crum points out, people who are exposed to fake poison ivy will develop rashes; given fake caffeine, they become more alert; and if given fake knee operations, they will report reduced pain and swelling in their "healed" tendons and ligaments. Just changing your mindset about how you are currently being physically active may give your body a much-needed boost.

Take Control of Your Engine

When life feels out of control, students have been shown to be more negative about the future and their ability to thrive in it. Incorporating physical activity into our life, no matter what else has gone haywire, can boost our confidence in the knowledge that we still have control over our decisions *and* our body.

In a study of over seven thousand undergrads across Europe, students who felt they had some control over their health were 40 percent more likely to exercise. But cause and effect can also be flipped: one of the benefits of exercise is the feeling that you are in control of something (namely, your body). The correlation between movement and a sense of control is powerful enough for therapists treating post-traumatic stress disorder to use surfing lessons and strength training as a way to help patients overcome the feeling that life is no longer in their hands. Feeling physically healthier and more attractive, more comfortable in your movements, and more poised (and sleeping better, to boot) leaves you feeling more in control over who you are.

The Student Body Is Not Going Anywhere

Undergrads shuffle an average of 7,700 steps per day. The recommended guideline is 10,000, meaning that most of you are getting—yikes—a C+. Whether it is in front of the television or computer or in a car, there is a whole lot of sitting going on. Even if you are doing everything right and following the national guidelines to exercise daily for thirty minutes, spending the rest of the day stuck in park puts you at higher risk for everything from weight gain, to diabetes, to heart disease. Regular motion is key when it comes to maximizing your physical and mental health.

Being your best in college should be a very moving experience. When you feel the urge to stay seated in the library, glued to your computer, or hunched over a microscope, think again. There's a reason President Obama took a break to shoot hoops and big-brained luminaries ranging from Aristotle to Charles Dickens were famous for their long walks (Dickens would walk twenty miles to his country house): movement enhances mental performance. When we stop moving for too long, we do not end up in neutral—we take two steps backward. A student body in motion can help you (and your beautiful brain) stride onward and upward, helping you thrive from your first step on campus through your walk to accept your diploma.

Opportunities for Action

Exercise: Putting the Movement Back into Your Life

Take a second to think: Is physical activity built into your daily routine?

It takes just five minutes: Quick energy breaks can make a huge difference during a long day of immobility. Many of us, exhausted by work, want to "do nothing" when we take a break, but in a study out of the University of Sheffield in England, psychologists Maxine Campion and Liat Levita compared undergrads who were asked to dance or do nothing. Those who got down for just five minutes increased their positive emotions and decreased the negative ones, leaving them more energized and more creative than their "do nothing" counterparts. When you sit down to get work done, it's easy to forget about taking a break or to feel it's a waste of time. But the payoff from doing ten pushups or taking a walk around the library comes in higher productivity. Don't let movement be an afterthought— instead, schedule it into your routine.

Standing rules: Although they are in their infancy, standing desks are gaining popularity fast. It's not hard to design a custom one for your room, and they are available relatively cheaply from IKEA. Studies show that people who move between standing and sitting are more productive than those who remain motionless. Many actors in our class tell us that when they want to learn lines, they head straight for the treadmill, elliptical, or stationary bike.

Exercise: Finding the Flow in Your Workout

A recent survey by the Centers for Disease Control and Prevention found that 65 percent of adolescents, 40 percent of college students, and 15 percent of adults exercised regularly. Many of us stop engaging in exercise because we have too much work and it's not convenient, and for some, it's just not fun. But being physically active not only makes us feel healthy and can potentially fill us with positive emotion, it has also been identified as a driver for engagement (remember that "optimal experience" from Chapter 3). Whether it's racquetball or Zumba, here are some ways to stay engaged with your exercise:

Set some goals: By setting goals, you are setting yourself up for accomplishments (the A in PERMA). Doing so will also help you avoid the dreaded workout burnout. If you are going to the gym but find that boredom sets in, you may not be challenging yourself sufficiently or varying the activity enough. Try asking these three simple questions to get you into the zone:

1. What am I going to accomplish (how far/long/intensely am I going to push myself?) at the gym/track/workout?
2. What am I going to do differently during this activity that I have *never* attempted before?
3. Did the challenge meet or slightly exceed my skill level (a sign of a good activity)?

Just as you wouldn't take the same class over and over again in college, try new activities when you exercise, keep things varied, and you will stay engaged with your body.

Make it social: If it's hard for you to make it to the gym, bringing a friend along may give you a boost and make it more fun. Working out can be intimidating, and the social support may allow you to get over your anticipatory anxiety *and* help the time pass more quickly and more enjoyably.

Exercise: Putting Your Mind Back into Your Body

For a moment, consider the hotel maids—what activities in your life might you already be performing that you can consider physical activity? Make a list. Whether you volunteer at a soup kitchen, return books to the shelves at a library, or work in a restaurant, you probably have a lot of movement in your life. Just considering how physical activity is already a part of your life may have its own health benefits. Break down the activities in your life with these questions:

1. How can I use technology to optimize my daily exercise routine? Every cell phone has the capacity to track the number of steps you are taking (and probably already is without your even knowing it). What number are you hitting regularly, and what goals would indicate progress and success?
2. Where can I incorporate physical activity into my life?
   a. Walking instead of riding?
   b. Riding (a bike) instead of driving?
   c. Stairs instead of elevator?
3. Where can I eliminate some sitting (or other sedentary behavior) in my life?

The Takeaway

The Big Idea

The optimal mind and sense of well-being cannot be achieved without physical activity.

Be Sure to Remember

- Physical activity leads to bigger brains and better moods; we don't need to run the marathon to find its benefits.
- Regular physical activity (at least once per hour) enhances our mood and cognitive capacity.
- Feeling that we have control over something in life is essential for our well-being. Daily physical activity confirms that, no matter what happens, we will maintain control over something: our body.

Making It Happen

- One of the best ways to stay physically active is to incorporate it into your day-to-day activities. Take the stairs, walk to work, find a volunteer activity that keeps you moving, or get a standing desk.
- If you want to maintain exercise in your life, make it self-reinforcing: make it enjoyable. Set goals for yourself, challenge yourself, and even better, bring a friend. Whatever you do, don't let it get boring—you will end up with workout burnout.
- If you were scarred by a traumatic gym class, consider shifting your mindset about exercise. Physical activity can be found in many forms—find the one that fits you best. Just do it.

CHAPTER 11

Nutrition: Feeding the Student Body

Life is a combination of magic and pasta.

—Federico Fellini

Maybe you're the foodie who brought a panini press to school and binge-watches *Chopped* on snowy weekends. Or the vegan who is on the hunt for the freshest produce on campus. For all we know, you could be subsisting entirely on Frosted Flakes or curly fries. We're not the food police and have no desire to be sworn in. If you are setting foot on campus determined to eat fast food for the next four years of your life, we wouldn't dream of stopping you.

Instead, this chapter will simply help you explore what is right for you. We will leave the choice—and the Oreos—in your hands. It's not about weight loss or looks, it's simply about the role nutrition plays in you being who you want to be. To get started, you'll need to "choose your own adventure."

Below are four ways to look at the relationship between your body and the food you eat. As you read them, consider which one fits you best.

I think my body is like:

1. A factory, because when we eat food it is broken down, transformed, distributed, and stored in different parts of the body, all in a very complex process.

2. A temple, because the body should be respected and food should be chosen carefully as an offering.

3. A tree, because it is a living thing that draws its nutrients from the soil, sun, and air to grow tall and full.

4. A car, because it needs fuel for energy just like the body needs food.

This list, used by University of Pennsylvania professor Paul Rozin to study how different cultures look at food and the body, has no right or wrong answer, but your choice speaks volumes about how you perceive your body and can help you gain perspective on how you treat it.

If you are a car, do you run on regular gas or need the premium stuff? Does your factory keep humming along efficiently, or do you frequently run out of parts and find production grinding to a halt? Are you the kind of temple that worships the body for physical perfection (think of the covers of almost any beauty magazine), or something more sacred? There is a good chance that you recognize yourself in more than one of the metaphors. Understanding your perspective can generate insights into how you will pursue the best version of your physical self.

Like anything that operates, moves, grows, or is nurtured, you need energy to get going—but the right energy is what matters. This chapter will help you understand how (and when and what) to eat for success in college, and how the choices you make (or don't, seeing that 75 percent of you most likely skipped breakfast altogether) will quite literally fuel your mind and body all day long.

You Are What You Eat: The Benefits of Eating Well

If you are what you eat from your head to your feet, how about from dawn until dusk? Nearly fifty studies support the idea that your mom was right after all: breakfast eaters do better. Morning meals improve cognitive function related to memory and result in better test grades.

One study looked at over a thousand undergrads taking Bio 101. Prior to the second major exam of the semester, students were asked if they had eaten breakfast before class that morning. The fact that only 65.5 percent of them had eaten wasn't the shocker. Whether they ate a Pop-Tart, a bowl of cereal, or a piece of couch pizza, what leapt out at the researchers was that of the 188 students who received an A on the test, 78 percent had eaten breakfast. In fact, while 72 percent of the breakfast eaters passed the test (with a C), only 50 percent of the students with empty tanks could say the same. (An added bonus is that even though breakfast eaters tend to consume more calories, they tend to weigh less. When we eat a good breakfast, we are less likely to reach for the quick fix later in the day!)

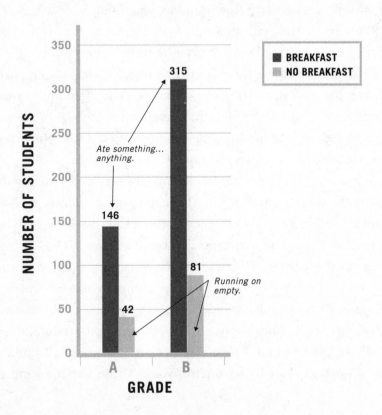

While the knowledge that a frosted Pop-Tart can give a positive boost will come as welcome news to many (Strawberry! yay!), there are, of course, reasons to consider the healthier alternatives (and we don't mean unfrosted Pop-Tarts. Boo). Long before clever marketers told us that a certain candy bar "really satisfies," humans knew that sugar gives us a bump in both mood and energy (and tastes delicious). But the carbohydrates that are broken down into sugar and raise the levels of neurotransmitters associated with a sunnier disposition are not all equal. Like Icarus, who flew too close to the sun, simple carbs (e.g., cane sugar, corn syrup, or even "healthy sugars" like brown sugar, agave, or maple syrup) hit you with a quick high before slapping you down with a plummeting crash.

On the flip side, the more complex carbs found in fruits, veggies, beans, and nuts ramp up slowly and let you fly high for longer. The right sugars in the right amounts will leave you feeling full and slightly better. In a study of over four hundred young adults, on days when they were eating their fruits and veggies, they also reported feeling more curious and having greater creativity. It might be worth letting go of the grudge you've held against broccoli since the infamous you're-not-leaving-this-table-until-you-try-it dinnertime showdown of 2005. No pressure, just saying.

While we may get an intellectual boost from fueling our tank with almost anything in the a.m., our emotions are—no surprise—more finicky. Over the course of four weeks, researchers tracked the daily fruit and vegetable consumption (F/V) and well-being of over a thousand students. Regardless of the rest of their diets, the more F/V they consumed, the higher their level of positive emotions. Many people consider employment one of the essential ingredients of thriving, but in a study of over eighty thousand individuals across England, F/V consumption had a bigger impact on life satisfaction than being unemployed. Those experiencing the

greatest amounts of positivity were consuming seven to eight portions a day.

Foods can bolster our mood, our intellect, and our pleasure in
life. What you eat and *when* you eat it can keep you moving, thinking, and happy as a clam (mmm…clams).

F(M)ood Matters

Food impacts mood, but our mood also has a say in the matter, often
dictating what and how much food we are going to eat. As our student Cathy discovered after completing the Food and Mood Journal
(the first exercise at the end of this chapter), she was far more likely
to get a double cheeseburger when she was feeling totally overwhelmed. The downside was feeling depleted shortly afterward.
Increasing her awareness motivated Cathy to experiment with alternatives. Greek yogurt with some granola, it turned out, left her feeling physically good and mentally fresh. Cathy still indulges in double
cheeseburgers, but it's a choice—not a reaction to how she is feeling
at the moment—and she can truly savor them. Cathy has come to
realize that making good decisions about what she puts in her body
is nurturing in every sense of the word—truly caring for herself in a
thoughtful and compassionate way is even more gratifying than the
juiciest cheeseburger.

Research shows that when it comes to our appetite, positive
emotions push us to go…both ways. Feeling great can encourage us
to reach for the healthy option, but people also eat to celebrate,
cement friendships, or increase positive emotions through the pure
pleasure of food. One of the major identified causes of overeating is
that people eat for reasons (including the ones above) that have nothing to do with their hunger. Tips for healthy eating often begin with
advice to pay attention to your belly and not your brain. Easier said

than done when a friend brings home Dunkin' Donuts or your roommates want to have a wingdown. Simply having some awareness can lead to very different choices and outcomes.

You may be capable of resisting a glazed doughnut after you've aced an exam, but if you find yourself chowing down on that fourth slice of pizza after a fight with your roommate, or you suddenly crave a cupcake after receiving a surprisingly low grade on a paper, it's no coincidence. Stress signals your brain to release hormones that tell you to eat more fat and sugar, so the desire to bury your face in a gooey cinnamon roll on a brutal day isn't just about good advertising, it's an internal marketing campaign that is very hard to resist.

A comforting food will at least momentarily tuck our stress into bed and elicit soothing memories to take its place (e.g., cafeteria lasagna brings you back to Mom's delicious home-cooked meals). Our senses of smell and taste are most likely the oldest senses, the ones we relied on before our ears and eyes took over. Smell is often considered the strongest sense because it is the only one with nerves exposed directly to the environment (shout-out to the nose). These nerves conduct the thousands of odors we are capable of detecting to the olfactory bulb, which—*quelle coincidence*—lives right next to our memory banks. Even if we're not consciously retrieving a specific memory (chocolate cake = seventh birthday = grandparents = Disney World), we're tapping into the good vibe surrounding it, instantly conjuring a time when we were perhaps younger, felt cared for and happier than we feel now (in the middle of finals).

What's important to remember, though, is that comfort food is more about feeling than flavor. Setting out to see what makes comfort food so comforting, Heather Scherschel Wagner and her colleagues at the University of Minnesota asked college students to identify their favorite comfort foods (accepting awards were chocolate, ice cream, cookies, and brownies), as well as foods they liked just as much but wouldn't describe as comfort food. The students were then shown disturbing videos to provoke feelings of anxiety and sadness. Immediately afterward, one group was offered their favorite comfort food, while a second group was given liked-but-not-comforting eats. A third group received a plain granola bar, which was considered a neutral food. After everyone had eaten, the psychologists used a twenty-question mood assessment to measure how much negative feelings had diminished. There was no significant difference bewteen the three groups: the act of eating—not the type of food—equally comforted them all. It turns out that a carrot stick has just as much power to comfort you as Dad's barbecue ribs with a side of Mom's mac 'n' cheese.

Craving something to eat is a natural response to stress, and the reason "food" is the instant solution for many of us rather than "classical music" or "exercise" is that food is the emotional multitasker: the ritual of eating reminds us of being happier at another time; the food itself stimulates all the senses at once, distracting us from whatever we were upset about; and, last but not least, the body responds to food by releasing dopamine, the pleasure neurotransmitter.

It's possible to reprogram your comfort foods. Think of three foods that both fill you up and keep you going, and make an effort to keep these foods handy. You can even make a ritual out of enjoying one of these at the same time every day. Alan takes a daily afternoon break with an apple and some nuts, chosen specifically to remind him of charoset, a traditional dish served on his favorite holiday, Passover. He even enhances the memory and amps up the good feelings by calling his mother for a quick chat. Alan ends up feeling full, comforted, and reenergized. Hitting the vending machine for a candy bar may be a quick and easy response to counter a midafternoon slump, but the momentary respite you get will ultimately leave you feeling hungrier and more tired (and possibly cranky). What your body would thrive on is some comfort food that will leave you feeling better not only in the moment, but in three hours as well.

The All-Nighter

It's bound to happen sooner or later: the paper you dreaded writing, the dense book you never got around to reading, the web page you neglected to design...and now the assignment you haven't even begun is due tomorrow and you have no choice but to pull an all-nighter. If your stomach is dialing 911 and FLAMIN' HOT Cheetos are answering, hang up! There's a better way to make it through the night.

The stress of staying up all night to hit a deadline puts you into urgent mode, and that may have you reaching for quick and comforting stuff, but too often, those choices have the exact opposite effect from the one you want and need in the moment. A little prepping and shopping ahead can fend off disaster.

To keep all systems running optimally for those extra six to eight hours when you normally would be hibernating, some protein (peanut butter), complex carbs (popcorn can be a good one), and a ton of water can help you not only stay up, but also stay on point. We expend an enormous amount of energy preparing for papers and exams; spend 1 percent of that considering the food that powers us and we just might make it through the night.

The Freshman Few (3.8, to Be Exact)

In August 1989, *Seventeen* magazine published an article that would change the way college students look at food. The author informed the world that during their first year, students gained not five, not ten, but yes, fifteen pounds. The Freshman Fifteen had been born, and it would spawn endless books, workout videos, and most importantly, concerns about eighteen-year-old waistlines across the nation.

There was only one problem: no studies or scientists were

involved, and the number had been pulled out of thin air. According to a survey of every study on the topic between 1985 and 2008, the average amount of weight gained for college freshmen (who actually do gain weight) is a mere 3.8 pounds. One study showed that up to 36 percent of students ended up weighing *less* by the end of their first year. *Seventeen* magazine's article was an epic example of why you shouldn't believe everything you read.

In case you're curious, the number one factor associated with putting on a few pounds during college wasn't eating at all; it was drinking. And we aren't talking about orange juice. (Hint: it's not called a beer belly for nothing.) If you are nervous about putting on pounds, there is a very simple formula: if it's weight you fear, stay away from the beer.

So, unless the idea of gaining 3.8 pounds strikes fear into your heart, there is no need to obsess about automatic weight gain in college. Instead of fixating on what foods you're served, consider figuring out what foods serve *you* best. The exercises below will help you create your own food profile to figure out your best fuels for every circumstance.

Opportunities for Action

Exercise: The Food and Mood Journal

Journals can help us identify patterns in ourselves that we don't realize in the moment. The goal of this exercise is to understand how your eating habits affect your mood and productivity, and vice versa. For one week, keep a log of the following:

- Where and when did you eat?
- What foods did you eat?
- With whom did you eat?
- Your mood before and after the meal

- How did you feel physically after the meal? Note how hungry you were when you began the meal and whether you felt more or less energetic when you finished.

Note anything of interest, but don't worry about the sodium content, fat, carbs, or calories. "Burger and fries" is description enough. Do comment on things like whether you overate (and how it felt), if you were hungry thirty minutes after the meal, or whether you ate sitting down or standing up.

A great way to identify patterns is to make some. When your journal is complete, grab three different-colored highlighters. Use one color to highlight the foods you enjoyed the most. Use another to highlight the foods that made you feel healthiest after the meal. With the final marker, try to identify the consistent contexts for your best meals: were you with friends (which ones?), did you have your phone in your hand, were you sitting or were you on the go? Finding emerging patterns will give you the opportunity to increase the frequency of those that help you to be your best. The more often you put yourself in a position to thrive, the more likely it is to happen.

Exercise: Enjoy Your Food (Mindfully)

Ivan Pavlov taught a dog to salivate whenever he rang a bell, simply by pairing the sound with the animal's meal. The dog didn't need to study salivation or understand the neuroscience of habit, he automatically learned that (a) I like food, (b) bell = food, thus (c) bell = drooling. This automatic form of learning is called classical conditioning, and it works just as well with the human animal.

We may not salivate at the sound of a bell, but many of us do at the sight of a remote control. In a culture where Netflix = unconscious snacking, people often find themselves elbow-deep in a bag of chips, barely realizing how they got there. A recent study at Cornell University found that most undergrads make over 221 food decisions a day, most of them unconsciously. In another study, given a larger bowl to eat from, 31 percent of students ate considerably more than their small-bowled classmates, but only 4 percent realized they were doing so. There is a lot to focus on in life and many of us make dietary decisions while on autopilot. If you want to get a glimpse of the automatic choices you are making on a daily basis—both good and bad—you will first need a tasty dollop of mindfulness.

A study of over four hundred college students found that those with more mindfulness—nonjudgmental awareness of what they're doing while they do it—were significantly more likely to eat healthier food. To try this for yourself, next time you sit down to a meal, hold off on diving in for just a few moments. Turn your TV, phone, or computer off. Make sure anything else distracting is put away. You should be seated comfortably, not standing or walking around. You are on a date: just you and your food. Take ten seconds to look at the food. Then take ten seconds to smell the food. For good measure, when you start, throw in another ten seconds to really chew and swallow the food mindfully. We dare you to "waste" the thirty seconds. In fact; if you have a piece of chocolate nearby right now, there's no time like the present to get started.

The Takeaway

The Big Idea

The food you eat will do more than fuel your body and mind, it will affect your ability to learn and perform at your best.

Be Sure to Remember

- Eating breakfast (any breakfast) has consistently been linked to better performance in the classroom.
- Our mood has a huge impact on what we eat, and what we eat has a huge impact on our mood.

- The Freshman Fifteen has no weight to it whatsoever. Average weight gain during your first year is closer to four pounds—and alcohol, not food, is the number one culprit.

Making It Happen

- Awareness is the first step when it comes to understanding and changing our food patterns. A one-week Food and Mood Journal can reveal what foods enhance your willpower, thinking, and positive emotions.
- Stress triggers your body and mind to search out sugar and fat, but healthy foods have been shown to be just as comforting. Keep nearby the foods that will truly empower you during times of crisis.
- Mindful eating can help you make better choices. Stop, focus on your food, and give your senses a chance to take in the wonderful aroma, appreciate the crunchy texture, and enjoy your meal.

CHAPTER 12

Sleep: The Student Body at Rest

A ruffled mind makes a restless pillow.

—*Charlotte Brontë*

In our 9:30 a.m. class, we've seen them all. The face-proppers—elbows on desk, chin resting in their hands, gazing at us without blinking (transfixed or trance? We're never sure). The mannequins—caps pulled down to conceal their closed eyes (um, you know your fingers have been motionless on your laptop keyboard for thirty-eight minutes, right?). The survivalists—half a dozen energy drinks lined up in front of them like tequila shots in Cancún (are those three Red Bulls just for the next hour, or all day?).

To be honest, we didn't need empirical data to convince us that students are getting less sleep than ever just when they need it the most—but we have it here anyway. Students today sleep an average of one full hour less than their peers forty years ago. Only one-third of undergrads think they consistently get a good night of rest. Twenty percent of students report pulling at least one all-nighter every month, but being able to survive the next day is not the same as thriving: inadequate sleep results in worse academic performance, greater anxiety, and higher incidence of depression. It also causes you to retain less of what you learn, which is why we say that students who don't get enough sleep are *renting* their education, not *buying* it.

How much sleep should you be getting? The definition of sleep deprivation is anything less than seven hours, and most authorities say the average adult should be sleeping between seven and nine every day. But that being said, what works for you? If you get ten, eight, or six and a half hours (which is the national collegiate average) and you feel you are at your best, that is how much sleep you should be getting. If you sleep six but then take a long nap during the day, that may be what works for you. In this chapter, we aren't going to tell you how much to sleep, but we will explain how to figure that number out for yourself. We are going to discuss the why and how of sleep, explain what is going on in your brain when you shut down your body, and cover how you can take advantage of the right amount of zzzs to feel, think, perform, and even look better.

A Riddle: When Do You Crash Because You Don't Crash?

When you find yourself nodding off mid-exam, it's no surprise that you awaken to a lower GPA, but imagine falling asleep and waking a few minutes later to find that you had spilled 38 million gallons of oil in the ocean. How about coming out of a sleep-induced haze to find that you had blown up a nuclear power plant? Sleep-related issues were the cause of the *Exxon Valdez* oil spill, Three Mile Island (worst nuclear disaster in the United States), Chernobyl (worst nuclear disaster in history), and even the explosion of the Space Shuttle *Challenger*. Now, you might be thinking that you are never going to drive an oil tanker or operate a nuclear facility, but you are probably going to drive a car, and the National Highway Traffic Safety Administration estimates that each year there are 100,000 sleep-related crashes, with an estimated 1,550 deaths and 71,000 injuries. If you are still wondering how this applies to you, one study found that 67 percent of undergrads reported being drowsy at the time of an accident, and 17 percent have fallen asleep behind the wheel of a car. Stopped at a red light while returning from an overnight shift during medical school, Alan fell asleep. It seemed like a blink, but when he opened his eyes he realized he had moved through the light into the intersection. Not only was he lucky to be alive, but so were the two passengers in his car. Alan never drove to his overnight shifts again, but he tells this story to his patients, asking them, "What will it take for you to take your sleep seriously?"

Check this one out, my all-night-driving friends: driving with fewer than four hours of sleep is the cognitive equivalent of driving while intoxicated. Just like some drunk fools think they are the funniest, wittiest, or cleverest folks alive, sleep-deprived people often think they are doing an awesome job when in reality, they are seriously impaired. Between the ages of eighteen and twenty-five, your body can bounce back from some serious sleep-induced damage, but your best judgment doesn't share that resilience.

Not getting sufficient sleep has some serious downsides. As Tyler Durden notes in *Fight Club,* "With insomnia, nothing's real. Everything is far away. Everything is a copy, of a copy, of a copy. When you have insomnia, you're never really asleep and you're never really awake." The physical and emotional harm caused by lack of sleep is so severe that sleep deprivation is considered a form of torture, outlawed by the Geneva Conventions.

We don't know exactly why, but all species, from insects to kangaroos to humans, need to sleep or they die. Death, oil spills, and lower GPAs aside, lack of sleep has a profound effect on your ability to thrive. There are many reasons to get a good night's sleep, but here are a few not to get a bad one:

- *Sleepy and Grumpy:* Sleep deprivation has a rather nastily selective impact on memory: you forget the good and remember the bad! When shown a list of both positively and negatively oriented emotional words, people who are then deprived of sleep remember 80 percent of the negative the following day, but only 60 percent of the positive ones. It is well known that depressed people sleep poorly, but it is now also understood that *if you don't sleep, you're more likely to get depressed.* So if you want to make the most of those precious positive emotions, go to bed.

- *Eyes wide shut:* Assessing reality is tough enough ("Does she really like me or was she just trying to be nice?"), but when we don't get enough sleep, our worlds can turn into fantasylands. One group of students at Bradley University was forced to pull all-nighters while the other half got a solid eight. When tested on the same material the following day, those who had been awake for twenty-four hours rated themselves as having better concentration, greater effort, and better performance than the group who had slept through the night, and yet the results showed the exact opposite: despite feeling more capable than the sleepers, the all-nighters scored 35 percent lower. You'll likely have to pull some all-nighters in college, but don't fool yourself: no matter what you think, you need to close your eyes to really open them.

Sleepwalking Through College

If sleep improves our memories, enhances our thinking, *and* benefits our health, why are so few students getting it? And it's not just college students who are suffering. Here are a few reasons Americans are sleeping two full hours less every day than they did just a century ago.

- *24/7 society:* With unlimited artificial light, people work longer, and with constant access to the Internet, they play longer, too. It's harder than ever to know when to stop. You may not realize this, but there was a time when the campus library actually *closed*. You couldn't get in even if you wanted to. Now if you're not there, you feel guilty.

- *Sleep machismo:* Some people (aka gunners) love to brag that they don't need sleep to kill it every day. Making yourself out to be a superhero or a martyr has become common in campus culture. But even though these folks are secretly suffering, they might make you wonder if you shouldn't try to push yourself further.

- *Fear of missing out:* College is FOMO incarnate. Opportunities ranging from partying to studying, playing it to slaying it, and everything in between just multiplied by roughly 895 percent. Try to take advantage of everything in college and you may end up sleepwalking through the whole adventure.

Sleep and Your Brain

Sleep is so much more than the cure for sleepiness; it allows our brain to create new memories, organize the old ones, and develop. Studies show that sleep has been associated with better judgment, eating habits, focus, learning, attention, and willpower.

Exercise may grow the brain, encouraging your neurons to multiply, but sleep allows them to connect. When you are taking notes in bio, listening to a lecture in English lit, or practicing a move on the field, your brain is encoding a memory; but this memory is like a Post-it note scribbled on and thrown into a basket with other Post-it notes you have scribbled on that day. When you sleep, your brain takes all these Post-it notes (called "unstable" memories) and puts them in the right order. It's only after sleep that you can make maximum sense of all that happened.

We've all heard that practice makes perfect, but it turns out that the phrase is missing a key element: sleep. Researchers at Harvard found that without the right rest, perfection may be even tougher to attain. Half of the subjects in their study were taught a simple finger-tapping task and were then tested on it and retested later in the day. The other half were taught the same task, but they got to sleep on it before being retested. While the first group realized mild improvement, the second group's finger-tapping skills showed a 20 percent increase in motor speed over the previous day, without loss of accuracy. Consider the outcome of another study done at Harvard, this one by Ina Djonlagic and her colleagues, which aimed to see how sleep propels our ability to learn. From childhood on, you are constantly categorizing objects and events, which enables you to better manage new material and experiences, both familiar and foreign. In this experiment, undergrads were shown how to categorize a series of cards, tested, and then allowed to sleep that night. The following morning, they were tested again, and their scores improved by 10 percent. Their improvement didn't come from just studying harder, it came from taking better care of themselves. Our learning is enhanced when we are given time to sleep on it. "Practice and then sleep make perfect" may not be as catchy, but it's the wiser strategy.

Say it's one o'clock in the morning and you have a big exam at eight. Should you stay up and cram, or shut down and snooze? Drilling that study sheet without sleep is like Snapchatting the info: one moment it's there, the next it has disappeared. In one study, students who reported sleeping well performed two grades better than their sleep-deprived peers taught the same information. Another study showed that students with consistent bedtime and wake-up times had an average GPA of over 3.5, whereas the GPA of more irregular sleepers was below 2.7.

Sleep and Your Body

It's not all in your head—sleep acts as a regulator for the rest of your body: your health, the way you look, and even your weight. If you've noticed the relationship between lack of sleep and how often you get a cold, that's the 50 percent reduction in your immune response talking. And beauty really is more than skin deep. In a Swedish study, subjects between the ages of eighteen and thirty-one were photographed after a night of good sleep, and then again after pulling an all-nighter. The photos were given to a series of untrained observers, who overwhelmingly found that when well rested, the subjects were significantly more attractive.

If you find that you eat more when you haven't slept enough, it's not just about a decrease in willpower. The right amount of sleep balances two specific hormones in your body: ghrelin, which is found in your gut and stimulates your appetite, and leptin, found in your fat, which tells your brain you are full. A bad night of sleep leads to a perfect storm: your ghrelin goes up 28 percent ("Hey, [yawn]... let's get some doughnuts"), while your leptin is down 18 percent ("Wait...just one more!"). If that isn't bad enough, it turns out that when you don't get enough sleep, you get a boost in your endo*cannabinoid* levels. Does anything strike you about that word? You got it, getting a bad night of sleep gives you the munchies without having done anything that is (in most states) illegal.

Adding the "How" to "How Much"

Think of a time when you got plenty of shut-eye and still woke up feeling groggy, and you'll realize that sleep is about both quantity *and* quality. To build a good night of sleep, you will need to understand the stages that make up your sleep architecture.

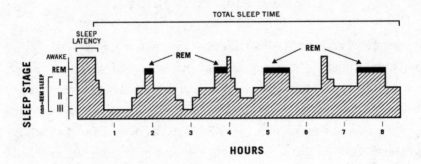

The graph above represents a solid night's sleep. (We know, we know…eight hours, haha…just come along for the ride.) The moment you shut your eyes, the timer begins. In a fantasy world, when you are well rested, the first stage is a ten-to-fifteen-minute period of "sleep latency," when your eyes are closed but you haven't yet begun to snooze. If you are out in less than ten minutes, there is a good chance that your body is overtaxed and craving sleep. If it takes you much longer, there may be issues to be addressed, and we'll have some answers for that in "Opportunities for Action."

As you see in the graph, after sleep latency you go into stage I, then stage II, and finally stage III of non-REM sleep: non–rapid eye movement sleep—your body moves but your eyes are still. Each stage is considered progressively deeper and harder from which to wake up. During non-REM sleep, your brain is in fully active mode, when you thread together and encode the facts you've learned since you last dozed.

After descending into our deepest sleep, we ascend back to our lightest slumber and then experience REM sleep: rapid eye movement sleep, where your eyes do dart quickly from side to side but the body becomes still. REM sleep is when you dream, as well as when you encode your procedural memory, that is, capture not just *what* you did, but *how* you did it. In stage I you might commit to

216

memory the facts you need for the written portion of your driver's test; in REM sleep you'll store processes like how to actually drive the car.

Like stage I, REM sleep is very light, and we are more easily woken up and less upset at the intrusion. In the figure on page 216 you will notice that our first experience of REM sleep is the shortest, but each successive period gets longer. We can dream up to four times every night, and for brief moments, often unmemorable, we almost come out of sleep. As the night progresses, we get shorter episodes of deep sleep and longer periods of REM sleep, so not getting enough sleep means fewer opportunities to tie things together from the day. This is why trying to catch up on sleep is like trying to turn back time: it's just not gonna happen. This is also why we can't "bank" sleep. Getting twelve-plus hours on the weekends may give your body some time to refuel, but all of those later and longer REM opportunities that were missed during the week mean that some stuff is just gone. Memories, learning, buh-bye.

Nap-Happy

Napping during the day is more than a recharge, it's a supercharge; it's not just restoring your cognitive powers but giving them a serious boost. Frequent nappers make up 52 percent of high academic performers. A twenty-minute nap between 1 and 3 p.m. may be the equivalent of an hour of nighttime sleep. Our levels of melatonin (a naturally occurring hormone that tells us to sleep) rise twice a day: once in the evening and another slightly smaller burst in the early afternoon. Pay attention to your melatonin and your brain will thank you.

An effective power nap is twenty to thirty minutes long (not including the time it takes to fall asleep). This brings you no deeper than stage II, helping you to avoid deeper sleep, where your brain does not want to be interrupted. If you're going to take a longer nap, you want to make sure you leave yourself enough time to go down to stage III and come back out of it (90 to 120 minutes), perhaps even making it to your first dream. We hope it's a sweet one.

Sweet Dreams

You can find out exactly how well you're managing your zzzs by taking a few minutes to complete the Epworth Sleepiness Scale in the exercises at the end of this chapter. No matter where you lie in the Land of Nod, here is some of the best expert advice to help you get the rest you need.

- *Larks and owls:* Larks thrive by hitting the sack early and waking at the crack of dawn, while owls do their best work well after midnight. During adolescence and into their early twenties, many people naturally become a bit owlish, which is why in 2013 the secretary of education, Arne Duncan, tweeted "start school later." Whether you're a lark or an owl, you still need a certain amount of sleep. Create a schedule around your sleep needs — try to avoid early-morning classes if you're a hard-core owl, for example.

- *Night light:* Television screens, computer monitors, the iPad, and even cell phones emit blue light, which decreases melatonin and thus dampens your desire to sleep. This is why you shouldn't be looking at any screens before bedtime. Content matters, too. If you are watching something particularly gripping, your brain will keep working long after your eyes are closed. If you don't want to power off, a program like f.lux can decrease the blue light emission (certain televisions and phones can also diminish their blue light). But ideally, you should keep gadgets out of arm's reach (yes . . . you *can* put your phone in the drawer across the room) to minimize temptation and maximize your shut-eye.

- *Too on to turn off:* Occasionally, our bodies are so fatigued or our brains are so overstimulated that they won't let us drift off to dreamland. When we become too tired, many of us become slightly activated (we feel a bit loopy or, in clinical parlance, hypomanic). We are so tired that we find it difficult to settle down for bed. We do not pay attention to the melatonin signaling the body to go night-night, and it can be hours before we get another chance.

- *If you are in bed for more than twenty minutes and can't fall asleep, get up.* Sit in a chair with low light and read a book (ideally, something that would normally help you nod off, perhaps something for class) until you are feeling tired enough to go back to bed and try again. It is helpful to associate your bed with falling asleep, not with the failure to do so.

- *Drinking yourself awake:* Whether it's Red Bull or coffee, these are called stimulants for a reason, and they keep you on your feet. Caffeine can be essential to staying on your toes — hey, college wouldn't be college without coffee shops — but with effects lasting anywhere from six to twelve hours, if you hit it too late, you'll never get to sleep. On the flip side, whether you are among the 10 percent of students who report using alcohol to fall asleep or like to party well into the night, don't be fooled: alcohol is no friend to sleep, either. It blurs that valuable REM sleep just like it does your vision, "fragmenting" it and wreaking havoc on your sleep cycle. If you ever wondered why you could sleep forever after drinking but still wake up feeling exhausted, bingo! — now you know.

- *Making room for sleep:* Trying to sleep in a well-lit room is like trying to study in the dark. Bedrooms that are dark, quiet, and cool set you up for successful and steady nights. If you are a reader, dim the light (forty-watt bulbs are about right for bedside tables). If it's noisy, go with earplugs. If it's hot (as in warm...we would never tell you to dismiss the other), cool it down.

- *A body at rest:* Hitting the tranquility button can be tricky at the end of the day. A long, hot shower might seem relaxing, but beware of staying in the steam too long—anything that raises your core temperature will inhibit melatonin. Likewise, exercise can wear you out, but doing it too close to bedtime will also heat you up. Ideally, you shouldn't exercise within two to three hours of going to bed. There is considerable evidence to support meditation as healthy bedtime prep, so give that a try. Settling in for slumber is like landing a plane: a gradual descent will give you the softest landing.

Opportunities for Action

Exercise: Epworth Sleepiness Scale

How sleepy is sleepy, anyway? The Epworth Sleepiness Scale is an objective assessment of whether or not you are getting enough shut-eye. As you imagine the following scenarios, ask yourself how likely you are to doze off or fall asleep right now. Use the following scale to choose the most appropriate number for each situation:

0 = would never doze
1 = slight chance of dozing
2 = moderate chance of dozing
3 = high chance of dozing

Situation/Chance of Dozing

1. Sitting and reading ____
2. Watching TV ____
3. Sitting inactive in a public place (such as a theater or meeting) ____
4. As a passenger in a car without a break ____
5. Lying down to rest in the afternoon ____
6. Sitting and talking to someone ____
7. Sitting quietly after a lunch without alcohol ____
8. In a car, while stopped for a few minutes in traffic ____

Add up your score. If your total is:

0–7: It is unlikely that you are abnormally sleepy.

8–9: You have an average amount of daytime sleepiness.

10–15: You may be excessively sleepy.

16–24: You are excessively sleepy and should consider seeking medical attention.

This scale gives you a tool to use, for example, whenever you get into a car, or just to get a sense of whether you should be getting more sleep. If your score is above 16, don't panic—maybe you just pulled an all-nighter. Remember, when we are tired, we aren't using our best brain; a little objectivity might go a long way toward making a better decision.

Exercise: To Hack It, Track It

While the majority of college students are at their cognitive best when getting between seven and nine hours of sleep each night, assessing what is right for *you* is key. This exercise allows you to look at your personal sleep patterns and determine what's best.

In a journal, for one week:

1. Record all the caffeine you consume each day.
2. Write down everything you eat, drink, and smoke within two hours of going to sleep.
3. Write down everything you do during the hour before you go to sleep. Be sure to note the timing of any exercise during that hour, as well as what you watch, read, or do online, and with whom you talk.
4. The next day, record whether and when you woke during the night, for how long, and what you did when that happened.
5. In the morning, note how your previous night's mood affected your sleep and how you feel on waking up. A good night of sleep should leave you feeling refreshed. Do you try to relax before bed, and if so, how? Does it help?

When you've completed a week, you'll have a rich resource at your disposal. What common themes emerge around both the good nights and the bad? Do certain people or conversations leave you restless before bed? Does it look like you're guzzling too much coffee? You might notice that you have particularly good nights (and mornings that follow) when you hit the sack with a book in hand or listen to chill music rather than club beats. This exercise can help you get a sense of what's working for you right now ... and what's not.

The Takeaway

The Big Idea

Sleep doesn't just return us to baseline, it is a cognitive enhancer and allows us to learn and perform at our best.

Be Sure to Remember

- Greater achievement in school isn't always going to involve more hours in the library—getting seven to nine hours of zzzs can make you smarter, healthier, and even more attractive.
- When the afternoon slump hits, a twenty-to-thirty-minute power nap can recharge your brain and solidify what you have already learned that day, and is the equivalent of one hour of nighttime sleep.
- Consuming caffeine or alcohol or exercising too close to bedtime can negatively impact the quality of your sleep.

Making It Happen

- To understand how to sleep better, we need to examine what we do while we are awake. Keep a sleep journal for one week and we can guarantee that you will get more out of your shut-eye.
- Reading is a fantastic way to help yourself drift off, but if the light is too bright, you might be, too. Dim the light or get a forty-watt bulb and you will find yourself where you want to be: asleep.
- The blue light emitted by electronic devices cues your body to stay awake. Try downloading the app f.lux, which blocks the blue light emission (comes standard on iPhones at this time as "Night Shift." Either swipe up from the bottom edge of any screen or go to Settings >Display & Brightness >Night Shift).

PART IV

POSITIVELY EXCELLENT

There is no real excellence in all of this world that can be separated from right living.

—*David Starr Jordan*

It's 8:45 on a Saturday night and I (Dan) am sitting on my living room couch. With the smell of freshly buttered popcorn wafting in the air (and the evidence glimmering tantalizingly at arm's reach), I have one arm around my girl and the other holding the TV remote and about to hit Play to finally complete our monthlong marathon of *Breaking Bad* (season five), when the phone rings. No caller ID. Now, as we all know, nobody picks up the phone if there is no caller ID, especially on a Saturday night (unless you're single, that is—which I clearly am not)—and yet, despite the warning sideways glance of said lady...I do. The last voice I expect to hear on the other end is the world-famous one that greets me with a sense of urgency.

"Hello," the caller begins, "you don't know me, but my name is..."

But I *absolutely* did know his name. Giovanni, as we'll call him here, is one of the most successful performers in classical music. He barely waited for my flabbergasted "Uhhh...hullo" before blurting out the reason for his call.

"Ever since I was a kid, my greatest goal has been to perform a solo concert at Carnegie Hall. I constantly thought about it in music school, I dreamed about it as I came up through the ranks, and it is what I told my agent at our very first meeting. And guess what...now I am finally doing it. I am giving a concert at Carnegie Hall."

"Congratulations," I replied, still stunned. "That's wonderful. When is it happening?"

"I don't think that you understand," he said, "I am doing it right *now*. It is intermission, and I am calling you from my dressing room because I finally achieved my dream. I finally made it, but I am totally miserable. What the hell went wrong?"

True story...and total cautionary tale.

My very first memories in life were of sneaking down the stairs after bedtime, hiding on the landing, and peeking around the corner to watch my parents play music together. What thrilled me the most, even at the tender age of three, wasn't the sweet sound of my father's flute and my mother's voice—it was the immense joy these two world-class performers exuded while sharing what they loved. My childhood curiosity would grow into a lifelong fascination with the relationship between excellence and well-being. Fresh out of college, I scored a coveted job as an assistant in artist management, helping young musicians develop their remarkable talents and careers. I was both exhilarated and dismayed by what I found.

Many performers were happy both onstage and off. They loved to perform, they adored their colleagues, and they found joy in the music, but it was clear that family, faith, or meaning came first. As one tremendously successful client mused when I asked how he kept the nerves at bay, "I care deeply about what I offer in performance, but if I crack a note, forget a line, or trip and fall onstage, I still get to go home to my kids and spend time with my friends. And you know what? None of them care about the performance: they love me, I love them, and that's what counts."

Yet many artists seemed profoundly unhappy despite great success in the music industry. During my first year on the job, I watched a renowned singer give a stunning performance in front of a sold-out crowd of thousands. With deafening applause and screaming fans pleading for an encore, her radiant smile dropped into a mask of annoyance the moment she walked offstage as she looked at me, put her hands on her hips, rolled her eyes, and groaned, "Jesus, why do I even do this?" I regularly received tearful phone calls from artists who missed their families, and angry calls from others who — despite ever-growing success and fame — were clearly frustrated with their lives.

Excellence and well-being, I discovered, did not necessarily go hand in hand. My parents, it seemed, had been the exception, not the rule.

A decade later, I left the management business in pursuit of the answer to a simple question: *What is the role of well-being in achieving excellence?* For the past ten years, I have followed this line of inquiry with some of the greatest performers and researchers in the world, and for the past five years with Alan and thousands of college students just like you.

The notion that success and well-being are mutually exclusive is well illustrated in our culture. Steve Jobs, Bobby Knight, and Kanye West — to name a few — have fed the idea that in order to be excellent we must sacrifice our well-being. But look at entrepreneurial icon Richard Branson, who penned *The Virgin Way: If It's Not Fun, It's Not Worth Doing;* author, poet, and civil rights activist Maya Angelou, whose resilience took her from the worst of upbringings to an extraordinary life; and soccer icon Pelé, who credits his great success to doing what he loves most. A distinct difference appears between those who trampled on friendships, positive emotions, and health on the path to success and those who not only allowed space for well-being, but also made relationships, family, happiness, and meaning priorities in their rise to the top. There are many roads to excellence. The choice of which to take is very much in your hands.

In this final section, we will show you what we have seen in our research, work, and teaching: excellence and well-being do *not* have to be mutually exclusive. We will explain how to set goals driven by passion, imbue your decisions with meaning, explore the pathways to well-being and success throughout life, and become what you are truly capable of becoming. We will help you define, craft, and live a life full of both well-being and excellence.

We began this book by stating "At its very best, college offers us the opportunity to turn dreams into realities." In this final stage of our journey, we will focus on moving beyond that, creating a springboard to shatter the ceiling of what you believe is possible in your life.

These final chapters are about you becoming your best.

CHAPTER 13

Excellence: Becoming Your Best

Be not afraid of greatness.

— *William Shakespeare*

Every single college student in America wants to be good at something, and many want to be truly excellent. As Oliver Wendell Holmes wrote, "Nothing is more common than the desire to be remarkable." Excellence may even be today's most popular spectator sport, where the action is so gripping that the Mark Zuckerbergs and Elon Musks of the world battle it out with insanely talented athletes, kindergarten-age violin players, and hot-dog-eating champions for a share of our attention. There is a reason why we don't clamor for tickets to watch *Battle of the Bands That Have Just Started to Learn Their Instruments,* eagerly set our DVRs to record the Libyan Professional Basketball League, or insist that our friends *must* check out the totally average show we saw the night before. Excellence thrills and amazes—it inspires and engages.

Developing excellence, however, is not a spectator sport. It ain't gonna happen just by watching. If you want it badly enough, though, and are ready to bust your hump in the most disciplined of ways, college is an incubator for taking huge leaps toward realizing your potential.

So how *does* one achieve greatness? In 1869, the eminent scientist Sir Francis Galton published *Hereditary Genius,* in which he studied experts of all kinds, from sheepherders to high court judges, and wrestlers to doctors. Galton's conclusion? You had to be born with it: your pinnacle of success was preset by your parents' abilities. If your father was a great surgeon, you had it in you to be one, too. If not, stick to whatever else your folks did well, be it bricklaying or astronomy, lest you be doomed to a life of genetically determined mediocrity.

For those who preferred not to carry on the family business, things started looking a bit brighter around the turn of the twentieth century, when University of Indiana researcher William Bryan and his colleague Noble Harter figured out that no matter their genetic imprint, people tend to get particularly good at what they practice right around the ten-year mark. Then, in 1947, Stanford University's Louis Terman and Melita Oden debunked the popular theory that IQ was the biggest game-changer in people's success. These studies did a terrific job of showing us what did *not* make the difference in expert development (genetics and IQ among them), but the question remained: How do human beings develop excellence in a field of their choosing?

In Your Hands

If you want to immerse yourself in the theory and application of expert development, a great place to begin is *The Cambridge Handbook of Expertise and Expert Performance*. The A–Z of developing young talent? In here. Hanging on to those mad skills when you're old? Bingo. The neurology behind expertise? Got it. The role of memory? *Schwing!* Chess, mathematics, music, acting, writing, ballet dancing, tennis, firefighting—if the expertise you are looking to develop is legal, the how-to can be found among these pages (and if it's not, the book will still help you figure it out).

There's just one minor snag: clocking in at 899 pages of prime grade-A scientific study (font size: "tiny"), this sucker is more massive and complex than you can imagine. So in the interest of saving you a little time and sparing you the risk of a hernia and/or chronic dry-eye syndrome, here's the money shot: what you need to learn is something called *deliberate practice* (DP).

The first thing you need to know about deliberate practice is that it works. It's been tested a hundred different ways from Sunday, on everyone from athletes to doctors.

What *we* find particularly cool about this idea—and particularly cool for you right about *now*—is not just the remarkable depth and rigor of the science supporting it, but what it signifies. Deliberate practice rejects the Galton theories flat-out, declaring: if you bust your ass to do something, you have a real shot at being extraordinary. And *that* is amazing.

Developed by psychologist K. Anders Ericsson, deliberate practice is based on the simple premise that realizing excellence is *not* about inherent talents or hitting the genetic lottery, but simply hard work—especially a certain *kind* of hard work.

So, how are you going to compete with that girl with the scary-high IQ sitting next to you? That guy who just seems to have a knack for getting As on everything (even though he "...like...*never*" studies)? The kid on your freshman hall who seems to skate by effortlessly on charm alone? Deliberate practice is how. DP doesn't simply level the playing field, it multiplies the opportunities that are now at your hardworking fingertips.

Whether you are striving for world-class skills or simply seeking to make the most of your potential, DP can be an enormously powerful and efficient bullet train to the next level of development. You may be looking to become the next John Mayer or Dave Grohl of the six-string or just shooting to lead memorably strong sessions of "Can't Feel My Face" around the campfire. Either way, DP applies.

Jumping from the top third of your class to the top 10 percent (or even 1 percent), becoming a working actress or an Oscar winner, a campaign strategist or a cabinet member—this is the place to start. DP is a path to improvement that goes as far as you are willing to bushwhack, no matter who your genetic predecessors may have been. The goal, motivation, and result of deliberate practice is improvement—period.

Here's an example of what DP might look like in action:

Two students enter college. They both sign up for the same schedule, aspire to similar professional goals, and set aside three hours to study every day. The first student goes to the library for those three hours, finds a quiet place to sit and focus, turns off their phone, and sets specific goals for what they would like to accomplish before they leave. The second student studies in the common area of their dorm (or in the quad if it's a nice day), with the door open and phone on, responding to texts and welcoming conversations with passing hall mates throughout. Both students work their way through the same amount of reading, but while the second student pushes through without stopping, the first student takes notes throughout (both for the class and on ideas that are of personal interest), pausing at the end of each section to reflect on what they just learned. The first student outlines questions for the professor (with whom they speak on a regular basis) and class discussions. They may even go back to revisit some of the material that was particularly challenging.

At the end of the semester, both of these students have earned very respectable grades. But are they likely to emerge with equally good educations? Will they make the same progress toward their professional goals? Heck no. They're both looking to acquire knowledge in the same field, but only one of them is on track to mastery. The secret to mastering a skill is not *that* you practice. It's *how* you practice.

In his work both as a performance coach and as a college instructor, Dan frequently turns to DP to help clients and students open new doors and maximize strengths they are either unaware of or underutilizing. He has found that three of the most helpful (and readily available) aspects of deliberate practice are goal-setting, mentorship, and feedback.

Goal Setting

Meredith was two years into the real estate career she had set her sights on back in business school. She felt lucky to have landed at a prestigious firm and was making a decent entry-level income, but she felt frustrated that she wasn't on the same radar screen as Peter and Audra, two peers who were seen as the rising young stars in the agency. "I feel stuck already," she told Dan. "They're halfway around the track on their way to the winners' circle, and I haven't even gotten out of the stable!"

"Forget the job titles for a second," Dan said to her. "What measurements of personal growth would mark your progress?"

"Building my base of knowledge," Meredith immediately replied.

"Great!" Dan said. "What do you want to learn?"

Meredith rattled off her list: sales, marketing, financing, managing a team...

Together, Meredith and Dan devised a four-month experiment, with Meredith choosing one topic from her list to deliberately practice each month, keeping a journal about what she learned. During her initial deep dive into sales, for example, Meredith asked to sit in on the highest-level sales meetings and presentations at work, and began reaching out to top agents for mentoring advice, studying their work styles and strategies, and getting specific feedback on her own endeavors. She read the memoirs and biographies of the greatest salespeople of all time, from P. T. Barnum to Meg Whitman. At the end of each month, she had filled pages of her journal with notes about all she had learned. She repeated her design-your-own-seminar approach in the following weeks with her remaining topics. At the end of the endeavor, her outlook had shifted from defeated to energized as she realized that she was fulfilling the very goal she had identified as her most desirable: she was learning and growing. Her bosses took notice of the change as well, and the more Meredith asked for fresh opportunities and learned from them, the more opportunities the higher-ups began throwing her way.

Mentors

Oprah had Maya Angelou, Zuckerberg had Jobs, Harry Potter had Dumbledore. And Dan's best college friend, Jonathan Mannion, had renowned photographer Richard Avedon. When it comes to developing excellence, working with someone who has "been there before" or who knows the path that will enable you to reach your loftiest goals is essential. The very community you cultivate in college can serve to stimulate, cajole, and encourage growth beyond comprehension.

Aspiring photographers at Kenyon College were lucky enough to have a direct pipeline to Avedon, the legendary artist who hired a steady stream of Kenyon grads as assistants. Dan's buddy Jon landed a gig as fourth (out of four) assistant right after college. It was long hours, hard work, and paid next to nothing—and Avedon was uncompromisingly demanding—but Jon loved learning from him every day. How did Avedon create a scene? Why this light instead of that one? How did he interact with the celebrities who posed for him? How did he run his business? The chance to soak it all in was worth absurd tasks such as finding a prizewinning rooster with the exact same plumage as the one a supermodel's husband's dog ate in the neighbor's yard (try doing that in under twelve hours pre-Internet!). Jon made it to number three assistant before he moved on.

Still, Jon considered his grueling year with the master worthwhile. Absorbing the wisdom of someone more experienced isn't about finding someone to meet your needs—Jon never made the rookie mistake of wanting a mommy instead of a mentor. The key, he realized, is to find what gifts the mentor has to offer and embrace them. Avedon never told him how to make it in the business, he never even gave him advice, but "the learning came from observation," says Jon. "The gift was to absorb everything I could," which is how he came to have a whole roll of candid portraits of Biggie Smalls and other rising hip-hop stars after crashing a Manhattan party hosted by Russell Simmons in the mid-1990s. With the right opportunity, the right advice, and the right equipment, Jon found his calling. Today, with more than three hundred album covers to his name and international gallery shows that have crowds wrapping around the block, Jonathan Mannion is what MTV describes as "hip-hop's go-to photographer."

Feedback

Your teachers and mentors aren't there just to help you set your goals. In deliberate practice, their steady guidance includes *very* honest feedback—both praising ("Very good, Daniel-san") and critical ("Show me paint the fence!"), so that you can make immediate adjustments when necessary to ensure constant growth in the right direction. Whether they are yelling at you from the sidelines, sitting next to you at a computer, or huddled over a car engine with you, it is their every tweak, twist, and slightest adjustment that will keep you constantly improving. Just as the greatest performers in the world still consult with their teachers, even business gurus have their own Yodas (see: Bill Gates and Warren Buffett). Sometimes just sitting with a pal or a professor to discuss your work and help you spot those little corrections can pay off in a massive way, and doing so now can get you into a lifelong habit that will pay off in the form of nonstop growth.

Natalie was flattered and excited when corporate recruiters plucked her from the bartending/waitressing ranks to put her on the management track at the restaurant where she worked. She loved the food industry, and being in the high beams of the restaurant owner could only be a good thing, she figured: after all, the guy had built an empire of over a dozen white-hot restaurants in New York City. He was an absolute superstar in the field.

He was also a world-class screamer and perfectionist. The napkins weren't folded right. The plates weren't centered properly. The servers weren't moving fast enough. The hostess was slouching, that busboy was chewing gum. Every directive and complaint came with a barrage of f-bombs and insults. ("They're frickin' GUESTS, not frickin' CUSTOMERS, you frickin' morons!") People in Natalie's class of trainees seemed to be quitting or crying every frickin' day.

Not Natalie.

For Natalie, the question at the end of each shift wasn't how she'd been treated, but what she had learned. She turned down the volume and filtered out the abuse to focus on the feedback. Day by day, the instructions the restaurateur was giving all added up to an incomparable handbook on how to structure and run a successful business. Knowing how to receive feedback helped Natalie deliberately practice the new skills she needed. She toughed out the boot camp and eventually become a senior executive.

We call DP forced evolution, because it's all about pushing yourself (and being pushed) further than you could possibly go without the goals, focus, feedback, tweaks, and timing that DP is all about. It makes the most of your every second, bead of sweat, and ounce of effort. It guides you to set habits that lock you into a rocketlike trajectory and helps you reach levels that you simply couldn't get to otherwise. The exercises at the end of this chapter will show you some other techniques for instilling DP.

Now That You Know the How, What About the How Long?

Some DP makes you better—more of it makes you great. DP was thirteen-year-old Mark Zuckerberg spending hour after hour at the computer while his father taught him programming, and it was also him giving his all in Facebook "hackathon" competitions well after he was worth a billion dollars. It was Georgia O'Keeffe drawing the same wildflower over and over again from different perspectives in her high school art class, and taking up clay sculpting in her eighties after her failing vision no longer allowed her to mix paints or see a canvas. John Hayes, a cognitive psychologist at Carnegie Mellon University, proposed that few (if any) of the greatest works of artists such as Mozart and Picasso were produced before they had been hard at work *for at least ten years*. That falls right in line with Ericsson's theory, which finds that ten thousand hours of deliberate practice is the key to becoming excellent at almost anything in life. Yup, ten thousand hours: that's three hours a day of DP for ten years.

How Mark Zuckerberg and Taylor Swift Ruined Your Life

Now, if you are sitting there thinking *"Ten years?? Who has ten years??"* you are in excellent company (provided that you find our students at NYU to be excellent company ...). Ten years of intensely focused work may not have felt like much to our hardscrabble ancestors in the Middle Ages (when this was the standard length for job apprenticeships), but fueled by the hyperearly success of role models like Zuckerberg and Taylor Swift, the burgeoning ranks of twenty-something zillionaires (whose age and net worth are easily accessible with a quick Google search), not to mention the seemingly overnight success of contestants on TV talent shows, by today's standards ten years is... well... forever. In truth, though, the average age of "groundbreaking innovators" has been rising steadily over the past century, and today 42 percent of today's wunderkinder are in their thirties, and 40 percent in their forties. You're likely just more aware of the phenoms in their twenties because their youth tends to generate more media exposure. While they may have seemed to just burst onto the scene to claim instant fame, chances are good that those who are the real deal put in years of deliberate practice that you never saw. Just because you hadn't heard of Zuckerberg until Facebook took over social media, or Swift before she released her first multiplatinum album at the tender age of sixteen, doesn't mean they weren't hard at work since they were kiddos. Zuckerberg began programming in middle school, and Swift first picked up a guitar at the age of nine. Talented? *Yes.* Hardworking for a long time before realizing success? *Very.*

The illusion that excellence comes fast and young can ratchet up the pressure you feel not only to hit incredibly high benchmarks, but to do so incredibly (perhaps impossibly) quickly. When the bar (or at least the timeline) is impossible to reach, the first things to get cast aside are often the exact things we need to thrive—like happiness, friendships, and sleep (to name a few). Consider the curious college career of James Madison, a Founding Father and the fourth president of the United States. After graduating from Princeton in two years (instead of the then-standard three), Madison was so exhausted that *he was unable to travel back to his home in Virginia for an entire year* (which prompts us to note the perils of premature matriculation... sorry).

Deliberate Practice Is NOT Fun

To qualify as DP, each practice session needs to be about nothing but single-minded improvement, and this is where the challenge of deliberate practice shows its true colors. Every single moment is the metaphorical dragging of a metaphorical bag of boulders up a metaphorically muddy hill while you nonmetaphorically suffer. Not fun. "Sucks" is not the official word that Ericsson uses (it's not very academic), but it gets the point across. If what you're doing is not at least *kind of* a pain in the ass, you're not engaging in DP.

Excellence Is Excellent, but What About Well-Being?

You may have noticed that nowhere in the description of DP did we mention any elements of thriving. Why? Simple—because nowhere in the literature on expert development is it mentioned, either. *The Cambridge Handbook of Expertise and Expert Development* concludes with a ninety-nine-page index listing 14,320 (yes, we have counted) topics. As you would expect, there are references to "mentors," "feedback," and "college students." There is even a reference to "anxiety," as well as one to "frustration." But a reference to, say, "positive emotions" or "relationships"? Nope, not one. "Passion," "meaning," or "purpose"? Zilch, zero, nada.

It is as if thriving and excellence couldn't possibly coexist.

The belief that one needs to make a choice between striving for success and thriving in life is increasingly driving students down a dangerous path, away from the very things that are essential to realizing their potential. We know that relationships are key to being and doing our best in both good times and bad, yet over the past twenty-five years, the percentage of incoming freshmen who spend at least sixteen hours a week socializing with friends has been cut in half, while the percentage of you who spend less than five hours a week with friends is at an all-time high of 38.8 percent. Is it mere coincidence that stress and anxiety for you and your classmates have nearly doubled in the same period? We don't think so.

No matter how it's spun, when you give your utmost to be your best, there are going to be some seriously challenging, OMG, arg-ghhh, I-just-can't-do-this! times ahead (for a hilarious example, Google "Daffy Duck yoiks video"). But positive relationships can help you deal with exactly these moments, serving as a buffer, decreasing stress levels both as you are charging bravely forward and after stressful things happen. The challenge of learning new skills through deliberate practice can be genuinely frustrating, but social connection predicts more individual learning behavior: you get to share your newfound knowledge with your crew, vent about the rough times, and celebrate the great ones.

The same elements that are key to thriving can offer huge advantages on the road to excellence. Positive emotions have been shown to foster faster cardiological recovery (hello, athletes and nervous test-takers!), increase levels of creativity (hello, artists, poets, writers, dancers, and you other creatives!), and set new and more challenging goals (hello, every single one of you who wants to improve at pretty much anything in life!). Optimism helps us overcome perceived limits, mindfulness can be used to deal with challenges, and resilience-related topics such as explanatory styles and thinking traps (all of which you can find in this book) offer strategies to overcome the frustrations that often lead to quitting or burnout. Developing excellence may be hard work, but it does not have to be miserable.

The Gray in Greatness

Okay, all right...everyone slow down for juuuust a minute. Can it really be *all* hard work and *no* genetics? That six-foot eleven-inch basketball star of a guy who towers over you in the cafeteria might beg to differ, as would the girl who aced AP calculus... *when she was in sixth grade.* The pendulum does seem to have swung from all nature to all nurture, without much room for possibilities between the two extremes. How can we possibly shake what our mamas gave us if it doesn't factor into the equation?

Just as celeb mags have attention-grabbing headlines, and even reputable news publications push the envelope for readership, the sharp-elbowed all-or-nothing arguments that help turn books into bestsellers (see Malcolm Gladwell's *Outliers* as an example of deliberate practice ruling supreme) echo in the halls of academia. Extreme positions can help establish someone's theoretical turf, but sometimes at the expense of reason, and in this case perhaps even common sense. It can't really be as black and white as "nature *or* nurture," can it?

Even the principal gunfighters in the high-noon showdown over the origins of expertise considered the numerous factors that go into developing greatness. Just a few years after Galton went all "if your mama's a sheepherder then so are you" on the world (we paraphrase, and please know that we are not talking about *your* mama), he acknowledged that extensive training *is* essential to reaching the highest levels of performance. One hundred years later, K. Anders Ericsson, Mr. Deliberate Practice himself, wrote, "One cannot rule out the possibility that there is something different about those individuals who ultimately reach expert-level performance," and he emphasized the need for "a better understanding of social and other factors that motivate and sustain future expert performers at an optimal level of deliberate practice."

Of course, then there is happenstance: You are born first (or last) and thus enjoy the fruits of your parents' undivided attention (or suffer the lack thereof). You are really, *really* tall: 17 percent of men over seven feet tall in the United States between the ages of twenty and forty play at least one minute in the NBA (in contrast, guys between six six and six eight have only a .07 percent chance of making it to the show). You happen to have a parent who shares your interest in ballet/Mount Rushmore/reptiles, so you get a leg up with trips to the theater/Black Hills/zoo, a shelf full of books and endless dinner table conversations on the topic. You possess the ideal body type, agility, and mentality to be a champion snowboarder but happen to have been born and raised in San Antonio. Science may like its simple formulas, but the combination of nature and circumstance has a way of creating some awfully complex situations.

And don't forget that some roads are just longer than others, so ease up and give yourself a break. Rudyard Kipling won the Nobel Prize for literature at the age of forty-one (and is still the youngest to have done so), Alexander the Great didn't conquer the entire known world until he was thirty-two, and four-time Ironman triathlete Chrissie Wellington didn't even begin competing until she turned thirty, so you have some time to figure things out and set yourself up.

An extraordinary number of factors contribute to realizing excellence, but this much we know: no matter what talents you were seemingly gifted with at birth (and perhaps a few of these have been integral to your successful path to college), there is no replacement for hard work, and deliberate practice is key to your becoming your very best. And for those of you who have yet to find that special skill, or who believe deep down that there is nothing at which you could be truly special, take heart—when you find your spark, the process of deliberate practice can fan it into a roaring fire and turn an underdog into a true champion.

Becoming great at what we do requires continually increasing levels of intensity and challenge. Yet while it may be essential to keep our eyes on the prize, keeping them open to possibility while simultaneously looking out for our well-being can lead us to even higher heights than we knew existed.

Opportunities for Action

Exercises: From Information to Transformation

You turn information into transformation by taking action. Whether you are shooting for good, better, great, or earth-shattering, opportunities are ripe for you to make the most of your efforts right now. Here are the essential questions to help you get a locus on your focus. Apply these questions to one area or several, but working through them right now can help you make the most of your goals in college:

- What is one area that you will focus on for optimal growth and development?
- At what time and for how long will you commit to practicing each day?
- Who are your ideal mentors, and what are three things you can do to create and nurture relationships with them?
- What are two ways in which you will gather high-quality feedback about your efforts (e.g., swapping papers with classmates, asking for specific feedback from professors, focusing on mistakes as opportunities for growth)?

Applying these questions to each area in which you are striving for improvement can help you make exponentially larger leaps toward realizing your potential!

Exercise: The Development Is in the Details

DP brings goal-setting to a whole new level of precision. Far from simply setting goals for ten years from now, or even the end of your semester, we are talking about setting goals for the next day, hour, or even minute. If you play the piano, it is not about playing an entire piece without making any mistakes, but about focusing a portion of your next practice session solely on finger speed *or* tone *or* the phrasing of one measure of music. For athletes, it is not just about running faster or shooting better, but rather getting your knees *or* arms positioned precisely, *or* developing a breathing technique, *or* focusing on one type of throw, move, or pass so that you can walk away knowing exactly what aspect of the technique you have improved during that session. When it comes to studying, you are not looking solely at the "A" at the end of the semester, but rather what you will have learned each and every time that you are ready to leave the library. If you are taking French, will you focus on better comprehension *or* a truer accent in your next study session? Goals in deliberate practice put your efforts under the microscope to track progress regularly and with finely tuned, measurable precision.

In the area(s) where you are most keen to see improvement, use the questions below to create a journal. The first page should list your development goals for the semester. Those will keep your eyes on the prize. The rest of the journal will set your weekly and daily practice goals. Finally, give yourself an opportunity to soak in your achievements: review your improvement each week and every night.

1. What skill developments would clearly indicate improvement?
   - By the end of the semester
   - By the end of this week
   - By the end of today
2. Which development best demonstrated your growth and development today, and why? What related goal achievement over the past week are you proudest of?

The Takeaway

The Big Idea

Achieving greatness in almost any domain is less about hitting the genetic lottery than it is about factors that are very much in your hands.

Be Sure to Remember

- Deliberate practice is a finely tuned, very precise way of developing your skills to their utmost and pushing yourself to higher levels than you would achieve otherwise.
- Just because it's hard doesn't mean it has to be unpleasant: integrating aspects of well-being into your developmental process can give you an advantage on the road to realizing your potential.
- The process of developing excellence is neither easy nor fast. Experts believe it takes ten years of deliberately practicing a skill to hit the sweet spot.

Making It Happen

- *Check the checklist:* When striving to raise your game by leaps and bounds, keep your checklist on hand, keep it current, and keep it full of challenges.
- *A goal a day:* To boost your skills *and* your sense of accomplishment, set tough, specific goals for each practice, rehearsal, or study session.
- *Pain, gain, and laughter:* Make sure to incorporate friends, laughter, meaning, and other aspects of well-being into your process. Striving for excellence is not easy, but doing so without positive influences is even tougher.

CHAPTER 14

Meaning: What Makes Life Worth Living

Life isn't about finding yourself. Life is about creating yourself.
— *George Bernard Shaw*

Dave Levin showed up for his first day of college without a clue about what he was going to study. Rather than focus on a set path, Dave used his curiosity as a compass, exploring the wide-ranging opportunities available to him intellectually, athletically, and socially. Although he had an inkling that physics would end up being his major, Dave took courses in economics, philosophy, history, and English. He held down three jobs, and when he wasn't working or studying, his broad-shouldered six-foot-three-inch frame could be found playing pickup basketball on the nearest court. Dave enjoyed his freshman year. He embraced learning, had great friends, and lived a rich, full life.

But Dave Levin was seeking more. He was looking for something that connected him to a larger world and a greater purpose in life.

Dave Levin was searching for meaning.

In a survey of a hundred thousand first-year students from over two hundred colleges, 75 percent of newly minted undergrads say they are searching for meaning and purpose in their life. In fact, the two times in our life when meaning is most important to us are at the ages of sixty-five and—you guessed it—eighteen. Many of you will search for meaning through courses ranging from philosophy to art, history to economics, and biology to mathematics. The key? You will most likely find meaning in the things that matter to you most.

Of course, not everything that matters is in the classroom. More than three-quarters of you report finding meaning with your friends, be it soaking up the sunshine in the quad or during late-night dorm sessions that delve into relationships, the direction of the world, and even the meaning of life.

Meaning can spring from experiences both joyful and challenging. You might find meaning through others—helping a friend achieve something wonderful, or supporting a roommate through a crisis. It may be found through the traumas or victories of your own, be it pushing beyond your perceived limits in school, losing a family member, falling in love...or out of it. Sometimes the most ordinary moments will present a doorway to a deeper understanding of our place in the world. Other times—often when you're not looking— meaning just comes knocking: there when you turn the corner to see a person in need, or at a random Friday-night concert in a crowd of dancing strangers.

Whatever gives your life meaning, studies show that finding meaning and purpose will have long-term benefits for you. People who report finding more meaning in life are more likely to enjoy greater well-being, increased resilience, and lower levels of stress and depression. In a 2010 study, undergrads who expressed a strong sense of meaning were considered more desirable friends—and more physically attractive—than those who scored high in happiness, self-esteem, and agreeability.

In this chapter, we will share the benefits of and pathways to meaning—how it can improve both your present and your future, keeping you afloat when the water is rough and carrying you safely past the obstacles in your way. We will explore the science and stories of how others have successfully identified the key stepping-stones to a deeper connection, and show how discovering your own meaning can provide a lifelong beacon to follow.

What Does Meaning Mean, Anyway?

There are few things more personal than what you find meaningful, so instead of attempting to define meaning, Colorado State University researcher Michael Steger has suggested that meaning provides us with three foundational principles:

1. Our lives matter.
2. Our lives make sense.
3. We have a purpose or a basis for our aspirations and pursuits in life.

These principles are easily applied to college. Think of the difference between the classes that give you practical tools for something you love and those that you take only because they are required. Maybe you are someone enthralled by fashion design taking a course on patternmaking, or a budding mathematician studying multivariable calculus, or an athlete practicing hard and improving at your sport. When we believe that our studies are enhancing our capacity to make a difference—or *matter*—in the world, it's much more likely that we will find meaning.

Finding meaning *makes sense* of your life. Meaning gives your choices clarity. It can help you decide which internship to go for, which extracurriculars to juggle, and which friends to spend your time with. When you are committing to something that is not feeling quite right, check your meaning meter and you'll probably find that it's dipping low. A student, Karen, was struggling with her decision to work in the film industry. She felt that much of her work didn't touch the lives of other people. Karen found meaning in helping children and decided to redirect her education to focus on writing stories meant to help bring families together. This made sense to Karen, and she is still pursuing it to this day. Understanding how our lives matter and make sense can serve as a guidepost for almost all of our actions.

Finally, meaning provides the springboard to finding your *purpose* in life. Purpose is your response to the question "Why are you here?" Identifying your purpose can help you to take the steps you need to achieve your goals. If you find meaning in kids, health, and the underprivileged, your purpose may be to provide medical services at a free clinic in a low-income neighborhood. If your purpose is to communicate with the world through physical expression, you may decide to become a dancer. If your purpose is to honor and serve your country, a life in the military might be what your future holds.

Not everyone identifies a single purpose in life. Our student Danielle felt that her purpose was to connect with the world through music and to pursue social justice. After graduation, she moved to Texas and began working in a sales job that left her empty. She held on for six months but knew that her connection to music was slipping through her fingers. When she switched to a job working to help others reduce energy consumption (which connected with her desire to pursue justice), she had more time—and more energy—to devote to her music. Whatever our purpose might be, it gives us a way to focus our meaning, harness it, and push through seemingly insurmountable obstacles. If meaning helps us know, purpose helps us do—and sometimes can propel us forward to truly remarkable existence.

During Dave Levin's freshman year in college, with his girlfriend's encouragement, he began tutoring two underprivileged local kids, a ten-year-old boy named Tyrone and his younger brother, John. As his weekly sessions with the brothers progressed, Dave felt depth in what he was doing—a feeling that what he was doing really mattered. He loved the puzzle of figuring out how to get the kids to learn, but it was the sense of accomplishment that really stood out—not his, but theirs. There was something special about those lightbulb moments when the boys figured out what a fraction really was—when their eyes lit up and the impossible became possible. Dave appreciated the value of tutoring. He'd faced his own learning challenges as a child and required a fair amount of assistance himself. He was aware that this had made a big difference in his life as a student.

Dave was also a passionate outdoorsman and spent the summer before his sophomore year at a National Outdoor Leadership School. He fell in love with the idea of combining his passions: enjoying the outdoors and working with kids to achieve their goals. Yet just a year later, Dave found himself doing what many of us do: rather than following his heart, he took the path that was expected of him. Despite the spark that was clearly present every time he taught or tutored, Dave followed his family's footsteps into the financial services sector, accepting a summer internship at the Tokyo branch of a major Wall Street firm. Undeterred by the grueling hours of the banking world, Dave found himself volunteering to stay ever later into the night to teach English to custodial workers in his office building.

By the end of the summer, he had fifty-three students.

It was becoming clear that teaching was Dave's destiny. But no one could possibly have predicted what he would go on to achieve.

Finding the Benefits in Meaning and the Meaning in the Benefits

Just in case you're thinking that all of this is a bit fluffy and touchy-feely, let us throw out a few reasons why you may want to be searching out meaning *right now*. In a study of over ten thousand people, University of Pennsylvania psychologists Stephen Schueller and Martin Seligman found that pleasure and meaning were both associated with greater well-being in life, but it was the latter that had the most profound effects. People who find meaning in their work enjoy it more, experience more positive emotions, and are more hopeful about life itself.

Meaning is also a powerful buffer against the toughest times of all, raising your levels of resilience and decreasing your stress and negative emotions. The heightened levels of self-control and personal responsibility that come with greater meaning increase your capacity to power through those tough times. For college students, finding that life is meaningful is connected with participating in a greater range of activities, like joining more clubs, taking classes that they might not have ventured into before, or—like Dave—reaching out to the surrounding community. Finding meaning can help you to challenge yourself and reinforces your willpower to strive for more. As you begin to nurture that sense of "why" you are here in the first place, the pathways to "how" are more likely to unfold before you.

Graduating with Meaning

The wall in Dave Levin's office holds no evidence of his Yale diploma, the honorary PhD that the university bestowed upon him a decade later, or the one he received from Duke University shortly thereafter. There is no indication of his national Jefferson Award for Greatest Public Service by a Private Citizen, his Thomas Fordham Foundation Prize for Valor, or even the Presidential Citizens Medal—the second-highest honor for a civilian in the United States—he received in 2008. Even without visible signs of the numerous accolades he has garnered in his twenty years since graduating from college, the path that he took to earn them is clear. Dave's wall is a giant collage made up of hundreds of photographs, each one featuring the beaming, proud face of a recent high school or college graduate, as evidenced by the rainbow of colorful caps and gowns that appear throughout. In every picture, there is Dave, standing right next to them, his smile just as broad and beautiful as theirs.

Upon returning from Tokyo, Dave continued to tutor kids throughout college, shifting his major to the history of education and writing a thesis about the mistreatment of minorities in America's educational system. Shortly after graduation, he joined Teach for America, working with students he believed had been disenfranchised. Dave continued to develop mentoring relationships and friendships around his work, and met Mike Feinberg, a fellow lover of basketball and education. In 1994, Dave and Mike created the Knowledge Is Power Program (KIPP). Today KIPP has two hundred schools in twenty states, serving nearly eighty thousand students, 90 percent of whom come from low socioeconomic backgrounds. National averages predict that only 34 percent of students in this demographic will go on to higher education; but to date, more than 80 percent of KIPP students have gone to college.

The path for Dave hasn't always been easy. Besides his learning challenges as a young student and his initial struggle to recognize his true path, KIPP certainly did not achieve its remarkable accomplishments without stiff resistance from local governments and powerful school organizations. But Dave's resolve and his belief in possibility have remained rock-solid throughout. A strong sense of meaning and purpose has helped him weather the setbacks and savor the victories, helping him build a life lived with great passion and joy.

Finding his meaning in life allowed Dave Levin to make a difference in the lives of those around him.

What will finding meaning in life do for you?

Opportunities for Action

Exercise: Where Is Your Meaning Right Now?

Dave Levin found meaning in the moments when he was tutoring, working with kids in nature, or playing basketball. You may find meaning in particular relationships, during a class with an inspiring teacher, or building a home with Habitat for Humanity. Write down three things that you have experienced or reflected upon that have resonated recently:

1. _____
2. _____
3. _____

Now that you have identified some of the experiences that bring you closer to meaning, let's think about the people and resources that are essential to those moments. As you revisit the list above, consider whether a certain friend or mentor is consistently present, or if these tend to happen in a place such as a lab, or an art studio, or simply when you are solo with a pencil and paper. Write down your observations:

1. _____
2. _____
3. _____

Finally, let's take action and list what three next steps will allow you to cultivate more meaning in your life. Whom might you spend more time with? What might you do with greater frequency? When will you do these things? Keep it simple, straightforward, and actionable:

1. _____
2. _____
3. _____

Finding meaning can seem daunting, but so is any journey without a GPS. Even once you know where to look for meaning, achieving it is the product of trial and error and will demand perseverance along the way. Now that you have some landmarks, though, you can figure out how to begin your journey, identify the people and things that will help you, and visualize what form your destination might take.

Exercise: Meaning Trumps Stress

Whether it's the ubiquitous Post-it note or a reminder set up on your cell phone, researchers from Stanford University can reroute your attention and direct your focus where it's needed. This exercise will give you access to what you find meaningful when you need it most.

1. Looking at the list of what you find meaningful in life, choose one that resonates most deeply with you. Spend ten minutes writing about how you connect with it in your daily life.
2. Now edit your message into one sentence, using the following format: "I find meaning in. . . ." (Example: helping others; caring for my family; creating cool art.)
3. Make your message accessible and sticky. Our students have used the background on their cell phones, made bracelets, and put their message on their dorm room mirrors. Some of our students even write a meaningful statement on their hand to get them through a stressful day.
4. Put it in your schedule to look at your meaningful statement twice a day. Get used to keeping this schedule (you might set an alarm reminder). When you practice this so

much that it becomes a reflex, you will have an instant source of strength, motivation, or reassurance when the going gets tough.

The Takeaway

The Big Idea

Understanding what we find meaningful is a path to finding our purpose and well-being in college and life.

Be Sure to Remember

- Meaning reminds us that our lives matter and make sense.
- College is a peak time in life when people report seeking out meaning.
- Those who consciously search for meaning find they have more of it in their lives.

Making It Happen

- Pursuing meaning requires action and often the support of our friends and mentors. Consider how you plan to pursue meaning in the future and spend time identifying who is helping you develop it.
- Writing about what is meaningful and keeping physical reminders around will help you on the days when the pressures of life obscure what really matters.

CHAPTER 15

Passion: Doing What You Love

Two roads diverged in a wood, and I—
I took the one less traveled by,
And that has made all the difference.

—*Robert Frost*

What Dan remembers most about his mother's voice isn't her soaring mezzo-soprano onstage at opera houses around the world, but her gentle whisper on the evenings when she wasn't performing but listening, the two of them sitting in the audience, entranced by the music that washed over them.

What do you hear? Mimi Lerner would ask. *What is it saying to* you?

Dan grew up in a house always filled with music. His father played flute in the Pittsburgh Symphony Orchestra. His mother was a renowned opera singer. The three of them would play chamber music together regularly. Dan sometimes traveled with his parents, hanging out backstage at a concert hall the way other kids did at a ballpark. It was a world he knew well and loved deeply. He could answer his mother's questions with clever insights about Bach and shared her heartfelt appreciation of the humanity to be found in Handel's operas. He was enthralled by the beauty of the human voice, the ability of a human being to seemingly communicate their very soul through music, and the timeless messages that seemed to resound as loudly today as they did two hundred years ago. But what moved him most, he would tell her now if he could, was this:

You.

While both fairly defined her, what Mimi Lerner embodied was more than just music or talent. What made this child of the Holocaust thrive wasn't that she was alive, it was *how* she lived her life.

Passion.

What do you think of when you hear the word *passion?*

Predictably (and understandably), many students equate passion with romance. A first love, a big crush, an intense summer connection. Moonlight, quickened pulses, the works. For others, "passion" prompts a related concept, with...shall we say...fewer articles of clothing, a little less innocence, and a bit more sweat.

Yet many define passion without mentioning any other bodies — clothed or otherwise. "Pursuing an activity I love," "Stuff that allows me to really thrive," and "What I hope will be my life's work" are common responses. One memorable answer came from a young man who sat through every single class in the same seat, with a fierce but silent intensity, his hat always pulled down low over his eyes and massive blue Beats headphones slung around his neck. When we called on him, he sat up straight, leaned in, and said slowly, almost lyrically, "Music. I love music so much. If I could do nothing but make music — swim in it, make it with other people, live and breathe it for the rest of my life — that would be all the passion I would ever need."

We wanted to hug that dude.

The seeds of passion can be found in a majority of college students — 84 percent of the 539 surveyed at the University of Montreal believed there was at least one thing in their lives about which they were passionate and in which they engaged for an average of eight and a half hours per week (both criteria for passion, as we will soon find out). When we ask our students if they believe that finding a passion in life is an essential element of being fulfilled, the response is unanimous. Passion, quite clearly, is highly valued, eagerly sought, and, when found, happily embraced.

Yet darker possibilities lurk, too, as evidenced by our students, who describe passion as "something that I can't stop doing even though I know I should," "an activity that is so intense that I forget other things in my life," and, along those same lines, "something I can't stop thinking about...like...ever." Passions can limit you just as surely as they can liberate you, either throwing your life wide open to possibility and potential or slamming the gate shut, making you single-minded and narrowing your focus to the point that you make lousy decisions and ignore important tasks.

College is a prime time to find, explore, and nurture your passion.

Before we show you the how and the when, though, let's get back to the what and why.

What Is Passion?

There are plenty of things in life that we are motivated to do on a regular basis, but only a few that genuinely qualify as passions. Poets, playwrights, philosophers, and even politicians have ruminated on the subject as long as language has existed, but when you cut through the thicket of words, the best definition is perhaps the simplest: "a strong inclination toward an activity that people like, that they find important, and in which they invest time and energy." You may pick up a guitar and take pleasure from playing it whenever you have time, but if the guitar is a passion, you will prioritize it, spend hours every week strumming it, and perhaps even look to challenge yourself and become better and better at playing it.

Being passionate about a subject will find you immersed, exhilarated (sometimes exasperated), and digging ever deeper. You might look for opportunities to discuss it with classmates, friends, and even your parents. You may look forward to a good pickup game a few times a week at the local courts or enjoy getting involved in intramural sports, but when you wake up early to take extra free throws, to stretch, to commit time to sport-focused workout programs, or to work with coaches and set specific and challenging goals, *that* is passion.

Your passion may become so incorporated into your sense of identity that you talk about yourself differently. Dan's son, Julian, used to say that he "did gymnastics." Now, with thousands of hours of practice under his belt, he refers to himself as a gymnast. You don't just enjoy programming, numbers, or writing—you are a programmer, a mathematician, or a writer. A passion becomes part of who you are.

The list of what psychologists qualify as passions is so vast that you may have one (or more) and not even realize it. They can range from traditional pursuits like cooking or running to reading, painting, hanging out with friends, watching movies, or listening to music. The idealism that's so fresh and exciting in young adulthood can morph into a passion-driven goal: ending world hunger, creating peace, human rights, environmentalism, education. Consider the passion that America's Founding Fathers must have had to risk their lives against all odds in the effort to win independence from Britain, or the passion that fed Harriet Tubman's courage and empathy as she led hundreds of slaves to freedom along the Underground Railroad. Passion can guide our days and even define our legacy.

Passionate Performances

Trailblazers from Oprah Winfrey ("Passion is energy") to Martha Graham ("Great dancers are great because of their passion") have cited passion as a key to their success, and psychologist Robert Vallerand's research supports them, finding that "100 percent of people who are experts are passionate." For you, the possibilities are as close as your campus: a 2007 study found that college drama majors with higher levels of passion for their art were assessed by their professors to have improved more throughout the year than their less passionate classmates. The same study found similar results for passionate college basketball players.

Passion compels you to work harder. Passion reminds you why you are grinding, sweating, and pushing, and it sustains your interest and focus through the frustration that comes with repeated failure. Vallerand believes that passion is *the* major motivational source underlying deliberate practice. In its own special way, passion can push you beyond your perceived limitations—in a sense, it too can help force your own evolution.

What will your passion be?

Passion: The Good, the Bad, and the Ugly

Passion comes in two distinct flavors: "harmonious" and "obsessive." Simply put, one good, the other...poison.

If there were ever a scientific study of the clichéd advice "Find a job that you would do for free," it would be the study of harmonious passion (HP). HPs drive you to activities that bring you joy and engagement. It's not about the applause, money, praise, or any social or parental pressures. It's about embracing the road rather than the destination, the process rather than the outcome. As the word "harmonious" itself implies, you know that your fascination with theater, medicine, law, history, finance, psychology, photography, architecture, animals, or airplanes is just one part of life and not the whole extra-cheese-and-guac enchilada. You make time for friends, hobbies, other interests, and may even share your passions with others, integrating them into the lives of your friends and family in a healthy way (as opposed to waiting for an opportunity in every conversation to jump in with "Yeah! That's just like with anime, where..."). You feel comfortable taking breaks from practicing, studying, or working. You welcome feedback; you see mistakes as opportunities for growth. You are in control. Your passion is in harmony with your life.

At its core, an obsessive passion (OP) is pursued for others or is driven by outside influences (what researchers call extrinsic motivators). You study, practice, or push yourself not because you find the pursuit engaging or rewarding for its own sake, but rather for the resulting promise of money, status, fame, applause, social standing, or approval from parents or others you long to please. OP pursuits can be so consuming that you leave friendships (and often family) in the dust. You may ignore emails, texts, and voice mails, and either don't respond or turn down invitations to hang out. It is guilt that anchors you to the practice room, field, library, pool, or lab. You fear that people won't love you when you trip up, get a bad grade, crack a note, or strike out at the plate. Even when you do succeed, the joy is short-lived and soon to be replaced by the need for more victories, bigger successes, and the flattery and praise of those around you.

Whether talking about yoga, studying, or Olympic cyclists (all areas studied by the University of Montreal's Vallerand), we find that OP is aptly named: it is about genuine *obsession*. People with OP might know deep down that they should get out more, take a break, hang with friends, maybe even (gasp) think about a different path, but they just can't stop the hamster wheel, even when it's flat-out dangerous to keep going. OP Olympic-level cyclists suffer more injuries (they've been found to train even when there is ice on the ground. Hello...ice, bicycle...), as have ballet dancers. Oh, and if your workouts are a bit less explosive, check this out: OP yoga practitioners experience more injuries as well. *Namaste.*

Harmonious vs. Obsessive Passion

Vallerand et al., 2005

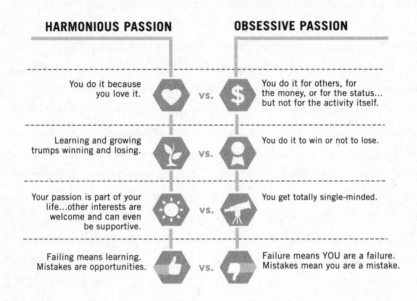

HARMONIOUS PASSION — **OBSESSIVE PASSION**

HARMONIOUS PASSION		OBSESSIVE PASSION
You do it because you love it.	vs.	You do it for others, for the money, or for the status... but not for the activity itself.
Learning and growing trumps winning and losing.	vs.	You do it to win or not to lose.
Your passion is part of your life...other interests are welcome and can even be supportive.	vs.	You get totally single-minded.
Failing means learning. Mistakes are opportunities.	vs.	Failure means YOU are a failure. Mistakes mean you are a mistake.

Passion, Performance, and Life

Like the path chosen by Robert Frost, the type of passion you cultivate makes all the difference. And when we say *all* the difference, we
are not exaggerating. We mean whether or not you make new
friends (and if you keep them); the quality of your relationships with
partners, pals, and family; how much you enjoy your successes;
whether you turn your challenges into opportunities to learn and
grow; what you do with feedback; and even how able you are to
focus fully on a task at hand. "All" includes which classes you choose,
how well you do in those classes, how much you enjoy a date, and
whether or not you go for a slice when your friends invite you out.

"All" means how you treat your body as an athlete, your mind as a thinker, and your heart as a friend, partner, sibling, son, or daughter. It means how enjoyable, engaging, stressful, healthy, and fulfilling your time is in college, and how you fare with your pursuits in the future. Yes, we do mean "all."

Only HP promises better concentration, greater resilience, and improved decision-making after mistakes and while you are under stress. Only HP improves relationships and leads to more mindfulness, creativity, and confidence, raising levels of performance, positive emotion, meaning, and engagement. What rates leap through the roof for people with OPs? Burnout. All that work, and then one day, *poof,* you just don't want to do it anymore.

A 2006 study found that after team practices, high school basketball players with an HP for their sport felt only more positive emotions—not an inkling of the negative at all. Those players with OP? No bueno, only the bad stuff. A more recent study went beyond sports teams to leisure activities and study groups, finding almost exactly the same results. In fact, whether in athletics, the arts, academia, or social pursuits, the differences experienced on a day-to-day basis when passions are harmonious vs. obsessive are truly eye-opening. One study of college students showed that engaging in a harmonious passion in the morning could raise levels of positive emotion for the rest of the day, yet once a student with an OP was away from their activity, negative emotions swept in as quickly as a dust storm at Burning Man.

Passions impact how we relate to one another on every level. In college study groups where classmates had not previously met, those with HP for the subject made both more *and* better friends. Ditto for new participants in a one-week basketball camp. Heck, even in the wide, wide world of online gaming (and actually in a study of the wide, wide *World of Warcraft*), HP for the game itself predicted better relationships with pals away from it.

Whether at dinner, at a concert, catching a movie, or just taking a stroll, harmonious passions gracefully allow you to turn your focus to your date, the changing fall colors, or whether the IMAX experience delivered enough bang for your hard-earned buck. People with OPs may pry themselves away from their obsessions for the same activities, but while they are physically present, all too often they are feeling so guilty for not studying/practicing/working that their minds haven't come along for the ride.

More Passions, More Benefits

So if it is indeed possible to have too much of a good thing, what can a passionate person do in their down time? How about filling it with other passions? A 2014 study by B. J. I. Schellenberg and Daniel Bailis shows that not only does an HP person allow room for more than one passion, but that those who pursue multiple passions report even higher levels of well-being. So for HP people, immersing yourself in French literature *and* Greek art makes perfect sense, and throwing yourself into building robots doesn't rule out picking up your guitar on a regular basis. Wu-Tang and water polo? The Snoop Dogg says fo shizzle. In fact, a 2012 study of college students showed that students who had HP for at least one activity also had a greater ability to focus on other things in their lives, passions or otherwise. Students with OP were on a one-track, blinder-wearing journey, missing a million amazing stops along the way. The good news? There are ways to lose the blinders and change course. Stay tuned.

Choosing Your Passion

We have yet to come across anybody—student, patient, or client—who didn't yearn to have a passion in life. Helping people pinpoint and develop what speaks to them most resoundingly is one of Dan's favorite challenges as a performance coach. When Andrew came to him, he was at a crossroads: he had quit a dream job as general counsel for a well-known corporation to take a chance on a new venture—a venture that didn't work out. He was clearly at his wits' end. "I would love to find something that I am passionate about doing every day, but I have no idea where to begin looking," he lamented. "Let's start simple," Dan suggested. "What are some responsibilities that you would most look forward to at work?" Andrew shared that he loved to wear a lot of different hats, and that was one of his problems. "Maybe that's more of a clue than a problem," Dan ventured. "What does that look like for you?" Andrew described how he was fascinated when he met a founder of a nascent brewery, particularly by how the fellow was responsible for everything from marketing to packaging, and even creating the product. "How cool is it that he gets to learn and be challenged in so many ways?" Andrew marveled.

Little did he know that he had just taken the first step to uncovering a passion.

Beginning with that first conversation, Dan and Andrew built a checklist that incorporated Andrew's interests and his signature strengths. As job opportunities arose, Andrew would not only consult his list to see how the opportunities fit, but also began to score each one, using the list. Positions that commanded a huge salary might score high for pay and prestige but fell out of contention because the organizations didn't value his strengths of humor, teamwork, or love of learning. The process continued for almost a year.

Many of us think passions are like lightning bolts or "love at first sight" moments, but more often than not, they can take months and years to develop. "The big shift for me came when I stopped doing what everyone wanted me to do," recalled Eliza, a student of ours during the very first year we taught The Science of Happiness. "I was 'supposed' to be a doctor, and while I worked incredibly hard, during class my eyes were on the clock and the rest of the time my mind was on the grade. I was *not* into what I was learning at all." That changed with her first psych class. "I was really interested in *why* my mind was doing what it was doing—and what it was doing in pre-med," Eliza explained. Psych 101 turned into a psych major. "I wouldn't say that Psych 101 was a eureka moment, but I definitely looked forward to my classes, so I just kept adding more of them until it was clear—my future lay in psychology."

Andrew finally whittled his choices down to two offers on the table. One was from a huge company that "would have been my dream job five years ago," he allowed. The other was a start-up, pretty much five employees and an innovative business plan. Despite the high risk of failure, the latter was clearly the route Andrew was meant to take. "Every box is checked for me—the law that I love to practice; they're incredibly funny, embrace the idea of team, and they need and *want* me to wear a whole bunch of hats." Two years later, Andrew is the general counsel for that start-up, now the super-successful Jet.com. "Even if it had failed in the first six months, I got to see that I could be passionate about what I do—the people, the culture, and the lifestyle were all realistic possibilities."[1]

Studies show consistently that college students who self-select their passions are far more likely to realize harmonious benefits. By stepping back to think through what really interested them and how they could explore those things, Andrew and Eliza each found theirs. You may not have pinpointed yours yet, but there's no better place to look than college. Following your interests and using your signature strengths are great ways to identify and develop an HP. Be sure to check out the exercise at the end of the chapter to work with these tools for yourself.

---

1. A few months before this book went to press, Walmart agreed to acquire Jet .com for $3.3 billion. Andrew's reaction was "The top questions that I got that first week were if I'm going to retire and what I am going to do with the money. But I'm not going anywhere. Jet was never just about the money. When we achieved this goal, I realized how I'm just incredibly excited to grow Jet our way and keep doing great work that I enjoy with great people that I respect and love." And he never stopped making time for friends and family. That, dear readers, is pure harmonious passion in action.

Pals, Professors, Parents, and Passion

Just because you find your passion doesn't mean the rest of the world is going to get on board for the ride. One of the biggest, and most frequent, challenges our students face is when their parents don't agree with the path their passion has set them on, whether it's a career direction ("Music is a nice hobby, sweetie, but you are sticking with pre-law. Period."), or a lifestyle move (say, when your passion for archaeology pulls you to spend a summer wandering solo across Egypt). Yet finding support of any sort is key to exploring passions and to a successful outcome. You already know how important relationships are for other components of thriving—the role of mentors in deliberate practice, for example, or using tend-and-befriend to get through stressful situations. A study of more than 1,300 participants found that when you're marching to the beat of your own drummer, you're more likely to develop an HP when your autonomy receives peer support. Getting your elders on board doesn't hurt, either. A 2009 study showed that athletes and musicians who had parents, professors, or coaches who supported their autonomous choices were far more likely to find their way to HP, and according to a 2014 Gallup Poll of recent college graduates, the greatest predictor of a fulfilling postcollege life was having "had a professor who supported their pursuits." Endorsement matters.

When Passions Change

Anson Dorrance, the record-setting head coach of the University of North Carolina's women's soccer team, once shared with Dan that he longed to understand why some recruits seem to lose all interest in a sport for which they once had so much passion. How was it possible that these young athletes, whose passion had seemingly fueled their drive to practice hard enough to be recruited by the best programs in collegiate sports, who had committed their lives to being dominant on the field, would choose to shift into cruise control and stop striving for excellence? Had their love for the game disappeared once they were no longer the very best, weren't scoring the most goals, or were no longer getting all the outside recognition? Had their passion hit the end of the line? And most importantly, what would they do next?

We have had students just like Anson's players, whose entire lives revolved around a focused passion, but who found that the passion faded once they hit campus, often leaving them feeling lost and searching for an immediate replacement. From your first day of freshman year to your graduation march, you will experience so much that is exciting and new, from eye-opening classes, to mind-blowing discussions, to different kinds of people with different perspectives, that the odds are very good that your passions will change along the way. If that happens, don't worry, you are not alone, and hey, you are in college, and there may not be a better time in your entire life to begin exploring anew.

Passion took many forms throughout the life of Dan's mom. A breath-holding, floor-pounding tantrum to get piano lessons at age seven was the first clue that music might be at the core, but attending New York's famed LaGuardia High School of Music & Art and Performing Arts sealed it. Mimi was well into her career of teaching music education when she found her way to vocal performance, stunning her instructors with a gorgeous tone, effortless dexterity, and an exceptional sense of musicality. She became an international success.

Yet Mimi Lerner may never have been happier than when she stopped traveling and settled back into her home in Pittsburgh. Not only was she with her family, nurturing a wonderful community of friends, and extremely active in the civic life of the city, but her passion was burning as brightly as ever. Having accepted a position as head of the voice department at Carnegie Mellon University, she took her students in as if they were her own children. There was always room for them at her table during meals, and she knew instinctively how to listen to someone's voice but hear their heart. Her students came to learn how to sing, but what she really taught them was something far more important: she taught them how to be human—she taught them how to live a life of harmony and passion.

Opportunities for Action

Exercise: Passion for the People

Psychologist Adam Grant has found that people work harder when their goals are linked to helping other people. For example, firefighters who were both interested in their work and linked their duty to concern for others averaged more than 50 percent more overtime than their colleagues. Related studies show that people who have a passion identify with statements such as "In choosing what to do, I always take into account whether it will benefit other people" and "I have a responsibility to make the world a better place."

When you find something that is of interest to you, ask yourself the following questions:

- How could this pursuit help make the world a better place?
- How could this lead to something that benefits other people?
- Who are some role models for me in this field, and what have they done to change the world?

More than think it out, write it out! Take fifteen minutes to write in your journal about these questions. Often, your chosen activity may not have an obvious answer, but if you keep at it, you may find a connection. Doing so can mean a leap in motivation and meaning and provide a beacon that offers you a terrific and exciting new direction.

Exercise: Making the Jump from OP to HP

If you recognize yourself as having an OP, all is not lost! Scott Barry Kaufman, the director of the University of Pennsylvania's Imagination Institute, recommends a number of ways you might make the leap to HP:

- *Harmonious scheduling:* Set time in the calendar for friends and family—and don't break those dates! Get some in during the day (go for a walk with a friend, meet a pal for coffee or a workout) and on evenings and weekends. The more consistently you schedule them, the more quickly they will feel natural and welcome. Plus, incorporating others is a key to success (and a classic attribute of harmony).
- *Fake it until you make it:* Kaufman suggests that speaking and thinking like someone with an HP can help you make the leap. Instead of using words and phrases such as "must" or "have to," try "want" or "would like to." It most likely won't feel natural in the beginning, but as your HP-related words feel increasingly normal, so, too, will your behaviors fall into line.
- *Add to the pillars:* At first, Dan's son, Julian, would cry if he didn't do well at a gymnastics meet. When he fell in love with acting, though, a less-than-stellar performance in competition would often be met with a response of "Well, at least I get to learn lines for that audition tomorrow!" Building a life on an OP is like constructing a building on one pillar. When you begin to develop other interests and hobbies, you lower the pressure and minimize the chances of burnout or collapse.

The Takeaway

The Big Idea

Passion has two pathways: Harmonious and obsessive.

Be Sure to Remember

- Harmonious passions are pursued for the sake of the activity. They are things that you truly love, feel in control of, and incorporate into your life with other interests and friends.
- People who pursue obsessive passions are motivated by external factors that take over, such as pressure from parents, status, money, and prestige. You feel no control over your need to work, feel guilty when you are not there, and do not make time for much else in your life.
- With the right strategy in place, an obsessive passion can be turned into a harmonious passion.

Making It Happen

- *Choose easy:* Finding your passion is not always a thunderbolt moment. Passions often take time to develop. Those things that interest you are a great place to start, and see where they go from there.
- *Peep the people:* Considering how your passion can help others or make the world a better place can be a great way to take an activity to the next level of interest and motivation.
- *Don't succumb to the dark side:* If your passion is obsessive, incorporating aspects of harmonious passion (i.e., friends, other interests) may help you craft a healthier pursuit.

Epilogue

The only person you are destined to become is the person that you decide to be.

—*Ralph Waldo Emerson*

As his students huddle around him, John Keating, the main character in the film *Dead Poets Society,* bends to one knee in the middle of his classroom.

There is pin-drop silence as Keating quotes Walt Whitman: "'O me, O life! of the questions of these recurring, / Of the endless trains of the faithless, of cities fill'd with the foolish, / .... / What good amid these, O me, O life? *Answer.* That you are here—that life exists and identity, / That the powerful play goes on, and you may contribute a verse.'"

Looking from face to face and slowing his pace, Keating repeats the last line, willing it into the depth of their hearts and souls: "'That the powerful play goes on, and you may contribute a verse.'"

The teacher pauses, rubs his thumb and fingers together, and takes in the moment. He looks around slowly before asking a question . . . the question. Both loving and daunting, hopeful and huge, the query is equally full of promise, possibility, weight, and gravitas. Keating tilts his head and intones:

"What will your verse be?"

This book has not been about happiness. This book has not been about relationships. It has not been about engagement, or willpower, or choice, or strengths, or nutrition, or sleep, or movement, or mindsets. This book has not been about mental health, passion, goals, choice, or even excellence. This book has not been about any of the topics we've covered, or even the sum of their parts. This book has been about something exponentially more powerful.

This book has been about you.

This book has been about how you can make the most of your experiences in college and in life. It has been about how you can succeed in the face of challenge and how you can thrive with the opportunities that lie ahead. The questions and exercises have been about you, when you have been at your best, when you have struggled, where you stand right now, and how you can move forward. Together, we have sought to more clearly articulate your path, your vision, your passion, your goals, and your dreams. This book has been about your experience, from the very first day you wake up to leave for school, through every day that follows. You can set yourself up to make the choices that will help you be the best version of yourself. This book has been about how you realize your potential, how you move beyond what you perceive as possible, and in doing so build a foundational experience that will see you thriving in college and for the rest of your life.

This book has been about the promise of what your verse can be.

Our final class of the semester is always bittersweet. Many students stay behind to have a last conversation with us, and those interactions are lovely but tinged ever so slightly with the sadness that comes from knowing that we won't see most of them again. Our hearts swell with the feeling we imagine mama birds must have when their chicks leave the nest. We always end up lingering in the auditorium for well over an hour as we speak with each student individually. They thank us for the course, many of them sharing the unique ways it has changed their perspective on college and life. In turn, we thank them for making the class what it is—a vibrant, open, interactive, supportive gathering, where students can share their thoughts about their challenges and opportunities, and hopefully realize they are not alone. We let them know that we, too, are grateful to have learned and grown throughout the semester. It's a meaningful experience for us and one of our favorite days of the year.

There are often a few students who prefer to wait until the line has dissipated before speaking with us. Sometimes they grab a seat in the front row, and other times they stand to the side, jacket off, bag on the floor, clearly waiting for a moment of privacy. These conversations can be quite personal and deserve to be given space. After our final lecture this past spring semester, one young man patiently waited nearby. When the crowd cleared, he approached.

Jon was a charismatic sophomore with a gleam in his eye and a quick wit. He and I had enjoyed regular postclass conversations throughout the semester, most of which were about how he was integrating the information and assignments into his life both on and off campus. An athlete in high school, he had returned to playing sports during the past semester, and as a result was feeling better and thinking more clearly than he had since arriving at NYU. His interests had broadened. He had realized how grateful he was for many things in life that he had taken for granted. We had a very comfortable relationship that always included a hearty handshake and a good laugh.

Yet something was different that day. Jon had always come bounding up, bursting with a question or observation, but now he looked pensive. He gazed over my shoulder and then quietly down at the ground before finally looking me in the eye. He seemed to be gathering himself for something much bigger. "I promised myself I wouldn't lose it," he said, his eyes beginning to well up. I urged him to take his time.

And then it rolled out: the pressures that he had heaped on himself since middle school, the expectations of his parents, peers, and teachers. He had been enormously successful in music and theater since grade school, not only scoring the leads in school shows but touring professionally. He had come to NYU specifically to continue his studies in the field, but had found the experience somehow empty, devoid of the pleasure and passion he once so enjoyed. It was in our class that he realized something he had not allowed himself to consider over the past decade: his opportunity to thrive might lie outside the theater. How could he possibly tell his parents? Music professionals themselves, they had supported and celebrated his path for as long as he could remember. They would surely be crushed.

But he had mustered his courage and shared his feelings with them. They were more understanding than he could have imagined.

What Jon's parents wanted most for him was a fulfilling life. They wanted him to thrive. And now he was thriving. Jon excitedly talked about other possible majors that he was exploring. He had even picked up the guitar again, finding that love of music that had been absent for far too long. The pressure to please others was gone. He was writing his own verse once more.

Having held it together the way he'd promised himself, he paused, taking a long, deep breath. The next words out of his mouth made *me* hold back the tears.

"I'm the happiest I have been in a long time," he said.

Then he opened his arms and gave me a hug.

Jon has been crafting his verse for nineteen years. The challenges he takes on and the opportunities he embraces continue to hone it each and every day.

For the past five years, the two of us have added to our verses as well. Teaching together has intertwined our passions and our friendship. We do what we love, with people we love, and for students we love. This book is the next stanza in our verse. We don't know what the next page holds, or even the next line, but we are sure that whatever it does, we will keep our families close, our friends by our side, and immerse ourselves in activities that are engaging and meaningful. That is the way we thrive.

The last thing that we do during the final class of each semester is thank our students for spending their time with us, trusting the process, and participating with such open minds and hearts. We hope that they might be that much better prepared to move forward toward being the very best—and the most fulfilled—they can be.

We would like to do the same with you. So thank you. Thank you for your time, your attention, your commitment, and your trust. It has been an honor and a pleasure to share all this with you. Just as we invite our students to reach out if they ever need help, we do the same to you. We are *all* still writing our verses: please, never hesitate to find us if you need a hand with yours.

This is the book we wish we'd had in college. Now it's in your hands. May it help you be the best you can be, and may you thrive in college and in life.

Acknowledgments

To every student who has ever joined us for The Science of Happiness at NYU—and all those who will do so in the future—words simply aren't enough to thank you. It is an honor and a pleasure to share with you, learn from you, and laugh with you. You are truly amazing and the inspiration for this book.

There would be no book without the course, and there would be no course without Jess Shatkin, the guiding force behind the Child and Adolescent Minor in Mental Health Studies (CAMS) and creator of The Science of Happiness. Jess, thank you for your mentorship, trust, and support every step of the way.

This book—indeed, the science of thriving—would not have been possible without the groundbreaking (and mind-blowing) research of Roy Baumeister, Alia Crum, Mihaly Csikszentmihalyi, Carol Dweck, K. Anders Ericsson, Barbara Fredrickson, Adam Grant, Kelly McGonigal, Scott Miller, Ryan Niemiec, John Ratey, and Barry Schwartz (to name but a few). A special thank-you to Drs. Howard Markman, Scott Stanley, and Galena Roades of PREP.

To Martin Seligman: the deepest and most heartfelt thank-you for helping us *all* understand how to thrive.

So much gratitude to all of the readers and contributors: Tamara Jones for herding the cats (and often saving them from themselves), Melissa Moore for her wonderful words and kind encouragement, Denise Clegg for making things meaningful, Drake Baer for his immense and immersive vitality, Andrew Soren for keeping us engaged, and Paddy Steinfort, who added fitness to our fitness. Dave Levin, thank you for allowing us to share your amazing story. Andrew Gasper, thanks for being your true self (and letting us relay it in print). Thank you, Anson Dorrance, for your passionate generosity and generosity of passion. Thanks to Nigel Holmes for making science beautiful, Scott Barry Kaufman for inspiring inspiration, and Jonathan Fields for turning doubt into fuel for brilliance. A very special thanks (and a hearty "Ayyyyyy...how YOU doin'!") to Dan Tomasulo and Reb Rebele, whose generosity of words, spirit, and friendship helped us to rediscover the path and forge onward during the most challenging moments.

Emil Hafeez and Chrissy Sandman were equally marvelous as research assistants and friends. Their brilliance is a part of every chapter you read. Karen Choe and Rachel Hettleman, your support was nothing short of awesome.

This book simply would not be without our brilliant agent, Richard Abate, who crystallized a vision, showed us what was possible, and kicked us into gear (repeatedly). To our amazing editor, Tracy Behar, and her whole team at Little, Brown and Company: We can't thank you enough for the guidance, wisdom, and (copious) patience in shepherding an unruly flock of ideas and turning potential into paperback.

It takes a very special village to write a book, and Dan is endlessly grateful to those who built it with him over the years: To Professor Ron Sharp, who shared with me The Gift of words. To Dr. James Pawelski for challenging me to aspire, doing so with immense kindness, and opening my eyes to the beauty and possibility of teaching. To Leona Brandwene, "Yoiks...and away!": thank you for showing me how to stand on the shoulders of giants (and pick myself up when I fall off them). To Dr. Nate Zinsser, thanks for teaching me to make the most of every performance. To the entire UPenn MAPP community—keep striving for thriving! To David Lavin, Charles Yao, and all the folks at the Lavin Agency: your guidance and support in helping me to explore these ideas in spoken word have been a true blessing. To John Hearn, Jonathan Mannion, Bill Powell, and Albert Imperato: thank you all for your friendship, insights, and gentle understanding of my absence this year; and of course to Miles: you will always be my boy. Julian, thank you for reminding me every single day what it is to laugh with abandon and love without limits — you are my heart. To my dearest Erin: without you there would be nothing — not this book, not this home, not this life. To Mom and Dad, you were the greatest teachers and most beautiful souls I have ever known: thank you for showing me the right road in this life, and walking it with me so tenderly and lovingly.

And then there is Alan. Hey, man...thanks for being my friend in more ways than I can possibly (or at least appropriately) express or ever have imagined. I love you, buddy.

There are many friends and family who made this book a possibility for Alan. Thank you, Mom and Dad, for supporting me: then, now, and always. Thanks to Professor Tony Connor, who taught me how to be a human being and helped me write my first story. I want to thank all of my patients who teach me on a daily basis how to find well-being during difficult times. I want to thank the people who cared for my mental health: Donald Cohen, Janet Madigan, and of course Karen Gilmore. I want to thank all my crew at Bellevue Hospital for their support, and of course our fearless leader, Jennifer Havens. Drew and Allison, thank you for putting up with me and reminding me of my many flaws. Tim Whyte, the other half of my brain, thank you for losing to me at backgammon. Nana Fran and Papa Steve, no son-in-law could ask for anything more. I want to thank my beautiful, caring, brilliantly talented wife, Carlyn, who is responsible for the wonderful graphics inside our book. What on earth would I do without you?

Finally, I want to thank Dan, my partner in far more than this book. You talk about how human beings cannot be defined by a single word — neither can our friendship and how much it means to me.

Index

Note: Italic page numbers refer to illustrations.

About the Authors

Driven by a passion for developing human potential, Dan Lerner and Alan Schlechter have taught The Science of Happiness together at New York University since 2012. Having shared the classroom with thousands of undergrads, they have created a blend of science and storytelling that has helped make the course the largest and most popular elective at the school. Dan and Alan integrate their individual expertise in the fields of traditional and positive psychology, striving not just to inform, but also to help each and every student create positive change by overcoming challenges and realizing the unique opportunities in college and beyond.

Daniel Lerner, MAPP, is a clinical instructor at NYU. He holds a master's in applied positive psychology from the University of Pennsylvania, where he has served on the teaching staff since 2012. In addition to presenting frequent guest lectures at universities nationwide, Dan is a keynote speaker and strengths-based performance coach, working with both established and high-potential musicians, athletes, and executives to leverage the advantage that a healthy psychological state can bring to their performance at work, school, and home. A graduate of Kenyon College, Dan lives with his remarkably tolerant (and equally lovely) partner, Erin, and their hilariously energetic son, Julian, in New York City.

Alan Schlechter, MD, is a clinical assistant professor at NYU Langone Medical Center and the director of the Outpatient Child and Adolescent Psychiatry program at Bellevue Hospital, where he has worked since 2007. In this role he seeks to provide mental health care to the most vulnerable children and families in New York City, to help individuals create change to overcome the challenges in their life. A graduate of Wesleyan University and Mount Sinai Medical School, Alan lives with his wife, Carlyn, and his two daughters, Maisie and Marlowe, in New York City's Greenwich Village.